Holy BURNOUT

Turning Brokenness Into Blessing, Through
The Power Of God's Restoring Love!

PASTOR
STEVE ROLL

Pastor Steve Roll is founder and president of Restoration Ministries, an organization dedicated to aiding pastors and their families in personal crises. He serves as an associate minister on the pastoral staff at Church on the Move in Tulsa, Oklahoma.

For further information about Restoration Ministries contact:

Pastor Steve Roll
Restoration Ministries
9837 East 96th Place
Tulsa, OK 74133

Holy BURNOUT

Virgil Hensley Publishing
Tulsa, Oklahoma

Holy Burnout

Dedication

This book is dedicated to the four most important persons in my life.

To my Lord and Savior Jesus Christ who has borne me on eagle's wings, lifting me to glorious new heights of God's grace. Through Him, I have come to know the wonder and joy of our Heavenly Father's unconditional love.

To my precious wife Jo Ann, whose unfaltering faith and steadfast support has kept me on course. Her unshakable, childlike trust in God's promises convince me that He is good, He is for us, and He is with us.

To Adam, my son, who is everything a dad could want in a boy. His delightful sense of humor and gentle spirit keeps me in touch with the lighter and tender side of life.

To my daughter Stacy, whose eyes sparkle and dance like diamonds. Her irrepressible enthusiasm for living keeps me dreaming and believing that nothing is impossible with God.

Introduction

I resign. Those two little words ended my first pastorate and plunged me into the black hole of depression where I lost my way and embarked on a frightening emotional free fall that nearly took my life.

I wrote this book for two reasons. First, it's a work about burnout in the ministry. It's my story — how a young minister crashed and burned emotionally and spiritually.

As a pastor, I loved serving the Lord and His people. My greatest joy was in preaching the Good News of Christ's redeeming love. Being a successful man of God meant everything to me. I dreamed of doing great things for Jesus. I was driven by a burning passion to build an outstanding church for the Kingdom.

I worked hard. Sacrificed. Burned the candle at both ends. I poured my heart and soul into the local church I served. I spared no energy in my effort to fulfill God's call and vision for my life.

My plans for successful ministry didn't include a forced resignation from my leadership role. Something inside of me died that Sunday morning when I stood before the church family and called it quits. My dream was shattered. So was the dreamer.

Resigning left me with a broken heart. I was devastated. I felt rejected. Abandoned by men. Maybe even God. It seemed to me that the whole world was screaming, "You messed up! Your ministry days are over! Steve Roll is a failure!"

As I began to believe those imagined voices, inner panic gripped me. My entire life spun out of control. No longer proud and confident, I cowered in fear.

Holy Burnout (collapse in the ministry) is something we would rather not deal with. The church hopes and prays this disturbing and disheartening issue will disappear while she looks the other way. But it doesn't.

Clergy burnout has become epidemic. According to Fuller Institute of Church Growth surveys in 1995, 50 percent of the pastors had considered leaving the ministry within the three months prior to the survey; 90 percent of the pastors surveyed felt inadequately trained to cope with the demands of the job; 80 percent felt their ministry affected their family negatively; 70 percent had a lower self-image than when they started the ministry; 70 percent had no one they considered a close friend. The average pastor works 50-70 hours a week; one pastor in eight has a second job; and most have spouses who work. Compassionate care for pastors in pain is critical if the burnout bogeyman is to be conquered.

I identify and empathize with pastors and church leaders who have been wounded in the ministry. I believe I understand the intense, inner agony of God's servants who are hurting and crying out for help.

This book is, second, a work about bouncing back from burnout — how brokenness can become blessing.

The Bible makes a wonderful statement about our God:

> *He heals the brokenhearted; and binds up their wounds.*
>
> Psalms 147:3

I write as a healed and restored man of God. Through a process of mercy and grace, the Lord has rebuilt my heart, revived my spirit, renewed my vision, and restored my joy!

The power of God's unconditional love has brought hope and healing to my hurting heart. The worst time in my life has given birth to the best time. Despair's darkness has given way to a sunrise of new life in the Spirit.

My mourning has turned into dancing! Rejoicing now reigns over remorse and regret. By His grace, my setback has turned into a comeback. Almighty God has used the very fires that threatened to destroy me to refine and restore me.

A new person is being raised up from the ashes of burnout. God saved me from myself and set me free to be the man I have always wanted to be, and this new kid on the block is excited about life and ministry again. Hallelujah!

Someone once said that we choose our pain. It's our choice to remain hurting or to secure healing. The price for both is pain.

Hurt's pain leads nowhere; healing's pain takes you somewhere. I didn't want to stay hurt the rest of my life, so I chose to get better. With the Lord's help, I made a series of decisions that set me on a course of action where the Holy Spirit could mend my broken heart.

I invite you to journey with me down the road to inner wholeness.

There is a future and a hope for you if you choose healing. It won't be easy — but the blessing is worth the pain. Your wilderness (burnout) can lead to a Promised Land (blessing).

I pray the Spirit of our loving Heavenly Father will touch you as you read these pages.

God bless you as you open your heart to His healing love.

Restored and Rejoicing!

Steve Roll

Chapter 1

Wounded in the House of God

For it is not an enemy that reproaches me; then I could bear it; nor is it one who hates me who has exalted himself against me; then I could hide myself from him. But it is you, a man of my equal, my companion and my familiar friend. We who had sweet fellowship together, walked in the house of God in the throng.

Psalm 55:12-14

I could hardly wait to pastor my first church. When God called me to preach, my entire life's focus became fixed on that future day when I would stand before men and proclaim the Good News.

There were a number of hurdles to overcome on the track to full-time ministry. My tour with the United States Navy. A college degree. Then seminary. I tackled each task with the unrestrained enthusiasm of a man obsessed with obtaining his goal.

Something sacred bonds seminarians together. My classmates and I became very close. We spent three years of our lives as comrades in theological trenches. We parsed Greek and Hebrew verbs and prepared piles of term papers. We prayed for one another to stay awake in the library as we poured over thousands of pages of collateral reading. Some of us played racquetball till the wee hours of the morning to relieve the stress of academia.

We picked each other up when times were tough. We planted dreams in each other's spirits.

As young couples in seminary, we looked forward to two blessed events: our first child, and our first church. The hallway in front of the campus bookstore doubled as an information highway. There friends and acquaintances proudly announced the news "we are expecting" or "we have accepted this church." The glow from expectant parents and expectant pastors was magical!

I have fond memories of that milestone day when my class walked across the chapel platform. The hard-earned diploma handed to me represented a significant personal accomplishment. I felt proud and relieved. The flip of the tassel meant we'd made it through the glorious grind of seminary training.

Degrees secured, it was time to celebrate. Upon cue from the class president, we tossed our caps into the air (reverently of course!) and the high-five's and hugs began.

Graduation was our green light to ministry. Now it was time to go. With joy in our hearts and tears in our eyes, we said our good-byes, packed up our U-hauls, and headed off into the sunset to pursue our God-given visions. It didn't matter where your church was located. What mattered was that you were on your way. A pulpit had your name on it. Soon you would preach the Word and people would come to Christ.

My first position was on the staff of a large, pace-setting church in southern California. I was blessed to serve under the dynamic leadership of a gifted, successful man of God. As my spiritual mentor, he taught me the practical side of ministry. He set before me an inspiring model of effective church management.

I knew God was grooming me for church leadership. I considered it my good fortune to serve as an assistant pastor at a church that was experiencing rapid growth. The Lord had provided a wonderful, real-life, hands-on setting for me to learn the ropes of how to grow a church. Each day was an absolute adventure!

The church was alive! So many good things were happening. People's lives were dramatically changed. Hope was born into the hearts of the hopeless daily. God's power transformed the impossible into the possible right before my eyes! It was exciting being part of a vibrant church.

My senior pastor instilled within me a positive attitude, a winning spirit and a confident conviction that God and I could not fail. I was certain my ministry would be successful. When the time came for me to take my own church, I believed that being a pastor was the greatest calling on earth.

Those three years deeply imprinted onto my spirit that this was the way a church should be. I determined in my heart to go out and build one like it. I found myself champing at the bit as I waited on the Lord for His appointment.

Our first church was pretty typical. Attendance and finance had been on the decline for some time. The facilities were adequate, but in need of repair. The members were nice people who were dreaming of better days. They were looking for a leader who could take them from stagnancy to growth.

I recall vividly the night my wife and I flew into town for our interview. It was mid-evening when our hosts arrived, late, at the airport. After we exchanged greetings and loaded our luggage into their car, they chauffeured us along dimly lit side streets of the city, through a section of town whose glory had long since departed, to the church. The foul odor from a sewage treatment plant filled the air along the way.

When we wheeled onto the property, our guides exclaimed, "There's the church!" I blinked a couple of times, then glanced at my wife. She looked somewhat bewildered. No lights illuminated the building against the black, wintry night sky. All we could make out was the shadow of a faceless structure.

So much for first impressions.

The next day, we toured the church parsonage. The decor was ten years behind the times. Huge holes dotted the grossly overworn, grass-colored carpet, giving the impression of craters in a lunar landscape. We did our best to dodge these dangerous depressions as we inspected our possible future home. The church leaders assured us they would improve the embarrassing eyesores before the next pastor moved in. I wondered why they had let the last minister live in those conditions.

The church building sat on a forty-acre tract of undeveloped land. When my feet first touched the property, the Lord gave me a vision. I saw in my spirit a seven-day-a-week, twenty-four-hour-a-day ministry center. I visualized warm-colored, brightly lit facilities beckoning people in. My spiritual adrenaline pumped and my heart pounded as I pictured tree-lined drives, gently splashing fountains, helpful parking attendants directing the overflow traffic, and friendly greeters manning the entrances.

Most importantly, I saw thousands of people. I envisioned a spiritual lighthouse where people could come anytime to meet with

God. Young and old. Rich and poor. All races. Hurting, searching, beaten-down people entering; smiling, joyful, hope-filled people exiting. God was calling me to that small midwest church.

We returned home to seek God's Will. In the natural, there were plenty of reasons to politely pass on this opportunity. Numerous negatives stood out like sore thumbs. But my heart was on fire! The outward shortcomings didn't matter. I knew God could change anything. I was ready to prove His promises. I felt prepared to assume the responsibility of working with the Lord to turn this church around.

The call came. We said yes. The movers loaded up our earthly possessions and headed east. We had a date with a dream.

Our pockets were empty, but our hearts were full of high hopes when the moving van pulled up to the parsonage.

It was one of those dog days of summer in the Midwest, the kind of August day when even playful puppies poop-out and plop themselves on the porch protesting the oppressive heat and humidity. Life slows to a snail's pace. The heat index blows the top off the thermometer.

Our new home didn't come equipped with air conditioning. As we opened the front door, we were greeted by a blast of super-heated air. It was hot. Horribly hot. The second story was steamy and stuffy. We cracked some windows and went to work. Sweat-drenched clothes and beet-red faces became the uniform of the day as we unpacked boxes and reassembled furniture.

Despite the tropical conditions, we had our entire house set up and fully functional within forty-eight hours, right down to every picture hanging in the perfect place. The natives may have been crawling, but we were running!

The sauna-like heat was unable to melt our enthusiasm. We were so excited we hardly noticed that the holey carpet was still in place.

Our excitement about pastoring our first church produced incredible energy. We were flying high on anticipation. There wasn't a minute to waste. After settling the family, I went to the church office. Entering the building, I felt like a little boy with a new bicycle. Today I was a pastor with his own church! They had even given me a key. Imagine that!

I was ready to take my shiny new bike for a spin. Stepping down the hallway, I slipped into the sanctuary. In the silence of that sacred place, I knelt at the altar and asked God to bless this church and it's rookie pastor.

I was confident we would have a fruitful ministry. Failure wasn't in my vocabulary. I planned on being successful. At age thirty-one, I was ready to charge hell with a water pistol if necessary! There wasn't anything the Lord and I couldn't do. I naively assumed that everyone in my church loved God, loved each other, would love their new minister, and would love reaching the lost.

I was prepared to be a great pastor who would lead these people to glory as we took our city for Christ. I believed everybody wanted to win. I was sure the church members would roll up their sleeves and make the sacrifices necessary to grow. I even expected them to work with smiling faces! Certainly change and growth would be welcomed. Appreciated. Applauded.

Our ministry took off like a rocket. Long hours of praying, planning, preparing, preaching, promotion and personal ministry to people paid off. Within nine months, the pews were packed. Offerings increased. Morale picked up. Members were excited about inviting their friends to services. The atmosphere was charged with expectancy! The Spirit was moving! The church had come alive!

Those were gratifying days. It was wonderful watching the Lord do His thing. The lost were being saved. The sick were healed. Captives were set free. Marriages were mended. Families were restored. People from all walks of life were falling in love with Jesus!

One of my early personal struggles as a young pastor of a growing church was how to handle the praise of the people. Things were going well. Church members expressed their appreciation to me. They told me how glad they were that God had sent me to be their pastor. They expressed their support for my leadership. They asked what was next, what they could do to help me carry out the dream.

I received pleasant notes. Lengthy letters praised my efforts. Some appreciative members took us out to dinner as a thank-you for a job well done. Others spoke highly of my ministry in the presence of their friends. Members bragged on their pastor out in the community. Once when we returned home from some much needed rest and relaxation, a hand-painted banner graced our garage door with the words "We Love You Pastor And Jo Ann."

The positive attention was great. I enjoyed it. I have to admit I liked being stroked. I have an ego like every other human being. Praise made me feel good. Important. Appreciated. Loved and needed. I relished in being recognized for doing a good job.

In my zeal, I interpreted the acclamation as approval. So I forged ahead. Taller mountains awaited conquest. I proceeded with some deeply held convictions that I had concerning Christians and the church.

I believed every Christian wanted to grow. Surely every child of God would want to mature and become everything the Lord wanted them to be. I thought every church wanted to grow after the pattern of the soul-winning churches found in the New Testament. Certainly every believer in Christ would want to reach the lost and would be thrilled when people were saved.

I was committed to church growth. I was prepared to lead the church to growth. What church wouldn't want to exchange empty nurseries for ones bursting with babies? Surely this church family would be excited about noisy young people coming on our campus in search of answers to life's questions. Wouldn't multiple services be welcomed so we could serve more people who needed the Lord?

I was convinced regular attendees would be more than happy to give up their parking places to visitors. Long-time church members would be glad to slide down the pew a couple of spaces to accommodate newcomers. Choir members would willingly step aside and welcome other soloists to share the spotlight on Sunday morning. Board members wouldn't mind stepping down for a season so others could serve in leadership positions. Sunday school classes would voluntarily surrender their rooms and shift to another space so growth could continue.

Success breeds success. Having done well, I was motivated to excel. Nothing seemed out of reach. I raced full-speed ahead pursuing that illusive prize of successful ministry.

But something happened on the way to the Promised Land. In the midst of the growth and victories, Satan launched a vicious attack against my leadership. Success came to a screeching halt.

Pastors understand they are engaged in spiritual warfare (Ephesians 6:10-20). Leaders are on the front line in the battle for souls. We expect opposition from the forces of darkness. Conflict with the world is predictable and inevitable if you're trying to do anything important for the Kingdom of God. Resistance from outside the church citadel comes with the territory. It's part of the fight. A united church can defeat the devil and push back the very gates of hell through the power of Jesus' name! (Matthew 16:18)

I experienced opposition from the community on several occasions. The wounds inflicted by unkind words, unfair representations and misunderstanding of my motives were painful. But I deflected these fiery darts of the enemy with the shield of faith. We were God's people. The victory was ours! I dealt with the world as graciously as possible, then shook the dust off my feet and moved on with my mission.

I was, however, ill-prepared for the fierce opposition that arose from within the four walls of God's house. Satan's strategy was simple: divide and conquer. The enemy was very smooth and subtle in the beginning. Little things popped up. Personality conflicts. Differences of opinion. Style preferences. Rumblings through the church grapevine questioning my decisions.

Petty matters took center stage. Why was the bulletin cover different? Who authorized rescheduling the morning service a half-hour earlier? Why were the new bathrooms painted off-white instead of gray. Why did the nursery get new carpeting and not the junior high room?

Changes that came with growth rocked the boat. The status quo had been turned upside down. New ways threatened the "we never did it that way before" mindset. As the new pastor, I became the target of attack because I was the chief boat-rocker.

I couldn't understand what the big deal was. The church had called me because they wanted to grow. Growth means change. The old ways hadn't produced desired growth, so new ways were implemented. Result: we grew. Pretty simple to me. I had been asked to lead the church to growth. I was delivering what I had promised. We were growing. I was keeping my part of the bargain.

We all experience pain. Everybody gets hurt in some fashion as we weave our way through life. Pain is tough enough. But often the source of pain stings deeper than the wound itself.

It hurts to take a hit from a tackle-hungry, 240 pound linebacker as you violate his space on the football field. But at least the hit is expected. The pain goes away fairly soon. (Until the next collision!) But it's quite another thing to take a shot to the heart from someone you love, in a place you thought was a safe. That hit comes unexpectedly. And the pain remains for a long, long time.

Satan's shots through the saints were hard to handle. I started receiving unsigned letters criticizing my leadership. "Concerned" individuals invaded my office, lists in hand, demanding the changes they wanted. Nice notes gave way to nasty, anonymous notes written on the back of attendance cards. Third parties got involved in the middle of business that wasn't theirs.

Suddenly, it was open season on the pastor. Little things mushroomed into big things. Personality conflicts escalated into power struggles. Political maneuvering took priority over pursuing our mission. Hidden agendas played hide and seek in the board room. Confidences were broken. Private information mysteriously made it's way to the fountain of public consumption. The gossip holes were well-watered by self-appointed watchdogs who believed it was their religious duty to keep the pastor in line. My authority was challenged. My motives became suspect. My character was riddled by innuendo and misjudgment of my heart.

I was a novice senior pastor with high ideals and high expectations. My training had been top notch. I thought I knew how to manage a church. But studying warfare and engaging in battle are two different animals.

Heaven knows I made my share of rookie mistakes. I am of good old German stock, which means I can be head-strong and stubborn at times! I confidently believed my way was the best way. I wasn't always right, but youthful arrogance and selfish ambition blinded me to the virtue and value of being a humble servant of the Lord. God would graciously work in my heart to correct my errant attitudes.

I couldn't understand how so much hurtful behavior could be found in the house of the Lord. Many innocent folks were wounded. I found that very disheartening. It tore my spiritual guts out to think that people were being wounded in the one place where they should be finding healing.

Power struggles belong in corporate board rooms. Hostile takeovers are par for the course in the business world. Union halls are notorious for brawls between brothers who don't see eye to eye. Mud-slinging is the sport of politicians, not the people of God. None of this shameful conduct should be found in the Father's house.

I hold a high and holy view of the Church. She is the bride of

Christ. She is to be spotless, without wrinkle. The church is a body of believers, a family of Christ's followers who are easily recognized as His because "of their love for one another" (John 13:35).

The church is a place that provides safety and protection from the harsh blows of life. A sanctuary. A refuge. A place to be healed, not hurt. A place of love, not hate. A place where people get better, not bitter. A place of giving, not taking. A place of submission and surrender, not self-promotion and selfish-ambition. Humble hearts, not proud ones. A place of unity, not division. Loyalty, not rebellion. Peace not war.

The war in our church produced countless casualties. I can only speak for this wounded warrior. Criticism cut my heart. Misunderstanding of my motives stung my spirit and slashed my self-confidence. Attacks on my character sliced gaping wounds in my self-esteem.

I felt like a person who had been jumped and stabbed repeatedly. With each wound, I bled emotionally. Cut, bleed. Slash, bleed. For a while, I managed to bandage the wounds.

I bounced back. I had some reserves to draw upon.

But the wounds got bigger and deeper. They bled profusely. Simple dressings no longer held back the gush of damaged emotions.

After five years of unceasing conflict, my emotional tank rested on "E." Leaving under pressure was the final blow that drained the last fumes of emotion and sucked the spiritual life out of my soul.

As pastor, the pain ran deep because the source was some of the sheep I shepherded. I can sense the sorrow in David's heart as he laments the fact that the wounds that hurt most came from those closest to him. In Psalm 55:12-14, he says his burden was heavy because men of his equal (brothers), his companions and familiar friends were who caused him trouble. He'd walked with them in God's house and had sweet fellowship together. Now they were at odds with him. Sweet fellowship turned sour.

I felt the same. How could it be that the sheep would strike out at the under shepherd God had sent to care for them?

Many times I walked the forty acres and wept before the Lord. I cried out to my Heavenly Father, wondering why brothers and sisters were at each other's throats. Why couldn't we love one another? Surely someone could hoist a white flag, negotiate peace, and then we could move on in ministry together.

During lonely hours of private prayer on the back side of the church property, I wrestled with God. I couldn't understand what was happening.

The majority of the church members were good people. Caring. Devoted to Christ. A few of them got caught up in the "feeding frenzy" concerning my leadership. But they didn't mean to create problems. Their intent was innocent. They got swept away in the current of conflict that wound its way through our fellowship.

It grieved me to be separated in spirit from those who really didn't understand what was happening. It hurt me to not be able to understand why they didn't have the courage to stand up and support their pastor.

Another group angered me. Their intent was far from innocent. They were antagonists. They were bent on control. Some were long-time, well entrenched church bosses. Others were spiritual drifters. Disruptive rovers who church-hopped, looking for a place of power to promote their personal agenda. I was frustrated and infuriated with the wolves in sheep's clothing. They were crushing my spirit, dashing my dream, and dividing my church.

Some days were so painful that I all but ran out of my study to the secret place to meet with the One who I was certain would understand what I was going through.

Pastors are posed with a real dilemma when they're hurting. Where do they go for help when their personal pain is overwhelming? Church members aren't a viable option. They expect the pastor to be a spiritual Rambo! Reverends can put to flight a whole army of demons with a flick of their faith. Ministers can conquer any crisis. Everybody knows pastors don't get sick, never need a day off, have perfect families, and don't have problems like other people do.

Isn't that right?

Members don't understand the unique stresses pastors and their families face.

Leaders who do share their needs within the church body when they are going through trials run the risk of members taking sides. Factions form and the feud invariably expands. They also run the risk of being perceived as weak.

Weak. That terrible little four-letter word that none of us want to admit is part of human life.

What will the people think if the pastor is perceived to be falling apart? The pastor must be the Rock of Gibraltar. No matter what storms crash in on the congregation, they expect the pastor to say "peace be still" and calm the sea.

When the battle was fiercest and I hovered on the brink of personal collapse, an incident took place that shattered all hope of help from inside the church. I needed some time off. I was worn out emotionally and spiritually. I shared with a brother that I didn't think I had the strength to preach on Sunday. He patted me on the back and said, "Pastor, you have to be strong for us. We need you behind the pulpit to keep us pumped up." How could I possibly keep them pumped up when all my tires were flat?

Though I kept up a good spiritual front, I was falling apart on the inside. I was disappointed. My dreams were dying. I felt as though I'd been bushwhacked in the house of God. A spiritual buzz saw was carving up me and my ministry.

The revival train had derailed.

I felt defeated. My faith began to falter. I began to wonder if God knew what was happening. Heaven seemed so silent. I pleaded with my Maker to answer my prayer for help.

My heart was torn. I was disgusted with those who were dividing the church. I loved my opponents as brothers, but I hated what they were up to. I believed better of them. I held out for a change of heart, hoping against hope for a cessation of hostilities. But that beastly black cloud that had settled over our fellowship just got darker and darker.

Disappointment was my constant companion. I had been taught that the people would get behind the pastor's vision. Own it as their own. Help make it happen. I envisioned the saints fanning the flames of the dream with their enthusiastic support.

Instead, at almost every significant turn, there stood one of Satan's sentries, armed with wet blankets. Each time the revival fire flared up, someone would toss a sopping-wet cover on the flames. Wet blanket here. Wet blanket there. Wet blankets everywhere. Smothering the fire burning in my spirit.

Disillusionment stalked me. Church wasn't supposed to be like this. I was experiencing a total reversal of my expectations. Gratifying, glory days had turned gut-wrenching and grief-filled.

The balloon had burst. Pieces of a once respectable ministry now lay scattered at my feet.

While David was King of Israel, his adversaries forced him out of the palace and pursued him to kill him. Out of the depths of desperation, with no other place to turn, he cried to the Lord:

> *To Thee, O Lord, I life up my soul; O my God, in*
> *Thee I trust. Do not let me be ashamed; do not let*
> *my enemies exult over me.*
>
> Psalm 25:1-2

When his woes only worsened, his humanity got the best of him. David's prayer shifted from "Don't let me be ashamed," to "Go get them, God!"

> *Contend, O Lord, with those who contend with me;*
> *fight against those who fight against me. Take hold*
> *of buckler and shield, and rise up for my help.*
>
> Psalm 35: 1-2

Fight them Lord! Rise up and help me. Take care of those rascals.

When Heaven's forces still didn't seem to be making headway, David ascended to a higher level of lament and implored the Lord to wipe them out!

> *Behold, God is my helper; the Lord is the sustainer*
> *of my soul. He will recompense the evil of my foes;*
> *Destroy them in Thy faithfulness.*
>
> Psalm 54:4-5

Track them down. Squash them under your Almighty foot. Erase their memory from the face of the earth!

I had studied those Scriptures before and wondered how this guy who was 'a man after God's own heart" and "the apple of His eye" could pray like that. Now I was starting to get a feel for it!

I had been raised to believe the guys in white win. But no matter what I did, black Bart was taking the town. At my wit's end, I screamed at God "Zap them! Nuke those turkeys, Lord! Can't you see that they're tearing up your church? If nothing else, I'd be much obliged if you would beam them to some galaxy far, far away!"

I found myself spending time searching those sections of Psalms where David sic'd God on his enemies. I wanted to be sure to pray biblical prayers! I came across Psalm 59:10 that inspired me with fresh hope for better days:

My God in His loving kindness will meet me;
God will let me look triumphantly on my foes.

Triumph! It struck a responsive chord in my battle-weary spirit. A legion or two of angelic warriors sent to wipe out my opponents would be just dandy. I was tired of being trampled by my foes.

But God didn't answer my go get 'em — take care of them — get them out of my life petition. I was praying in the wrong direction. I needed to triumph over another foe. I wanted God to work on them. God wanted to work on me.

An unholy war in the house of God set the stage on which the most important drama of my life would be played out. During the desolate days when my spirit dried up and I lost sight of what life and ministry is all about, the Lord moved to rescue this heartsick soldier.

But before I found healing, I passed through a valley of pain I never knew was possible. From disappointment, discouragement, and disillusionment, I sank into despair, defeat, and finally to an enemy that threatened my very life. Depression.

This formidable, frightening foe mocked the wounds inflicted in the house of God.

Chapter 2

A Nightmare Named Depression

My heart throbs, my strength fails me, and the light of my eyes, even that has gone from me.

Psalm 38:10

My resignation marked the end of one fight and beginning of another. The battle for the church was over. The smoke cleared. I was out. Someone else would take my place. Little did I know that I would now face the fight of my life.

My duel with depression started when I returned home from church, shed my suit, and realized that I was a minister without a ministry. I wouldn't be preaching next Sunday. No more salary after sixty days. We would have to move out of our home in the middle of winter. Cold, hard facts hit me head-on. What could I say to my wife and children, who were waiting for me in the family room?

I looked in the mirror for a long time, trying to summon the courage to tell my loved ones it was over. Staring back at me was a dejected figure, stripped of dignity and self-respect. Shame and humiliation perched on my slumping shoulders. Fear tormented me. Questions I had no answers for sent tremors of terror through my heart. When would I preach again? How would I support my family? What would we have to do to survive this unexpected transition?

I was numb. Shocked. Could this really be happening to me? Surely this whole scenario was just a bad dream. Soon I would wake up from this nightmarish slumber and the sun would be shining. A new, pain free day would have dawned. Confidence, strength, and togetherness would be mine. I would be in control of my world again, in touch with the things that made me who I was.

But the sun didn't shine. It hadn't even risen. Rays of hope disappeared over the darkening horizon. Somebody else enjoyed their warmth.

Depression is an awesome adversary. As a counselor, I had witnessed despair descend upon others and had done my best to console and comfort those captured by this crippler of healthy emotion. But I had never personally experienced it's paralyzing power. Now something unfamiliar to me was happening.

I found myself unable to keep despondency's black clouds at bay. In the past, I had handled emotional hits better than most. People close to me were amazed at how speedily I rebounded, regrouped, and pressed on. God and I could conquer anything! There was no way this proud, self-sufficient servant of the Lord was going down in defeat to an emotional upheaval.

But this time I was in for a big surprise. Depression became a personal foe. It kicked in the door of my emotional defense system. Past "fix-it-formulas" now failed. My ten easy steps for defeating depression weren't even getting me to first base.

I was scared because I wasn't me. I didn't like what I was feeling. I was adrift on a sea of uncontrolled emotions. Wave after wave of denial, disbelief, anger, fear, sadness and sorrow rolled over me.

I felt like a sailor trapped in a sinking submarine. The watertight seals blown, workspace flooding fast, he expends all his strength struggling to keep his head above the invading sea. Water keeps rising. The air pocket, his only hope of survival, grows smaller and smaller. He'll drown unless he's rescued.

Like rising water, depression kept coming. I cried. I prayed. I screamed. I spoke God's Word. I took authority over the devil. I did everything I knew to do. I expected relief. None came. My best shots didn't stop despair's advance. My emotional air pocket was collapsing.

For the first time in my life, I couldn't cope. My ministry lay in ruins. My self-esteem was in shambles. The three most important people in my life anxiously awaited me down the hall. They would be watching for that familiar bounce in my step that signaled we would weather this storm and be all right. But there would be no bounce this time.

The parsonage was only four blocks from the church. So close, yet so far away. The emotional confusion I was experiencing was disturbing. My heart was engaged in a titanic tug of war. On one hand, I desperately wanted to be at the church as I had daily for five-and-a-half years. On the other hand, I couldn't bear the thought of seeing the place where I had given so much of myself.

The night I drove over to the office to pack up my library, I chose to go after dark. I wasn't sure how I would handle running into someone from the church.

As I turned into the parking lot, the headlights shined on the spot where my name...*used to be.* It had only been a few days, yet my name had been scratched off the church sign. Just like that — gone! Gazing at that blank space, I felt erased. Just a memory. Forgotten.

Boxes packed, files collected, I snuck home feeling like a man without a country.

The isolation began. A congregation that once welcomed us, was now divided and in a state of shock. The church had, in reality, become two churches. There were those who were for us and those who were against us. Those who wanted us out worked hard, pushed the right buttons, and got their way. Those who wanted us to stay waited too long to fight, and watched us leave. Those who supported us grieved. Those who succeeded in forcing us out gloated. We grieved over both groups.

In the midst of the hurt and confusion, both gloaters and grievers left us alone. Our friends didn't mean to desert us. Some of them just didn't know what to do. But we needed loved. We felt abandoned in our hour of sorrow.

Isolation is difficult for people persons. As pastor I thrived on interacting with others. Suddenly, we were cut off. Few familiar faces came to the door. The phone seldom rang. Strong shoulders to cry on weren't available.

There were no hugs, no angel of mercy to comfort a family in mourning. We became outcasts. Exiled to a prison of personal pain. Shipwrecked and stranded on an island of agony.

Depression tortures it's victims by dragging them into the past. As I sat in our home trying to put the pieces of our life together, today was overshadowed by yesterday. My mind rewound and replayed yesterday's tapes. The spirit-piercing words that had been said against us, and the shameful deeds that had been done to us, kept playing over and over again like broken records. Mercilessly, they drove the dagger of despair deeper and deeper into my heart.

I observed an injured robin one day in the woods behind our home. His right wing was damaged, bent and hanging limp by his side. He was on the ground but his heart was in the sky.

I watched him as he took a couple of steps and then thrust himself skyward. He wasn't airborne very long. His broken wing just wouldn't flap. He slammed to the ground, tumbling in the tall grass.

But this brave little bird was determined to give it another try. Birds are born to fly. Instinct commands them to flap their wings and soar into the sky. He taxied down the weed-infested runway, getting up a head of steam that should have propelled him into the stratosphere. He took off, even went a little farther this time. But the result was the same. He crashed to the earth. Grounded.

Poor bird. I wanted to rush to his aid, lay hands on him, pray for healing and see the lame fly! Even though he wanted to fly, and robins are supposed to fly, he couldn't. His damaged wing needed mending. This gutsy creature needed time out for healing.

God's people are meant to soar, too. My favorite soaring verse in the Bible is found in Isaiah 40:31:

> *Those who wait on the Lord will renew their strength; they will mount up with wings as eagles. They will run and not be weary, they shall walk and not faint.*

My spirit has always responded well to the Holy Spirit's invitation to soar on the high places with God. I was flying when my wings were broken. Soaring on to success. And even though my wings had been clipped, I wanted to fly again.

Driven by desire and necessity, I accepted a position as pastor of a church in Baton Rouge, Louisiana. Prior to moving, I took Jo Ann and my then four-year-old daughter to the airport. They were going ahead to secure housing. We hugged and said good-bye. They boarded the plane. I waved to them through the terminal window, walked away, and wept.

What was happening? There I was out in public, sobbing uncontrollably. A tremendous surge of sadness sprang up from deep inside. People watched me as I staggered out of the airport. It didn't matter. I couldn't stop the flow of emotion.

For nearly eight weeks, I had done my best to hold back the

tears. But now the dam had burst. I could no longer restrain the raging river of pent-up feelings that filled my heart.

I was out of control! Frightened! My wife and little girl were on a plane destined for a strange city. They were going without me. What would happen to them there? What was happening to our family?

Reality hit me square on the jaw. We were really having to leave the place we called home. This wasn't a bad dream. We were actually moving somewhere else. We were really going to have to start all over again.

I realized as I returned to my car that my wings were indeed broken. I couldn't fly. Soaring was out. My heart was grounded. I was emotionally and spiritually crippled.

As I walked into the house that afternoon and surveyed the sea of unpacked boxes, nails where pictures used to hang, and a six-year-old boy sitting on his bed snuggling up with his favorite stuffed animal, something invaded my soul. A heaviness came over me.

I found myself unable to think clearly. Simple decisions became monstrous challenges. Life as I once knew it came to a standstill. I sat down and didn't move for moments that seemed like eternity.

Despair permeated every fiber of my being. I felt I was sinking deeper and deeper into a bottomless hole each day. Fear invaded our home, immobilized me. I lost all my energy. I couldn't get off the sofa. I felt as though I was carrying a 500-pound weight around my neck.

Thank God for a boy and a beagle puppy that depended on me. Caring for their needs forced me to get up.

Emotionally, I was free-falling without a parachute. I had no idea where I would land, or if I would even land at all. Even the Savior that I loved seemed far away. Was anybody out there who could rescue me before it was too late? I wasn't sure.

Days later, twinkling stars dotted the black, pre-dawn sky as I loaded my son Adam and our dog, Rusty, into the car to leave for Louisiana.

I reluctantly hugged our overnight hosts for the last time and, teary-eyed, started a trip that I wasn't sure I could complete.

As the street signs of familiar neighborhoods receded in the rear view mirror, I felt displaced. What was I doing in my Chevrolet with my boy and dog, fleeing the town I had dreamed of winning to Christ?

I'm not blessed with a good sense of direction. I'm one of those guys who can get lost on his own driveway if conditions are just right. I can become all turned around without even trying. Just ask my wife. It amuses her to see her highly-educated husband unable to remember which way is north. I enjoy traveling with Jo Ann because I know when she's on board, we'll at least find our way back home!

Yet here I was setting out on a thousand-mile journey down unknown highways without my trusted navigator. And the spunky, red-haired, blue-eyed boy sitting in the back seat, looking forward to seeing his mommy and sister, was counting on his daddy to take him to his new home. Depression became so intense I could barely hold on to the steering wheel.

This trip spelled fun for my son. Life for six-year-olds is a never-ending adventure. He pleaded with me, as only little boys know how, to stop at every resting place — especially the ones with junk food. Like all good fathers, I gave in. He was in his glory devouring Doritos, crunching away on Kit-Kats, gobbling Gummie Bears, and washing everything down with Dr. Pepper.

The journey was far from fun for me. An unwanted exodus was more like it. I felt like an exile. Banished. A refugee, fleeing to who-knows-where; heading to a place I might like to visit, but not live. A beast called rejection had run me out of town.

I had left my heart in Michigan. My dream, now dead, was buried in some dirt behind a church building. I hadn't even been allowed to visit the graveside to grieve.

My grief became overwhelming. As the driving rain drenched each long, lonely mile we traveled, my heart overflowed with sorrow, and tears of despondency spilled down my face.

Our trip required one overnight stop. We found a suitable roadside motel, called it a day, and turned in for the night. The next morning we packed and prepared to continue our journey.

When I took the dog out back, it was raining hard. Suddenly, from out of nowhere, a pack of wild dogs charged us. I was terrified for my son and pet. The protector in me knew it was fight or flight time. Rusty, Adam and I were no match for this marauding band of predators. I grabbed Adam, held on for dear life to Rusty's leash, and ran to the car as fast as my feet could fly. Just as we scrambled into the car, our would-be assailants slammed, growling, into the doors, visibly disappointed that they had not taken a bite out of our hide. We were soaked and shaken, but safe.

It took a moment for me to gather my wits; then we pulled away from the motel, the preying dogs no longer a threat to our well-being.

The incident set loose memories of another predator. I had been attacked in Michigan. My character and reputation had been attacked by a pack of misguided people. Thoughts of the assaults haunted me as I drove down the road. I could hear their bitter barking. I felt the terror of their taunting. They had taken bites out of my emotional flesh. I fought for a time, but ultimately had to flee. Though I had left my adversaries behind, as we headed down the highway I did not feel safe. I still felt threatened. My wounds were open. My heart was hemorrhaging.

Only by the grace of God did I make it to the Wal-Mart parking lot where we met Jo Ann and Stacy. This should have been a happy day. Reunion. Hope of a new beginning. The next step in our service for the Lord. When my wife saw my face, she knew something was wrong. My heaviness of heart was visible.

I had quit fighting, surrendered to something we could not put our finger on. We had never been down this emotional road before. Nor did we know what would be forthcoming in just a few days.

The people of our new church were very kind, good folks who showered us with Southern hospitality. They brought pizza and helped us unpack the moving van. Soon the truck was empty, the move complete.

For me, inner panic moved in with our belongings. A feeling of doom and gloom overshadowed our first day in our new home. Reality sunk in again. We had moved. This was permanent. Good bye Michigan, hello Louisiana. There was no going back. All hope of reconciliation vanished as the moving van drove away.

What would I do now? I wasn't ready for a new ministry. I was still mourning the last one. I didn't want to say hello. I was afraid of Baton Rouge. It represented a new beginning I wasn't equipped to handle.

I found myself withdrawing from people. I didn't want to be in public. I felt everyone was staring at me. I was sure they knew I had failed — a huge scarlet "F" must have been flashing across my forehead like a brightly-lit neon sign.

We live in a throw away society. If someone or something doesn't work anymore, is out of style, doesn't agree with us, or doesn't entertain us anymore, we chuck it. Spouses, children, employees, leaders, authority figures, men of God — all are subject to discard.

I had been rejected, and I felt like a reject.

Rejection hurts. One defense mechanism against rejection is withdrawal: If I retreat and hole up somewhere, you can't hurt me. If you can't find me, you can't reject me. Emotional hide and seek — I hide; you seek; and I pray you never find me.

Withdrawal had never been my thing. Up to this time it had been my style to initiate conversation with everyone I met. My smile and warm greeting brought sunshine to others. My enthusiasm for life had always prompted me to interact with people. No more. I now found myself in unfamiliar territory. I was afraid of people. Distrustful. Insecure in the presence of others.

I didn't want to talk with anyone. I went to the grocery store at times I knew few people would be shopping, because someone might ask how I was doing. If I said "great," as I always had, I would be lying. If I told them the truth, I would fall apart for sure. That being the case, I was certain they would think ill of me, and withdraw. So I settled for "fine." I'm fine. Just fine.

You gotta be kidding! How could I say I was fine when my emotional and spiritual insides had been ripped out? How could I say I was fine when my soul was dying a slow death? How could I say I was fine when I was afraid to live, and at the same time, afraid to die?

No, I was far from fine. I was in big-time trouble. I rejected myself. Therefore, I walked in terror that others would reject me, too.

I assumed my duties as pastor. Gifted, skilled, and very good at what I do, I knew how to grow and prosper the work of God. I'd done it once, already. But now, I didn't seem to have a clue about how to get a small, struggling church off the ground.

Feelings of frustration overwhelmed me. Energy for the simplest ministerial task was nonexistent. Fear of failure sapped all of my strength and vitality. Deep down, I worried that this ministry might end up like the one I had left behind.

Depression is an intimidating intruder that forces it's way into every facet of your life. It profoundly affects your thinking and feelings. You view things differently, as though you have been given a pair of glasses tinted with despair.

In the past I had always enjoyed going to the church office. My wife's tasteful decorator's touch had transformed my study into a warm, comforting, safe haven for searching souls.

I'd witnessed miracles in the office. God had moved in powerful ways as people opened their hearts to His love and grace. Tears of repentance. New birth. Shouts of joy. Hugs of reconciliation. Healings. Deliverances. Victories. Laughter over the silly things of life. Serious prayer that touched the throne of God. It was wonderful watching the hand of the Lord at work. Though I dealt daily with things eternal, the office was a joyful place.

Those first few days in Baton Rouge I went to my new office hoping to establish another happy working environment. But each day, after I'd been there for about an hour, the crying would start. Tears flowed for no apparent reason. I'd sit at my desk, trying to compose myself, but with only me in the office, the quiet became deafening. The walls began closing in.

I'd phone Jo Ann. When she'd answer and find her distraught husband on the other end, it scared her.

It scared me. I was afraid to be alone. Even in God's house.

Throughout my ministry, the sanctuary had been a special place. I'd sneak into the auditorium, early and late, to be alone with my Savior. I could always go to the sanctuary, kneel before the Cross, and find help in time of need.

But as I prayed in this sanctuary, I found no peace. Before, it had been God and me. Now it was God, me — and depression.

The place of comforting had turned into a place of condemnation. The evil one's dark presence was powerful. It had infiltrated the holy place. The accuser hammered me with guilt. He tried hard to convince me I had failed. Satan even suggested my pain was punishment from the Lord.

My distorted view of what had happened hindered me from connecting with the Lord. I desperately wanted to run to God and be held in His loving arms. Yet I found myself pulling away from Him as depression brainwashed me into believing He no longer loved me.

I had always been a dynamo. Mr. Enthusiasm. A fireball with endless energy, able to get up and go no matter what. I could work circles around anyone. I could even work circles around my circles!

I was the kind of guy who, when he had a horrendous headache, went out and worked it off. I couldn't stand the thought of lying in bed with a throbbing head! Get up, get out, and do something is the motto of my life.

Yet one morning I woke up and I couldn't get out of bed. It blew me away. No matter how hard I tried, I couldn't crawl out of the covers. Worse yet, I didn't want to get up!

Anguish gripped my heart as I glanced out the bedroom window. Fear paralyzed me. I closed my eyes, clutched the blankets firmly and wished someone would announce that today had been canceled.

Then the sobbing started.

In our supposedly sophisticated society, we have perpetuated a life-limiting lie. We communicate to our young men, through words and actions, that it is not macho to cry. We put impossible pressure on our males.

As a result, most men resist the urge to cry at all costs. We can be hit on the shin with a 95 m.p.h. fast ball, writhe in excruciating pain, utter some not-so-righteous expletives, and not shed a tear. Curse — but don't cry. By all means, don't let anyone see a tear leak from that little hole God put in the corner of your eye. Be tough! Suck it up! Shake it off! Don't be a wimp!

Well, I cried. Bawled like a baby. Body-wrenching weeping. Hour after hour, rivers of tears streamed across the pillow. My grief glued me to the bed. Until then I hadn't known a person could cry unceasingly for days on end. Yet David wrote about weeping in Psalms 69:1-3:

> *Save me o God. For the waters have threatened my*
> *life, I have sunk in deep mire and there is no foothold.*
> *I have come into deep waters and a flood overflows*
> *me. I am weary with my crying; my throat is parched.*
> *My eyes fail while I wait for my God.*

I experienced what the Psalmist was saying. I too became "weary with my crying," my "throat was parched", and my "eyes failed as I waited for God." I was in deep waters — struggling to survive.

Jo Ann comforted me. She cradled and rocked me like a baby as I poured out a seemingly endless ocean of sorrow. It was humiliating to be totally out of emotional control and curled up like an infant in my wife's arms.

Jo Ann asked me why I was crying. It was hard for me to admit that I didn't know. The man who used to have all the answers didn't have any idea why he was overcome with such sadness.

My heart was like a saturated sponge. Something was squeezing the water out. There was so much! Would this deluge ever end?

Would my heart dry out? When would the day come when the sobbing would cease?

When I did manage to get up, I found myself sneaking around the family to beat it back to the bedroom. Assuming the fetal position under warm blankets provided a hideout from hurt. Warm. Secure. Protected.

At thirty-seven years of age, I was regressing. Trying to return to a place where pain had not reached me. I hoped curling up in a little ball would protect me from further pain. I just didn't want to hurt anymore.

Other strange things started happening. One afternoon I sat in a stupor, trying to figure out how to write a check. I had easily managed our money before. Now I was lost in a world of dollars and cents that made no sense to me. Another area of my life out of control.

Another afternoon, I ventured to the garage to organize the there-isn't-anyplace-to-put-this stuff from our move. I'm a neat freak. Bona-fide, obsessive-compulsive, a place for everything and everything in it's place kind of guy. Disorder disturbs me. If it's messy, I mess with it until it's tidy.

I approached the job with great hopes of achieving noticeable improvement. An unusual thing happened. Nothing happened. I stood immobile in the center of the garage floor.

Jo Ann came out to check on the progress. She inquired as to what I was doing. I grumbled some mumbo-jumbo. She attempted to motivate me to action. No response. Numerous verbal efforts proved fruitless. It was evident I was out of it. Her reservoir of patience exhausted, she tossed one of Adam's nerf balls toward my head. (I thank God there are no bowlers in our family!) The soft missile sailed past me. I didn't budge.

My wife possesses a sincere, positive faith and an unconquerable, optimistic spirit. She believed that I would come out of this valley and start climbing the peaks again. She had married me because of my strength of character. She had leaned on me and my self-confidence for years. She thought I had it all together.

That day in the garage convinced her that this problem I had wouldn't go away with two aspirin and a good night's sleep. She had never seen me like this before. She began to realize that her husband needed help. Much later, she told me that it really frightened her to see me weak and out of control.

For four weeks I tried to proclaim the Good News. Each Sunday was a struggle just to get to the church, let alone stand before people as God's spokesman. Walking through the sanctuary door required a Herculean effort. Unbelievably, the church, the place I loved, had become hostile territory, a painful reminder of rejection and abandonment.

I sensed no anointing as I stepped behind the pulpit. It seemed as if a veil hung between the people and preacher. A thick, black curtain cut us off from each other. I couldn't open the dark drapes that separated me from the sheep. There was a heavy curtain between God and me, too.

With each successive week, the strength to preach diminished. I was exhausted before I started. Words came out, but they were void of visible impact. I felt embarrassed, ashamed that I could not preach the Word of God with power.

Jo Ann knew that preaching is my life, that I love sharing God's Word more than anything. In the past, I had told her that she would know I was in trouble if the day ever came when I was unable to preach.

Then it happened. A minister's worst nightmare! One day I could not preach. I shut my Bible and shuffled off the platform. As far as I was concerned, I was done as a preacher. If a preacher can't preach, what's left? It was over. Finished. I had now failed in my life's calling.

I had lived in several regions in the United States, but nothing like Cajun country. Although I didn't realize it then, God in His wisdom, had sent us to Louisiana for a specific purpose. He put us in a place where the healing process could begin. Baton Rouge became the intensive care unit for a family in critical condition.

He graciously provided a location for us where it was okay, and safe, to unload our pain. He even supplied a house that didn't have neighbors on either side. The privacy proved invaluable as we started our journey to inner healing.

The Lord had His reasons for sending us to Louisiana, but I didn't like Baton Rouge. It wasn't my idea of paradise! After the beautiful northlands of Michigan, I felt we'd been banished to the wilderness.

The thought of alligators, water moccasins, copperhead snakes, and who-knows-what-else slithering beneath the slimy, brown water of the bayous sent shivers up and down my spine!

Emotionally, I saw myself sinking in a swamp of scary feelings. Everything within hinted at danger. I was certain calamity crouched around every corner. Who knew what was lurking in the darkness waiting to get me!

The people were pleasant, but different. Their language contained jargon I didn't understand. They ate things like jambalaya, crawfish, and gumbo. The sweltering heat and oppressive humidity didn't seem to phase them. How they could eat blackened fish with cayenne pepper an inch thick on those hellishly hot days baffled me!

Nature's own set of novelties caught my attention — creeping things that gave me the creeps. Bugs as big as B-52 bombers buzzed by my head whenever I dared to stray outside. Truck-sized roaches, were everywhere; I had to watch where I walked so I didn't squish them under my sandals.

Fire ants let me know that little things can carry a big wallop when you step on their house. Swamp moss hanging from towering cypress trees, twisted vines dangling overhead, green, musty-smelling mildew, and the ever-present, oily odor of the refineries provided a backdrop that intensified my already panicky disposition.

We did our best to become acquainted with our new town. Not long after our arrival, we took a tour of the sites. One of the main attractions is the state capitol, the tallest capitol building in the country. Elevators whisk visitors to the top of it's thirty-four stories. On a clear day, you can see for miles from the open-air observation deck. The view is breathtaking.

The Mississippi River, in all of its meandering majesty, gently rolls by on its way to the Gulf of Mexico. Steam-powered riverboats, proudly paddling by, provoke images of southern belles and gentleman gamblers of another era.

Lush vegetation covers the landscape like a soft, green blanket. Magnificent, century-old magnolias in full bloom, Civil War monuments to Confederate heroes, and nostalgic plantation houses restored to their original grandeur, paint a picture-postcard setting.

In so many ways, a beautiful place — unless you're depressed. Depression doesn't take a vacation. An uninvited and unwelcome traveling companion, it goes where you go.

Depression even accompanied me to the observation deck twenty-seven stories above ground.

My view from the top turned from terrific to terrifying. While my family cruised around the observation deck, oohing and aahing, I battled with a messenger of death.

Something urged me to jump from the building. A force coaxed me to leap. "Go ahead," a seductive voice whispered in my ear. "You know you've been thinking about it. Why not get it over with? Nobody knows you. Here's a quick and easy way to end it all."

A dark presence nudged me to the edge. Only six short inches separated me from certain death.

As I peered over the restraining rail, the people on the marble steps below were tiny specks. The longer I looked, the closer the concrete came. I grabbed the safety rail, white-knuckled. My flesh was poised to jump. My spirit frantically resisted. Time stood still. I froze, frightened to move even an inch.

I had to gain control. If ever I needed to be master of the situation, now was the time. But I was being manipulated. My thoughts were stuck on taking my own life. At the lowest point of my life, atop the highest building in the city, I was tempted to leap to my death.

It troubled me tremendously to be entertaining thoughts of suicide. How could a man who loved life, lived life, and preached life become absorbed with thoughts of self-destruction?

As the battle raged in my mind, my son Adam darted around the corner, distracting me for one life-saving moment. I stepped back from the ledge. For the moment, death released it's icy grip on me.

Taking advantage of the break in the cycle of suicidal impulses, I gathered my family, hit the elevator button, then breathed a sigh of relief when the door opened on the ground floor. As we headed toward the parking lot, I looked over my shoulder at the towering edifice, wondering whether or not my encounter with death's messenger was over.

Satan sells a lot of lies when you're depressed. He distorts truth; falsehoods appear to be reality. He plays upon your fears. My greatest fear was to be out of control. I loathed the thought of failure. I wanted to please God. I craved His love, acceptance, and approval more than anything else.

I had always been a man of purpose, a self-starter with tons of drive. Consumed with God's mission for my life, I had always set my sight on a goal and pursued it with all my might. I seldom, if ever, drifted from the course I set. The debacle in Michigan threw a monkey wrench in my plans. I began to wonder and then I began to wander.

Each day I descended deeper and deeper into the abyss. Friends tried valiantly to perk me up. I followed each one's advice. I did what I thought and hoped would open the parachute that would stop this frightening free-fall. I tried and tried, but I couldn't locate the ripcord. I had fallen so far and for so long that I was certain nobody could ever stop me.

Finally, one Sunday afternoon I was in the kitchen alone battling once again with the messenger of death. Despair was winning this round. I was accepting the invitation, actually formulating suicide plans.

I was ready to write the note, step into my car and drive to the foreboding building that kept calling my name, drawing me like a magnet.

I had convinced myself that I was even out of God's reach, that He had more important matters to attend to. Kingdom work had to go on. I was on my own. There was no one to care for my soul.

Depression had deceived me into believing my Savior had abandoned me; that God had taken a hike. That He was nowhere to be found in my hour of deepest need.

But God doesn't abandon His children. He never fails or forsakes them (Hebrews 13:5). He is faithful to His promises to stick with His kids (Psalm 55:22), especially when their hearts are broken and they're in trouble:

The Lord is near to the brokenhearted. And saves
those who are crushed in spirit.

Psalm 34:18

I thought God hadn't heard my cry for help. He had; I just didn't know it. Depression had worked its way between me and my Heavenly Father, obscuring my view so much, I lost sight of the One who loves me, and of His promises. But He didn't lose sight of me! He had a great plan of rescue and restoration!

God used some dear friends to save me from self-destruction. Ken Cochrane, one of my very best friends from way back, had spoken to me on the phone a few days earlier. He sensed then the deep despair surrounding me.

That Sunday morning, as he stood before his congregation to preach, he burst into tears. Excusing himself, he went to the basement of the building and cried out to God. The Holy Spirit told

Ken I was in serious trouble, near to ending my life. Ken prayed and returned to his pulpit, where he poured out his burden for me. The people joined him in praying for my protection and deliverance.

After the service, Ken phoned my mentor, John Maxwell. He shared with John that I was in deep waters. Ken's action literally saved my life. His sensitivity to the Spirit of God was the difference between life and death.

John called while I was sitting in the kitchen making my plans. He talked with me, then Jo Ann. He told my wife I had a few "good" hours left, and that she needed to get me to a hospital as soon as possible. I rejoice in friends who love you enough to intervene in times of trouble. Intervention is never easy. But love requires that we respond to cries for help.

Things moved swiftly. Phone calls were made. Some brothers in Christ came over to help us decide on a course of action.

Even as they talked about how to help me, I was afraid this day would be my last on earth. I was lost in an emotional fog. I couldn't help myself out of the pit. Jo Ann didn't have the resources either.

In the end, the decision was heavy, but not difficult. I was in grave personal danger. Depression had pounded me into a pile of emotional rubble. There would be little left to salvage if we didn't act soon.

We agreed that I would voluntarily commit myself to the care of a psychiatric hospital the next day. I went to bed that night wondering what that decision would mean.

When Monday morning arrived, I dressed and packed a bag. We took the kids to school and I kissed them good-bye. Then Jo Ann and I went to Shoney's for brunch. I affectionately call this meal "the last breakfast."

We had no idea what lay ahead of us. What would happen? How long would I be hospitalized? What would be the consequences? What did the future hold for us?

There we sat. Two thirty-something adults. Very much in love, very much in trouble. We looked tenderly into each other's eyes hoping and trusting God for better days.

Chapter 3
Face to Face With Failure

A joyful heart makes a cheerful face, but when the
heart is sad, the spirit is broken.
                                    Proverbs 15:13

I had been in psychiatric institutions before to visit patients who requested a pastor. This time was different. I was the patient. I was emotionally ill. Instead of giving care, I would be receiving it.

None of the counseling courses I had taken in seminary taught about pastors and depression. The implication was, ministers don't get depressed! With the title "pastor" comes a lifetime guarantee of immunity to emotional burnout. Theological degrees are backed by unconditional, unlimited bounce back ability to resurrect oneself from discouragement in thirty minutes or less. Pastors are the Clark Kents of religion. When people are in trouble, the pastor climbs into the confessional booth, changes into his clergy garb, and out pops Super pastor, ready to rescue another perishing soul! Mission accomplished, he goes home and collapses on the couch, another notch on his ministerial belt.

So why doesn't it feel like a victory? Overworked, over-whelmed, and overrun pastors must keep on keeping on, no matter how they feel. Depression isn't allowed. Church boards don't authorize pastors to experience bouts of melancholy. It's not in the job description.

Even so, it happens.

Pastors suffering various degrees of depression serve Sunday after Sunday in churches across the country. Depression is nonde-nominational. No pastor is immune to its devastating effects.

But we don't call it depression. We clergymen dignify our low times by saying spiritual-sounding things like" "I'm just under attack from the devil. Pray for me." That's true, but not all the story. Or how about this familiar line of clergy rationalizing: "It's just a heavy time of year. Budget committee. Christmas pageant. Election of officers." Who are we trying to kid anyway? Pastors' ministry plates are loaded all year long!

Then there are those pseudo-heroic lines we use to hide our holy lies. When we're disappointed with the growth of the church we say things like, "Oh no, I'm not discouraged. Everything's fine. This is just a phase in our congregation's life. Plateau time. A rest period from our last growth spurt. (Even though they've have been resting for five years!) No big deal. I know I look worn out. A couple of rounds of golf will perk me right up."

When it comes to depression, there's a double standard in the church. If members become despondent, we call out the troops; surround the downcast-in-spirit with lots of love; get them in counseling; relieve them from their church duties during their time of distress. They're hurting people who need help.

Not so for pastors. Someone somewhere, sometime, somehow, decided pastors and their families cannot become emotionally spent. Those who do suffer censure.

Parishioners feel good and secure when their leaders are on the sunny side of Proverbs 15:13. Members expect that "joyful heart" and "cheerful face" from their leaders. But "sad hearts" and "broken spirits" elicit another response — something is wrong with the pastor.

Love seems to be in short supply when the pastor's depressed. If he discusses it with someone, he's exhorted to fast and pray, confess the Word, make sure all of his relationships are right so the anointing will return and the cloud of despair will disappear into thin air.

Instead of asking how they can help their leader, the church usually ignores the pastor in pain. The troops aren't mustered and called to duty.

Counseling for clergy is considered an admission of weakness. God forbid that a man of the cloth might experience a "weak" time in his life. Time out and time off to seek appropriate help is out of the question.

I was too numb to be afraid as we walked through the clinic door. A cordial staff person escorted us to a conference room for my evaluation.

They determined I posed a genuine threat to myself. We signed some papers and, with the stroke of a pen, I surrendered my freedom and submitted to their care.

A ward nurse took Jo Ann and I upstairs. The long, baby-blue corridors seemed to stretch for miles. I can still hear the sound of the heavy oak double-door closing behind us. One door can really change your day. This door shut out one world and ushered me into another.

As we stepped off the elevator onto the second floor, a warning flashed in my mind: You are about to enter a restricted area where your life will no longer be under your control.

I hesitated for a second, but it was too late to turn back. Parkland hospital would be my home for thirty days.

I was reminded of a time when I was in seminary. I had served as an assistant pastor for three country churches located about an hour's drive from our home. The road we traveled wove it's way through vintage Kentucky countryside. Small mom-and-pop farms dotted the scrub-oak covered rolling hills. Framed by whitewashed fences, horses and cattle grazed on legendary bluegrass. Hefty hogs slopped in the mud, chickens scratched in the barnyards and hard-working farmers baled hay into huge, round cylinders.

We enjoyed our weekly trip through the eye-catching scenery. Each season staged it's special magic. Winter, spring, summer and fall found us in our Dodge Colt heading down the road to preach God's Word to some very wonderful country folk.

Our journey took us across the Kentucky River. The road descended to a gorge where a concrete bridge spanned the water-way. One wintry morning, we made our way across the bridge. Just as we reached the far side, the steering wheel spun out of my hands and I lost control of the car. We'd hit a patch of black ice. We hadn't seen it, but it was there. As we started to slide at the mercy of the ice, I told Jo Ann, "Here we go!"

Our "sleigh-ride" ended when we slammed into the bridge abutment. Thankfully, we escaped injury. Examining our vehicle, we knew our trip for the day had been terminated. The right front fender was wrapped around the tire. The car wouldn't move. We couldn't fix it. We had it towed to a repair shop where those who know what to do would restore our automobile to usefulness.

Now, as they checked me into the nurses station, I once again thought, "Here we go!" For thirty-seven years, I had cruised down the road of life, in control of my destiny. Then came the black ice. I never saw the failure of my ministry, and the subsequent depression, coming. I slid and crashed. My emotional fenders were crumpled, my tires locked up, and I was out of service.

I recall two distinct feelings when they placed the patient identification bracelet around my wrist. First a concern: How extensive was the damage and would they be able to repair it? Second, a desire: I really hoped I would drive again and re-enter the journey of life. For the moment, though, I wasn't going anywhere.

They took me to a small room where I was indoctrinated to the ward routine. I received a copy of the rules and code of conduct. A structured daily schedule was to be strictly adhered to. Morning status reports, individual and group therapy sessions, recreation, and meal times were all laid out for us. They searched my personal bag and confiscated sharp objects, double-edged razor blades, and a hair dryer with a long cord.

My wife and I were taken on a guided tour of the ward. A social worker led us to a large, square area called the community room. Patients' rooms were located on both sides of this "living-room" like space. Upon entering, I noticed the dense cloud of cigarette smoke hovering overhead and thought how difficult it would be to spend time in this atmosphere.

My gaze moved across the room. The television blared while some residents slouched on the sofas, soaking up the afternoon soaps. Another group of patients was playing games at a card table.

I was moved by some of the individuals I observed. Alone in a corner, a gray-haired gentleman worked a crossword puzzle. He could have been anybody's grandfather. He was a picture of isolation and loneliness.

An unkempt, middle-aged woman puffed on a cigarette and stared vacantly at the wall. She looked like "no one was at home."

A young man sat fidgeting with the newspaper. His hands shook. He seemed so frustrated.

A girl about eighteen years old paced frantically back and forth. She had lost her baby. She had been on suicide watch the day before. She paced and paced and paced. Like a caged animal, she retraced her steps over and over again. I wondered what was going on in her tormented thoughts.

As we headed down the hallway to my assigned room, another new patient was being transported on a gurney. She was curled up in a tight, fetal position. She was very well dressed but totally helpless. What happened to her that she would end up like this?

My roommate was lying flat on his back, lost in thought, when we entered the room. Pulling himself together, he rose, asked my name, and then asked what I was in for. Even though it was an innocent, normal question for the hospital setting, it threw me for a loop.

Why was I here? I knew I hadn't committed any crime. But "what are you in for" sounded like I had been sentenced for something. I managed to mutter the word "depression." I told him I was a preacher who had lost his church and lost himself.

At that moment, I came face to face with failure. Were all of these sad, broken-spirited people, including me, in here because we had failed? It made sense to me that if we had been successful, we would be out there, not in here. Soul-searching questions started surfacing: Where had I gone wrong? How had I failed? Did failing mean I was a failure?

Jo Ann and I spent a couple of minutes in the room alone. Privacy would be minimal. We talked about things at home that she needed to do. Soon, too soon, visiting hours were over. Hand in hand, my wife and I walked down the hall. As the elevator came into view, my heart chilled. She was going home. I was staying in the hospital.

Until now, Jo Ann had been by my side during this bout with depression. We had slugged it out together. There was comfort in fighting as a team. Now I would battle by myself. Who would I turn to when it hurt? Who would hold me close and assure me it would be all right? Who would listen? When I became frightened in the night, who would turn on the light?

It was difficult for me to let Jo Ann leave that first night. Not only would I be here alone, but she would be home alone. I should have been there for her. But I wouldn't.

My wife carried her own heavy load of personal pain. Hers was as significant as mine. My anguish had erupted and bubbled to the surface. Her hurt was still submerged. She had witnessed so much cruelty and ugliness. Her character had been maligned also. She'd watched her mate's dream turn into a nightmare. She'd been ejected from her home. She'd been forced to stand by helplessly as depression consumed her husband.

I worried about her. How was she handling this? Was she okay? Could she manage the day-to-day family responsibilities and carry the weight of my hospitalization as well? Was she embarrassed over our situation? Worried about our future?

I had this sick feeling in the pit of my stomach. I wasn't there for her. I was her husband. Protector. Provider. Spiritual leader. Companion. It was my job to tuck my three redheads in at night and secure the dead bolts. My role was to provide security and stability. But our whole life had fallen apart. My wife and children needed attention too. It troubled me to know that my family would be out there without me.

I watched her go. I had witnessed a lot of exits lately, but this one was a biggy. This was my beloved wife, my life's partner, God's gift of love to me. We were supposed to be together.

Failure and depression had deprived me of my ministry, my home, my friends, my children, and now my wife.

I walked back to my room very much alone.

My first meal at Parkland was memorable. That evening, when it was time to depart for the dining facility downstairs, I proceeded on my own. An aide stopped me in my tracks, and informed me we had to leave the ward as a group. Someone with a key would lead the patients through locked passageways to the cafeteria.

Imagine my shock. My life of independence, coming and going as I please, eating pretty much when I wanted, making my own decisions, was temporarily over. Now I couldn't even go to get a bite to eat without a keeper and a bunch of others in tow.

I resented being controlled. Sure, I needed help. I was unsteady and unstable. But something inside of me wanted to rebel. I wanted to stretch my wings. Be free! But I'd signed away my freedom when I entered the hospital. My choices were now being made for me.

That first night I was grateful for a sleeping pill. For a few hours, I escaped the eerie emptiness in my heart.

Upon awakening the next morning, the sea of sadness surrounding me seized my attention. A sense of sorrow permeated the ward. It was as if we had all just returned from a loved one's funeral. Everyone was grieving.

Each morning the daily routine began with the patients gathering in the community room. There were no smiling faces as we found our places for the morning status reports.

My fellow patients wore their pain on their sleeves. To me they looked like I felt inside — hopeless. The shepherd in me wanted to reach out and comfort the Good Shepherd's hurting sheep. I wanted to help them. Let them know somebody cared.

My heart said yes, but my head said no. I couldn't be the caregiver this time. I didn't have enough energy for myself, let alone anybody else. I knew from the very beginning of my stay that I was there for me. Maybe one day I would return for them. But at this moment in time, I was critical. It was touch and go. If I were to get better, I would have to zero in on me.

The charge nurse directed the status report session. One by one, we shared in our own words how we were doing.

It was interesting hearing what was going on inside the others. Some of the patients shared freely. They were open, honest, and to the point. You knew where they were coming from. Others shut down when their turn came. They closed the lid on their heart. No chinks in their defensive armor. They hurt so much they couldn't talk about it. They were afraid to let others see the real person.

Then there were those who tried to fake their feelings. You could tell when someone was trying to convince you they were all right when they weren't. It was like a game. I don't want you to know how I really feel because you won't like what I have to say, and you may not like me. If I tell you my true status, you'll hear how much I hate myself for being where I am. But I want you to like me. So I'll try to buffalo you. Let you think I am better than I really am.

This was their attempt to try and convince themselves they were okay. They were looking for a vote of confidence. Desperately needing someone to affirm them. Hopefully, if they could find some approval, they might lighten up on themselves. All of us were suffering from severely low self-esteem. Our sense of self-worth was shot.

I understood the game being played. I, too, wanted to be better than I was. I longed for others to accept me and find value in me as a person.

I sat in the session listening to status reports feeling increasingly threatened as my turn approached. What do you say on your first day? How open should I be? How much of my shattered soul should I bare? How would my report impact others for the day? What would the staff think if I wasn't having a particularly good morning?

What would they think if I told them how I really felt? I felt like a piece of human hamburger. Ground round. Beaten to a pulp.

I was so angry. Rage welled up inside. Resentment boiled when I thought how easily others had rejected me and abandoned me on the scrap heap of human wreckage. My thoughts were ugly.

I wanted someone to know how badly I hurt. I wanted to scream at the top of my lungs. "How could they do this to me? It's not fair. I don't deserve this."

All I could do was sit on the lid and not unleash the outrage I felt. In truth, everyone sitting in the circle wanted to scream. Life had not been fair. None of us deserved this. But we were too afraid to reveal the deep sense of failure that haunted our hearts. So we danced with each other. I won't let you know how I really feel as long as you don't let me know how you really feel.

But I'm not a very good dancer.

My feelings erupted and spilled over during my status report. I stumbled through my first public admission that I was in trouble and needed help. Thirty-five people now knew that this pastor was in crisis, struggling to survive. How humbling it was to confess that I didn't have a clue as to how to escape depression's grasp.

In a strange, yet real way, I felt more welcome and accepted by this group of wounded warriors than I did by people in the church who considered themselves whole, needing nothing, and beyond the grasp of emotional collapse.

Bless their hearts. There we were, each wrapped-up in our own world of hurt, absorbed with pain. Yet they felt for me. They sensed my deep discomfort. Personally and professionally I was devastated, mortally wounded by a double-barreled shotgun called failure. I felt I had failed in living and in the ministry.

They hadn't seen a man of God in this condition before. My presence raised a lot of questions in the days ahead. How did this happen to a pastor? Why did God allow it? Why hasn't he gotten better? How does a man of faith lose his way? Where is God for him right now? If a pastor can't handle a hit like this, how can I?

My unique situation provided an opportunity for my "temporary family" to see that men of God are human too. We aren't Incredible Hulks that never hurt. We're not immune to pain and suffering. We're far from perfect. We have real feelings. Our dreams can be dashed, hopes smashed, hearts broken.

They discovered that depression knocks on clergy and layman's door alike. The clergy gets sad. We cry. We get angry. Frustrated.

We laugh. We pout. We shout. We hope. We win. We lose. We like warm-fuzzies too! We ask questions. We even wonder about God sometimes. Pastors have fears. We worry. Rejection rips our hearts out. Betrayal and abandonment scares the daylights out of us, too. We're flesh and blood people who seek love, acceptance, and approval as much as the next guy.

I had been afraid that when my ward mates found out that I was a pastor, they would seek my counsel. I'd been terrified at the prospect of attempting to help a lost person find himself when I, myself, was lost. How can you give directions when you don't know where you are? How can you help someone find the way out when you don't even know where the door is? It's like the blind leading the blind; both fall into the ditch.

My fear was relieved by the sympathetic attitude shown me by the others. Sufferers understand suffering. They can relate to those undergoing trauma. There's an unspoken sharing of pain. They understand because they've been there. A strong bond of empathy motivated by love develops between fellow sufferers. Because they know pain, they feel the pain of others. Sufferers possess a kind of pain-radar that picks up on the anguish of others.

One element of our treatment program was group therapy. A counselor and six to eight patients met daily. I had already formed my impressions of group therapy — from Bob Newhart's show. I viewed the group process as no more than a humorous platform for divulging silly secrets and sharing the latest psychological shop-talk.

To me, people sitting in a circle spilling their emotional baggage resembled a "can-you-top-this-one" convention. I thought it was a big joke. How could anyone receive significant help in a setting where everyone dumped their garbage? What about privacy, dignity, self-respect? How could the heart heal in an environment where personal feelings became public domain? Could one find safety in a group of people hurting as much as, or more than, you? I was skeptical as I signed in for my first session.

Bob Newhart made group therapy fun. Everyone laughed. But I wasn't laughing when I entered the room. No one else was, either. Nevertheless, the Lord has a tremendous sense of humor. Imagine my surprise when I walked into my first group session and discovered I was the only male present. The therapist and other members were all women. All the patients were quiet and withdrawn. It was as though we had pulled down a shade over our hearts: "Out to Lunch."

I had no idea what to expect as I occupied my chair in the circle. I felt out of place. Humiliated. Weren't men suppose to be strong? Have their act together around women? Emotions are for women, right?

As an outgoing person, I usually find it easy to converse with anyone. I have seldom, if ever, felt threatened sharing my feelings with others. Yet there I sat. Shattered. Devastated. Wiped-out. Staring at eight women who were staring at me.

God knew that I needed to be broken. In His wisdom, He had appointed this arrangement for the purpose of unmasking my arrogance.

As I was asked how I was feeling, I choked up and was unable to respond.

The therapist remarked "Steve, you look so sad." The others nodded in agreement.

It didn't take long for the floodgate holding my emotions back to give way. The word "sad" triggered an emotional outburst of sorrow that swept away every barrier I had hidden behind. Unloading my grief, I wept like a baby in a circle full of women.

For the first time in my life, I was stripped bare to the emotional bone. Nothing to hide. As a man and leader of men, I found myself broken and humbled, telling a group of ladies I was a failure.

Over the next several weeks, the Lord used this group of sensitive, sympathetic women to humble me. Pride flew out the window as I poured out my pain to them.

God showed me that a humble heart is a prerequisite for wholeness. Arrogance blocks the healing power of the Holy Spirit. Healing must always be preceded by humility.

I learned that in reality, group therapy succeeds through patient participation. Members are encouraged to share their feelings. In an atmosphere of acceptance, each person is shown respect and dignity. The group becomes a surrogate emotional family where love and support are the order of the day. Permission is granted to be real. It's okay to open up and be yourself.

Individuals are challenged to dig deep into their emotional reservoirs. Members help each other discover and deal with who they really are.

It requires courage to open up in a group. Most people find this process intimidating. Even in healthy settings like small-group Bible studies and cell groups in homes, people struggle to share their inner feelings. We erect many barriers to our true selves.

From our earliest, formative years, we build elaborate fortresses around our hearts. We seldom let down the drawbridge and allow others to cross the moat to enter our private castles. We resist transparency. We don't like being vulnerable. If I let you into my heart of hearts, you might find that I'm less than perfect. You'll discover my cracks. See my warts. Find I have faults.

I can't risk exposing the real me to you. You might take advantage of what you learn, and break my fragile heart. So we keep one another at bay. Each of us safe and secure in our forts, raising a flag once in a while to let others know we're home. But no invitations to dinner.

Group process assists people in lowering their drawbridges. Walls come down when you're accepted for who you are.

Though my group was conducted in a secular setting, we instituted some Biblical principles of unconditional love and support that enabled God's healing process to penetrate our pain-hardened hearts.

We were coached to be ourselves in group. No charades. No acting. No condemnation. No finger pointing. No blaming or shaming. No passing judgment. Group therapy was a place to share. A refuge from the storm. A safe-haven for battered souls.

Through these sessions, as the emotional and spiritual healing process began, the Holy Spirit brought me face to face with five areas in which I saw myself as a failure.

Relationships

The most important things in life are relationships, and the closest relationships are family. Every time I thought of Jo Ann, Adam, and Stacy, I felt like a failure as a family man. What kind of a husband and daddy was I, sitting in a hospital, deeply depressed, out of touch with "normal" life?

My family's security meant everything to me. I had grown up in a broken home where insecurity greatly impacted my life. While growing up, I told myself that when I had my own family, we'd always be together, stable, secure, and happy. But look what had happened. Life for the Roll family had fallen apart at the seams.

I couldn't look my wife and children in the eyes because I believed I had let them down. Our future was uncertain. We'd lost everything families count on to provide security and stability. Ultimately, our strong love for each other and commitment to one another proved to be the stabilizing factor in our world turned upside-down, but my depression stressed our emotional and spiritual bonds to the max. God's gracious love and faithful provision carried the Rolls through this stormy season of life. But at the time, I felt ashamed that I couldn't lead my family when they needed me at the helm of our home.

Before I was hospitalized, Jo Ann and I had traded off driving Adam and Stacy to school. Round-trip took about forty minutes. As my depression advanced, early mornings were particularly difficult for me. Pre-dawn darkness and hectic rush-hour traffic raised my panic level significantly. I found my emotions on edge as I tried to get the kids off to a good day at school.

After dropping Adam and Stacy in front of their classrooms, I would pause for a moment to watch them. They were so cute. Precious, innocent. Deserving of the very best.

As their little figures disappeared into the building, my heart sank. Tears freely flowed. I hurt for my children. They were fine. But their daddy wasn't. I felt like such a failure. If I hadn't been forced out of my ministry in Michigan, they would still be in school with their friends. My failure had taken them away from friends and familiarity.

One morning I barely made it back to the house. Crying all the way home, I remembered a tough moment just before we moved to Louisiana. Adam's first grade class had a farewell party for him. Jo Ann and I attended. I was doing all right until his fellow students said in concert, "Good-bye Adam. We'll miss you."

I bolted from the classroom to the bathroom where I burst into tears and bawled like a baby.

The incident had struck a raw nerve. It took me back, for a brief moment, to when my folks divorced. We'd had to make some adjustments. I knew personally how it felt to leave familiar neighborhoods, schools and friends. Since that time, it has always been hard for me to be the one to leave.

It tore me up to take my son from his little buddies. Because I had been rejected, I felt my son was being rejected too. That wasn't true. But I thought it was.

The church people in Michigan stayed. They kept their jobs. Their children continued in their schools. They didn't have to move out of their homes. The swing sets stayed in the backyard. Life went on as usual.

But we had to leave. With one decision, everything turned topsy-turvy. Everything secure in my son's life became insecure. What I never wanted to happen in my family had happened.

I never wanted to fail as a father, but that day I began to see Adam and Stacy Roll's daddy as a failure.

Professionally

Americans are known for being performance oriented. We're a nation of human doers instead of human beings. What we do supersedes who we are. Making a living is more important than how we live our lives.

If you don't think so, when was the last time you went to a social gathering and were introduced to the other guests as a wonderful, gentle-spirited, caring person who believes strongly in the sanctity of life? Most likely, your host said something like this: "Please meet Dr. Jones who is a surgeon at Memorial Hospital." When getting acquainted, people don't ask who you are, what you believe, or what you feel. They ask what you do.

Unfortunately, in the American culture much of our identity is wrapped up in our work. We're judged a success or failure based on how well we do what we do.

I'd graduated from college and seminary with highest honors. I'd set high standards of performance for myself. My expectations were lofty. I'd elevated ministry to a place of prominence just below the throne of God. For me, excelling in the Lord's work was the name of the game.

I'd wanted to be known as a successful man of God. People flocked to my church to hear me preach God's Word in a communicative style that touched their hearts. Our church's growth steadily headed upward. A group of pastors from out of state had toured our facility and picked my and my staff's brains for keys to church growth.

Professionally, I had been headed to the top. A plaque hung on my office wall commending me for outstanding spiritual leadership and church growth.

Then the bottom fell out.

When the dust finally settled, I found myself a minister without a ministry, a pastor without a parish, a preacher without a pulpit, a shepherd without any sheep. I was embarrassed, humiliated. And when people learned I was a minister and then asked me what church I pastored, I was ashamed. I didn't have a church anymore. What was worse, I interpreted my leaving as failure.

A good friend who is experienced in the ministry told me, when I was down on myself, that every pastor has his first church. That's true. I knew what he was saying. But at the time, his kind words brought little consolation. I had branded myself a failure in the Lord's service.

I couldn't watch television preachers because they were doing what I was not.

As I sat on a hospital ward wondering if I would ever preach again, I wrestled with feelings of envy, jealousy, and bitterness.

Even shortly after my release from the hospital I was still battling the problem. The first time I sat in a worship service after treatment for depression was when our family traveled to Ohio to visit dear friends who are in the ministry. As the congregation sang hymns and praise choruses, my heart sang it's own song. A song of lament. I felt so low. I didn't want anyone to know I was a minister.

As the service proceeded, I grew more and more uncomfortable. Question after question popped up in my mind. Would I preach again? Would I ever again know the joy of leading someone to Christ as Savior? What did my fellow pastors think of me? What church would call a rejected pastor to fill their pulpit? Would I ever be respected as a spiritual leader again?

As the questions kept coming, and the only answer I could muster was "I don't know," a sense of worthlessness and uselessness washed over me. There I sat in the house of God, an out-of-commission minister of the Gospel. Tears of shame and humiliation stained my new silk tie, a visible reminder of the pain I felt.

We were sitting in the middle of a row of seats, so I couldn't escape. But I wanted to. I wanted to run as far away as I could — far away from the sense of failure I carried underneath my three-piece suit.

Financially

It's a scary thing to think you've failed your family financially. The material demands of daily living require financial resources. There's no way around it. It takes money to live.

I hadn't been without a paycheck since before high school; but now, for the first time in my adult life, I had no visible source of income.

For me to suddenly be without a predictable paycheck, not knowing when and how I would put food on the table for my family was frightening.

The devil accused me incessantly that I wasn't a good provider. I knew the Lord was my Source and promised to meet our every need (Philippians 4:19), but I felt responsible for the bills that would soon be coming due. I wasn't sure how they would be paid.

A man is supposed to bring home the bacon. How could I do that when I had been released from my employer and I was a patient in the hospital, having no idea when I would return to emotional health and be able to pursue gainful employment once again?

The depression trapped me into the compete and compare game. I looked around at other families. They had good salaries and benefits. The Smiths down the street had just purchased a gorgeous new car. The Jones family was planning a vacation to Disneyland. Dads and moms were taking their children out for kids meals and good times in the play land at the golden arches. Couples were stealing away for romantic moments at nice restaurants and hotel suites.

When I compared myself to the other breadwinners on the block, I came out looking like a big zero. It destroyed my ego to have to say, "No. We can't afford that right now." Inside I kept beating myself up because we would have been able to afford it if I still had my position at the church. My seeming failure in the ministry had deprived my family of financial security.

Financial security was very important to me. I'd grown up in a home whose main income had been state welfare. We'd received a monthly check and voucher that entitled us to pick up staple food items from a food distribution center. A basement room, lined with shelves, served as a pantry where we stored powdered milk, bags of beans, boxes of cheese, and sacks of rice, flour and oatmeal.

Being the oldest son, I took it upon myself to keep the supply pantry in order. I operated it like a store. Each item had a place. I stacked everything in neat rows. I kept inventory, accounting for every bag and box.

The days I enjoyed most were the first of the month. That's when we stocked up and my pantry shelves were replenished. I took pride in seeing the shelves bulging with groceries. I knew that we'd have food to eat as long as the pantry shelves were full. I remember feeling very secure knowing that behind that basement room door sat an ample supply of food. I likewise felt extremely insecure when the supply diminished as the end of the month approached.

To this day, I feel secure when the refrigerator and pantry are well stocked. It seems silly, but I become agitated and feel insecure when the Rolls start to run low on groceries.

Each day of treatment in the hospital cost eight hundred dollars. We didn't have that kind of money. But God does! And He knows how to deliver His miracles in the most surprising ways.

When we left our church, our health insurance policy technically should have been dropped. But grace prevailed, and the powers that be allowed us to remain covered until we came under another program. The hand of the Lord was in this, because our policy was unusual in that it provided 100% payment of in-house psychiatric care. Just like our awesome God to provide nearly $24,000 for this need when I was totally unable to do anything about it! Hallelujah!

The Lord does not forget His servants! The Bible gives us these wonderfully reassuring words from Isaiah 44:21:

> *Remember these things O Jacob, and Israel, for you are My servant. I have formed you; you are My servant O Israel, you will not be forgotten by Me.*

My fear of monetary failure was rooted in looking to myself and men as my source of provision. When men pulled the financial rug out from under me, I fell hard because my source was in the wrong place. God's plan of restoration for me included teaching me to trust Him alone as my Source of material provision. Plenty of opportunities for me to believe Him for financial miracles would present themselves in the days ahead.

Spiritually

My greatest grief and deepest sense of failure was spiritual. I hadn't turned my back on Jesus, but I felt I'd let Him down. He'd called me to preach and build a great church. He'd entrusted me with precious souls for which He'd given His life. He expected me to fight valiantly and come out victorious against the enemy. But things hadn't turned out right.

The church body lay in ruins. The devil danced with delight as his demons dragged me away to depression's dungeon.

From the moment I realized I was finished as a pastor, I began a frantic search to try and discover what went wrong spiritually. I'd prayed, preached, believed, battled — and lost.

I started a soul-search that turned me into a spiritual schizophrenic. Part of me believed I had done my best and the Lord would take care of this mess. A compassionate voice reassured me that He loved me no matter what, and He would restore me to usefulness. I would learn the lessons He had for me and I would do better next time. I had not failed — I was being trained in spiritual warfare. I liked that side of me and tried to hold on to that perspective with all my might.

But another part of me conducted a merciless inquiry that resembled a medieval inquisition. A condemning voice charged me with the sole responsibility for everything that happened. It was my fault, and my fault alone. I had failed as a man of God. I was spiritually worthless, of no use to God anymore. The greatest failure in life has to be failing God. If we fail Him, what's left?

In Luke's Gospel, chapter 22, Jesus had been delivered into the hands of the Jews. Judas' betrayal had set up the arrest of the Master. Peter followed Jesus from a safe distance as they led Him to the judgment hall. Having sworn earlier that he would be willing to die for his Lord, Peter now denied Jesus three times. In verses 61-62, we find these soul-piercing words.

> *And the Lord turned and looked at Peter. And Peter remembered the word of the Lord, how He had told him: "Before a cock crows today, you will deny Me three times." And he went out and wept bitterly.*

When the Lord's eyes met Peter's, and the fisherman-turned-disciple realized what he had done, he went out and wept. Peter's bitter weeping was prompted by a sense of having failed the Lord. When his Master needed him most, Peter dropped the ball. He failed to stand for Jesus. I believe from that moment until his personal restoration (John 21:12-17) and the infilling of the Holy Spirit at Pentecost (Acts 2:1-13), Peter felt like a spiritual failure.

Peter had let the Lord down. He'd never intended to. He'd pledged he never would, even if others might. But in the heat of a fiery trial, he didn't come through for Jesus.

I'm sure Peter spent many lonely hours asking why. I did too. I couldn't bear the thought of looking into the eyes of Jesus. When

I met with Him in prayer, I felt ashamed, unworthy to come into His holy presence.

I believe Peter saw compassion in Jesus' eyes when the cock crowed. The Lord loved Peter in his hour of personal disgrace. But Peter didn't love himself.

Nor did I. I felt unlovable because I had failed to fulfill my mission in Michigan.

Personally

When our children were younger, they loved to go to Chucky Cheese's. It's a fun place for kids and those young at heart. The pizza is tolerable, and kid noise is unbelievable, blasting the decibel scale out of sight. But the real attractions at Chucky Cheese are his animated musical variety show and the game room. A parent can become poor in a hurry feeding tokens to those insatiable, magical machines that draw little ones like a magnet!

One game in particular captured my kids' fascination. It consisted of a table with a dozen or so holes in it. From inside those underground silos sprang puppet-like kittykats. They appeared randomly and suddenly. The object was for my darling children, hammer clutched in hand, to clobber as many of those jack-in-the box kitties as possible as fast as possible. It blew me away watching my sweet, innocent children pounding the daylights out of those tantalizing targets!

At slower speeds, the cagey cats never had a chance. As soon as their Cheshire smiles surfaced, Whomp! Boom! Gotcha! Headache City and a quick retreat to their dens!

Depression affected me the same way.

I could identify with those kittens at Chucky Cheese's. Something very powerful was going on in my heart. Steve Roll kept trying to surface emotionally. Without warning, I kept trying to pop up and live in the light again. But each time I raised my head, the hammer of failure walloped me, driving me back down into the den of depression. Though I tried every way I knew, I couldn't escape the despair of heartache city.

To me, sitting in a psychiatric hospital, depressed, suicidal, and out of touch with real life was ultimate personal failure. That's why I thought death was the only way for a failure like me to atone for his disgrace.

A righteous man named Job once surveyed his life. In a very

short period of time, he had lost his children, his wealth, his health, and the respect of his peers. He questioned his own faith. In Job chapter 3, verse 25 this suffering servant of the Lord laments:

> *For the very thing which I greatly feared has come upon me; and that which I was afraid of has come to me.*
>
> KJV

When I inventoried my life, I felt like Job II, sitting on an ash heap of defeat, grieving over relational, professional, financial, and spiritual failure. That which I feared most in life, failure, had come upon me. The only conclusion I could arrive at after assessing my condition was that I was a failure as a person.

Not only had I failed people and God, but I had failed myself. Steve had let Steve down. That was the toughest pill to swallow. How could it have happened? What was the matter with me? How could I have ended up like this? Was there something wrong with me? Was I a defective human being?

But thanks be to God for the unspeakable gift of His unconditional love! I would go through a painful process of death to self in the months ahead, but I would be rescued and restored to self-worth and human dignity.

Failing is not failure. It's important in life that we understand the difference between messing up and being a mess up. Someone once said that life is one long lesson in humility. There is no greater teacher than mistakes. Humility, the meek and gentle spirit of Christ, inhabits us when we face our failures and learn from them.

Falling down doesn't make you a failure, but staying down does. Proverbs 24:16 tells us we can expect to fall. It also tells us what to do when we stumble:

> *For a righteous man falls seven times and rises again.*

A survey of Scripture reveals that God's shining heroes of faith were successful failures! Every great man or woman of God failed at some time. Many failed big time. But they weren't failures. They were people who walked by faith, turning their stumbling blocks into stepping ' ones to success.

The prophet Micah stated boldly and with holy determination

the position of the victorious child of God whom the enemy has tried to keep down.

> *Do not rejoice over me, O my enemy; Though I fall,*
> *I will rise.*
>
> Micah 7:8

My heart cried out to rejoice over my enemy, but depression had so crushed my spirit that all I could see was failure. The line between failing and failure had become blurred. Day and night, the enemy of my soul taunted and tormented me with the thing I feared most — failure.

Failure is a formidable foe. Man was created by God for success. Male egos, in particular, are motivated by an insatiable thirst for success. Fear of failure keeps more people from achieving success than any other factor in our performance-driven, results-oriented culture. To be labeled a failure is to be branded a loser. We don't tolerate losers. We discard them. We aren't as gracious or as merciful as our Heavenly Father who is in the business of making winners out of losers.

A key turning point in my healing came the third week of my treatment when the Lord tenderly spoke to me through Psalm 118:17-18:

> *I shall not die, but live and tell of the works of the*
> *Lord. The Lord has disciplined me severely, but he*
> *has not given me over to death.*

My lame spirit leaped with joy! Fires of hope rekindled because God was watching over me. He would teach me how to turn failure into success.

Chapter 4
Confessions of a Controller

He must increase, but I must decrease.

John 3:30

I was settling down in my room for the night when a soft knock on the door broke the evening silence. After I invited the unscheduled visitor to come in, the door opened and Zahn Martin walked into my life.

My first thought was to wonder what I looked like to him. I must have been a sight. Depleted, demoralized, disillusioned, deep in despair. In a word, depressed.

Zahn introduced himself. After we exchanged pleasantries he looked directly into my hollow eyes and, smiling, said three things. "Steve, God's anointing is all over you. You will get better. The issue is control."

My response was immediate and equally straightforward. "No it isn't; it never will be; and you gotta be kidding!"

That brief encounter began a life-saving relationship. Zahn was my age. He loved God, and cared about people. He'd experienced emotional pain in the ministry, himself. He was a trained, licensed, therapist assigned to me. But in reality, he was an angel sent by God to help me find myself.

It was easy to dismiss my counselor's assessment that God's anointing still covered me. Shame and humiliation had done a thorough job of erasing any sense of the Spirit's unction. The notion that I would get better totally eluded me. What I was feeling inside seemed hopelessly incurable.

But the phrase "the issue is control" wouldn't go away. I couldn't shake it from my mind. Everything in me revolted against the thought that I was a controller, yet something stirred deep down inside when I dwelt on the possibility that control was a key culprit behind my emotional and spiritual collapse.

Aided by the Holy Spirit, Zahn began focusing his attention on uncovering the causes for which control had become the dominant, driving force in my life. My answers to his questions proved his diagnosis to be right on target.

Our running dialogue developed into the following list of characteristics of the controlling personality.

Controllers Have to Be in Control

It's hell for a controller's life to be out of control. That's why I was in the hospital. Everything I held dear had been wrenched from my control. What I feared most in life, not being in charge, had come to pass. I didn't know how to handle that.

God created man to be under His control. Father does know best! (See Genesis 1 & 2.) Man's rebellion was all about control — who would call the shots, creator or creature? Sin is simply man living under Satan's control, out from under God's control. The devil deceives us into thinking that being in control is more fulfilling than being under control. (See Genesis 3.)

As our sessions continued, I came to realize why I was so determined to dominate and dictate every detail of my life. I didn't know until God graciously intervened, but the arguments I gave for needing to be in control were the very things that were cutting me off from the freedom and blessing my Creator intended for me to possess.

Controllers Are Made, Not Born

The most significant event of my hospitalization occurred halfway through my treatment. Jo Ann and the children had come to the ward as they did each night, hopeful that I would be doing better and would be ready to go home.

As we sat in the community room dunking Oreo cookies in chocolate milk, my loved ones could see that this day had not been a good one for me. Our visit didn't go well. Hopes were dashed again in my son and daughter's hearts when I told them I didn't know when I would be returning home.

Visiting hours over, we shuffled down the hall. A kennel full of basset hounds probably looked happier than we did!

We rode the elevator in silence to the ground floor. When the door opened, Adam hurried ahead of us. As we said our good nights, he ran out the hospital entrance. I went after him. I pushed the door aside and grabbed my son as he slumped to the floor. Tears streamed down his little face. He thought his daddy was never going to get better. He was certain his father wasn't coming home.

I sank to the floor and scooped Adam up into my embrace. Nothing could have loosened my grip on my boy.

As I held him close and tight, something snapped inside of me. I broke down and wept with him. We sat in the doorway and cried our eyes out. I looked my precious son in his tear-reddened eyes and told him I loved him. That I would never leave him alone. That I would get better; his daddy would come home.

That's when it happened. As I looked at my young son, I saw another six year old. Me.

A voice from deep within my soul said, "Steve, meet Steve."

I held on to Adam for all I was worth. My son's fear of losing his daddy triggered a deep-seated emotion in me. I came face to face with the little boy that got lost when his mother and father called it quits on their marriage and went their separate ways.

My parents divorce had shattered my security. For thirty-one years, I had buried the pain of rejection. As Adam and I sat on that cold marble floor, clutching one another for dear life, I flashed back to a time when all another boy of six wanted was for his daddy to come back through the door, hold him, and say, "I love you son, and I will always be here for you."

Wiping away his tears, Adam kissed me and said good night. As he walked off with his mother and sister, I looked at the back of his head. No big deal, except I had this sense that I was looking at the Steve Roll I had lost in the scramble to survive. The kid I had always longed to be.

That night the cleansing process began. The little boy I had never been in touch with finally surfaced. The boy I craved to know and make peace with was now knocking on my heart's door.

Out of His loving kindness for me, God did two things that evening. First, He introduced me to myself. The real reasons behind my broken heart could finally be addressed and attended to. Second, He bonded me to my son in a way that only a Heavenly Father can.

In the days ahead, the Lord reunited me with a part of myself that I had lost track of for three decades. Zahn helped me understand that I had unconsciously become a controller at age six. I didn't choose to be a controlling individual, but the spirit-crushing conse-

quences of my parents' parting propelled me onto a path of protecting my broken heart at all costs. I was an emotional casualty, a
negative byproduct of a broken home.

People become controllers because early in life something got
out of control.

Dads, moms, and kids — families — are supposed to stay
together. For me, the pain of my family's breakup was so severe I
had to bring it under control. Subconsciously, I set out on a mission
to control the hurt. Driven by insecurity and the fear of rejection, I
unknowingly established a plan of damage control based on controlling my life so that no one could ever hurt me again.

My three-step plan consisted of resisting rejection, avoiding
abandonment, and trusting no one. Little did I know that it would be
a mission of misery for me and those lives touching mine.

Controllers Are Insecure

I have a little card taped to my computer. It shows two penguins
standing facing each other. A big fish has swallowed the head and
shoulders of one of the penguins. The unaffected penguin remarks
to his half-swallowed friend, "Relax, God's in charge." I love that
humorous little reminder of how we're to look at things out of our
control.

Prior to burning out, I had preached that God was in charge. I
acted in such a way as to make people think God was in control of
my life. I talked positively, walked boldly, and lived decisively. I
presented a picture of personal strength and power.

People thought I had it all together and I knew where I was
going. But it was all a facade. Behind the always-trying-to-look-
good, seemingly-secure, self-confident Steve was an insecure man
who was pretty good at faking everybody out, including himself!

God wasn't really in charge. Steve was. It was vital for me to be
on top of everything, influence every decision, direct every program, because then I felt secure. My internal security was based on
external performance. That's why I pushed myself to be perfect. My
modus operandi of "I must," "I have to," "I need to," never allowed
me, or anyone around me, to relax. Life was a duty to be endured,
not a journey to be enjoyed.

When my mom and dad split up, I thought something was
wrong with me. Young children assume that something they did

caused their parents' divorce. Because they don't understand that dads and moms make personal decisions that can split a family apart, they think they're at fault. Somehow children of divorced homes take the blame for the breakup upon themselves.

When my dad moved out, an intruder named insecurity moved in. From that point on, my thirst for security drove me to attempt to control every element of life, innocently thinking that I could create security by barricading pain out.

Controllers Fear Failure

Those who feel they must control life delude themselves with the mistaken notion that outward success will prove to others that they are a valuable human being.

For me, success became an obsession. I was driven to make straight A's, graduate near the top of my class, excel in sports, make a lot of money, be recognized for accomplishments in my profession etc., because then my parents and other significant people in my life would realize that I was worth loving.

I feared that if I didn't succeed, my feelings of low self-esteem, self-rejection and my negative self-image would raise their collective voices in a chorus of, "See, we told you. You're a nobody."

As a controller, I was afraid someone might find out that I was human, imperfect, and insecure. So I erected an emotional wall to guard my heart and became pseudo-Steve, that super-human, practically-perfect-in-every-way, totally-secure gift to mankind!

Controllers Have to Be Right

You can win a war without winning every battle, but controllers believe they have to win every battle to win the war.

The insecurity (prompted by pride) that lurked in the deep recesses of my heart wouldn't allow me to lose. To feel secure, I had to win. Always. At all costs. Ties were not acceptable. Win-win was a foreign language to me. I win-you lose was the only acceptable scenario for keeping my secure (should I say insecure) world from collapsing.

From earliest childhood, all I had known was lose. Everybody lost when the family broke up. Welfare wasn't a winner. Constantly struggling with poor self-image wasn't winning. I recall very few role models in my formative years who were win-win people.

To defend my turbulent emotional turf, I had to be right. My selfish, sinful nature kicked in high gear here. I could not, would not, admit I was wrong. The controller, who was guardian of the gate to my heart, wouldn't allow that. When I was wrong, saying "I'm sorry, will you please forgive me" was next to impossible.

Obviously, having to be right all the time puts tremendous stress on relationships. Controllers frustrate people. They don't mean to, but they do because they don't know how to give. Because they've been taken from in some significant manner, they erroneously assume that they can't give ground because they will be taken again.

Most people will give when you give. But that requires risk — the risk of opening yourself up to the possibility that you might be hurt again.

"No way!" the controller within commands. Watchmen to your posts. Close the gates. Man your battle stations. Maintain your positions. Don't budge, even if it means driving a potential future ally away. Remember your mission — keep the fort intact at all costs.

Denial is a powerful force in life. Diseases go untreated because people deny they are sick. Relationships remain strained because the parties involved refuse to recognize a problem exists. God's miracles get hung up in Heaven because His children don't think they really need His help.

James 5:13-16 is a Biblical antidote to denial. This well known, often-referred-to passage gives God's prescription for dealing with suffering, sickness, and sin. The Bible tells us that if we're experiencing any of the above, admitting our need is the first step to healing (verses 13 & 14).

Then we're to take action by calling upon the elders of the church to minister to us. "Prayer offered in faith" and "anointing with oil in the name of the Lord" will restore the sick (verse 14). "The Lord will raise him up, and if he had committed sins, they will be forgiven him" (verse 15). That's Good News! Hallelujah!

But verse 16 holds the key to healing. It reads:

> *Therefore, confess your sins (faults, KJV) to one another, and pray for one another, so that you may be healed. The effective, fervent (white-hot) prayer of a righteous man can accomplish much.*

Healing (cleansing and restoration) begins with confession. The exhortation is for the sick or suffering person to confess his sins/faults to his brothers.

Most of the confession of faults that goes on in the body of Christ today is the confession of another's faults, not our own. Faultfinding and revealing to other people what's been found is a grievous sin in the church.

The purpose of the personal confession of our shortcomings (the Word calls them sins and faults) is so that we can receive prayer. Unless he knows the need, how can a righteous man pray a fervent, effective prayer that accomplishes much for anyone? Prayer can be made when we know what to pray for. God's goal for the confession and prayer for one another is clear: "So that you may be healed."

Could one of the reasons we see so little divine healing in the church today be because we don't practice in a loving and edifying manner the injunction to confess our faults to one another and pray for one another? I'm convinced it is.

Note that confession and prayer is a mutual exercise. I confess my faults (not yours); you confess your faults (not mine). Then we pray for each other. Fervent, heartfelt prayers, prayers full of faith for our brothers' healing, will obtain results. God promises to hear and heal those who obey these instructions.

Biblically, to confess is to agree with God. It is to acknowledge that what He says about a situation is what is right.

Zahn spent a lot of time those first few days giving me permission to unload on him. Boy, did I unload. My humanness rose to the occasion. I protested vehemently that what had happened to me was unfair. Name by name, I confessed the faults of my adversaries. I pleaded for Zahn to rule foul ball.

After a couple of days of dumping my grief, it dawned on me that God had not brought me to the hospital to confess the faults of others and work on their healing. I was there to agree with Him concerning my own faults so we could work on my healing.

Out of His goodness, God put His gentle finger on the areas where my heart needed healing and my character needed correction.

Zahn was a masterful listener. When someone listens and lets you spill your guts, you start to hear what you're saying. Through the tears, I began to see that certain things in my life needed to be straightened out if I was to get better. I'd struggled with some of these things in the past, but denial always carried the day. Now I was broken, stripped of any reason for denying what God would show me.

As we informally put James 5:16 into practice, Zahn played the role of "the one another" that I would confess my faults to. Prayerfully, I agreed with God before Zahn that the following factors had contributed to my burnout.

- I'd been arrogant, thinking I had all the answers.
- I often acted out of anger fueled by frustration.
- I'd been afraid to admit when I was wrong.
- I hadn't heard what people were really saying.
- I didn't know how to sincerely give and receive love.
- I valued results more than relationships.
- I'd been impatient with people and process.
- I didn't trust people because they might let me down
- I'd attempted to control everyone and everything so they wouldn't hurt me.

Quite a list for a guy who thought he had it all together!

A few months after I was born again in 1972, I came across a prayer of a saint from the middle ages. It was deeply introspective and very inspiring. Near the end of his prayer, this wise warrior of the faith said, "Above all Father, save me from myself."

In Hebrews 12:5-11 we read about a father's discipline.

> *And you have forgotten the exhortation which is addressed to you as sons, "My son, do not regard lightly the discipline of the Lord, nor faint when you are reproved by Him: For those whom the Lord loves He disciplines, and He scourges every son whom He receives."*
>
> *It is for discipline that you endure; God deals with you as sons; for what son is there whom his father does not discipline? But if you are without discipline, of which all have become partakers, then you are illegitimate children and not sons.*
>
> *Furthermore, we had earthly fathers to discipline us, and we respected them; shall we not much rather be subject to the Father of spirits, and live? For they disciplined us for a short time as seemed*

best to them; but He disciplines us for our good,
That we may share in his holiness.
All discipline for the moment seems not to be
joyful, but sorrowful; yet to those who have been
trained by it, afterwards it yields the peaceable
fruit of righteousness."

I must have prayed for God to "save me from myself" a thousand times in twenty years of walking with Him. I'd also prayed "break me" time and time again.

There's an old adage that says, "Be careful what you pray for — you just might get it!" I know that to be true. I got what I prayed for!

It would take trust and time before I fully understood what God was doing through this excruciating experience. I was confused and concerned about what was happening. But the Lord wasn't! He knew exactly what He was doing. He was answering my prayers (and those of others who loved me and were concerned for me).

My loving Heavenly Father had a son who needed correction. He would "break me" and "save me from myself" through a painstaking process of spiritual discipline.

Believe me, correction is not fun! The Hebrews writer is right when he says in verse 11 that "all discipline for the moment seems not to be joyful, but sorrowful."

A hearty Amen and Amen to that! Discipline hurts. Sorrow was my constant companion. There is no joy in the moments when God is spanking your spiritual behind. I had fallen so far and was hurting so bad that I thought I was being punished. I thought my Father in Heaven had withdrawn His love.

But not according to this passage.

The Lord loves whom he disciplines.

God was disciplining (correcting) me because He loved me, not because He hated me! I'm His son. Fathers who love their sons, discipline them. I understand this because I am an earthly father with two wonderful children whom I love with all my heart. But occasionally, (too often in their eyes I'm sure!) this loving daddy has to correct my heirs because they have erred in living. The process is painful for them and dear old dad.

Does this scenario sound familiar, dad? Convincing your child with some assistance to bend over, you prepare to apply the board of education to that padded spot God wisely provided on their posterior side. Then you blurt out those words the kids love to hear. "I'm doing this because I love you. This is for your good. This hurts me more than you." Sure dad! Give me a break! Better yet, give me the paddle and let's reverse this discipline thing and see who hurts most.

Kids don't understand those phrases (until they have to correct your grandchildren one day), but they are Biblical. In this scripture, our Heavenly Father disciplines His sons (not illegitimate children) because He loves them (verse 6). It's for their good (verse 10). The purpose is so that they "may share in his holiness" (verse 10). Our discipline training will then "yield the peaceable fruit of righteousness" (verse 11). Holiness and righteousness is the goal of spiritual discipline.

Because of the form (depression and hospitalization), it was hard for me to accept that this was for my good. But God was perfecting me through the pain. He was bringing me to the end of myself so he could save me from myself. Out of burnout and brokenness, He would raise me up to a new, powerful Spirit-controlled life!

The book of Job records in chapter 5, verses 17-18:

> *Behold, how happy is the man whom God reproves, so do not despise the discipline of the Almighty. For He inflicts pain, and gives relief; He wounds, and His hands also heal.*

I must confess that in the early stages of recovery, I despised the Almighty's discipline. Happy is hardly the word I would use to describe my attitude in those initial days of the Lord's reproof. Disgusted was more like it.

But God was very patient with me, and the day would come when His loving hands would heal me and I would be happy and blessed because of His correction.

Confession paved the way for cleansing. After David confessed his sin, he prayed for a clean heart.

> *Wash me thoroughly from my iniquity, and cleanse me from my sin. Purify me with hyssop, and I shall be clean; wash me, and I shall be whiter than snow.*

Create in me a clean heart, oh God, and renew a
steadfast spirit within me.

Psalm 51:2, 7, 10

I had not sinned deliberately, as David had, but my heart was cluttered with lots of "stuff" that needed to be cleaned out. I liked the idea of God creating a clean heart in me. I had tried to make my own heart clean for years.

Once, when I was despairing over my failure, a good friend shared a great insight with me. He said we all travel down the road of life and run into potholes. We fall into the holes because we didn't know they were there. We find our way out and head on down the road. Sure enough, more potholes. Maturity and success comes, my friend said, when we watch for the holes and avoid them. Immaturity and failure are ours when we keep falling into the same old holes.

For years, I kept falling into the same holes. It really frustrated me. No matter what I tried to do to improve my hole-missing skill, I found myself falling victim to the same traps. Something, or some things, were impairing my ability to journey through life without crashing in some crater.

The issue was control. Steve, not God was driving the vehicle. I had performed as a controller for so long, that even God couldn't get in the pilot's seat. Somehow, I had decided that I had to control everything, including God, so that even He wouldn't mess up the trip!

John the Baptist understood who was to be in charge and dominate in life. As the forerunner of the Messiah, his role was to prepare the way for the coming of the Lord. All eyes were fixed on the fiery prophet from the desert who proclaimed with spiritual authority, *"Repent, for the Kingdom of Heaven is at hand"* (Matthew 3:2).

The locust-and-wild-honey-eating man of God pointed out *"the Lamb of God who takes away the sin of the world!"* (John 1:29) He baptized Jesus in the Jordan and bore witness that this *"is the One who baptizes in the Holy Spirit"* and *"is the Son of God"* (John 1:33-34).

John was popular in the beginning. Then, Jesus began ministering, and people started coming to Him (John 3:26). A question arose about doctrine. John's disciples approached him. The prophet could have drawn attention to himself, but he didn't. Simply, and powerfully, he said that Jesus was everything. John's position was clear. *He (Jesus) must increase, but I (John) must decrease* John 3:30.

My crisis brought me to a valley of decision. I had to make a choice. Who was going to control Steve Roll, Jesus or Steve? Brokenness brought me to the place where I could humbly and sincerely agree with John, "He, (Jesus) must increase, but I (Steve) must decrease."

That crucial choice started the cleansing process that would forever purge the controller from my heart and purify me so I could be controlled by the Holy Spirit.

Chapter 5

Hurdles to Healing

*Why are you in despair, O my soul? And why have
you become disturbed within me? Hope in God, for
I shall again praise Him. For the help of his presence.*
Psalm 42:5

Controllers die hard. At least this one did. It took the death of my dream to bring this dreamer face to face with who should be in control.

Jesus taught that *"unless a grain of wheat falls into the earth and dies, it remains by itself alone; but if it dies, it bears much fruit"* (John 12:24). He also said, *"For whoever wishes to save his life, shall lose it; but whoever loses his life for my sake, shall find it"* (Matthew 16:25).

As the "clutter" tumbled out of my heart, Zahn and I were able to identify three hurdles that stood between me and healing. I would have to "die" to these hindrances if I were to be cleansed and delivered from the curse of a controller and find freedom!

Hurdle #1: Abandonment

According to *Webster's Dictionary*, the word "abandon" means "to withdraw protection, support or help; to give up with the intent of never claiming a right or interest in; to desert or forsake."

Abandonment. The awful agony of someone turning their back on you. Walking out. Leaving you behind. The Lord Jesus's deepest cry came from the Cross.

"My God, My God, why have you forsaken me?"
Matthew 27:46

God turned His back on His only Son in that hour of hours when Jesus became sin for us. He was left to die on the Cross all alone. As God's Son faced death and the grave alone, Satan poured out his cruel fury. The mocking crowd, the merciless soldiers, the iron nails driven through His holy body, and Heaven's silence screamed at Jesus: "Look, you who claim to be the Son of God. Men have rejected you and God has forsaken you. You're by yourself. Suffering! Bleeding! Dying! No one's standing up for you. No one to rescue you."

The Cross was a place of brokenness. The Son of God's body was broken for men. Jesus was abandoned at Calvary, left to accomplish the Father's Will without the Father.

In America today, many homes are places of brokenness. When the father leaves, children are abandoned physically, financially, emotionally and spiritually. A sacred relationship is severed. A trust is broken. A relationship designed by God to provide security disintegrates, leaving behind insecurity's debris.

When Jesus died on the Cross, He chose to become sin for us. He willingly became the sacrifice for sin (John 10:15-18). He knew it would mean temporary separation from the Father. He also knew that death would be destroyed, the devil would be defeated and resurrection day would come! Jesus and the Father would be reunited — together again for eternity in the unbreakable bond of love!

Children don't choose to be abandoned. That consequence becomes reality for them when their parents choose to get a divorce. Dad and mom sin, but the children become the sacrifice.

Little ones, and not so little ones, don't understand why mom and dad can't live together under the same roof. Dads and moms are supposed to love each other. Stay together. Grow old and become grandpas and grandmas together. Parents are supposed to provide a home that is secure, stable, and full of love, acceptance, and approval. A place where dependent children are cherished and nurtured.

When dad leaves for the last time, something happens. Insecurity invades the heart of the innocent. The thought of daddy going away for good is too much. Children kick, scream, cry and literally run after their dads. Some have to be pried from his pant legs as he walks out the door.

The trauma is tremendous. This isn't an adjustment to a new living arrangement. Children perceive it as abandonment, pure and simple.

Dad is leaving the family. Turning his back on them. Getting in the car. Driving down the street. He won't be coming home. This is no short term, temporary separation. Not a business trip. It's a permanent severing of emotional security when a father's love, acceptance and approval leaves with his luggage.

Little minds begin to wonder. Why is daddy leaving...Why can't he stay...Why did he push me away when he said good-bye...Why did he have tears in his eyes, too...Why was he upset...If he felt like I did, wasn't there another way...But he got in the car and drove away.

I don't know all the reasons my own folks didn't stay together. That's their business. But my dad's leaving profoundly affected me.

My father is a good man whom I love very much. He wasn't typical of many dads today who leave their families for parts unknown, never contacting their children or caring for their needs.

My brother and I spent every fourth Sunday with dad. We ate ham sandwiches and drank cream soda on the lake when he took us fishing. He got tickets to the Harlem Globetrotters when they dribbled into town. We played ping-pong, shot pool in Grandpa Wunderle's basement, threw baseballs around the yard and always watched The Ed Sullivan Show before returning home.

Dad never missed one child-support payment. He provided nice presents on birthdays and Christmas. My hat goes off to the special man who did his best to meet the needs of two families he was responsible for.

But once a month wasn't enough time to develop the nurturing relationship a father and son are supposed to have. Boys need their dads every day.

I really missed not having my father around the house. I remember playing basketball in elementary school. Dad had another family to raise, so he couldn't be as intimately involved in the details of my life as I wanted him to be. It hurt to look up into the stands and see my teammates' dads cheering them on. Hoot'n and holler'n for them when they made a good play. Consoling and encouraging them when they blew the shot, communicating the belief that they would sink the winning basket the next time.

My dad's spot in the bleachers was always empty. I felt left out and abandoned as I exited the gym alone after the game while the other boys rode home with their dads replaying the game.

My heart a had dad-sized hole in it, one only my father could fill. Nobody could take his place. That's the way God planned it.

I needed God's man in my life to show me how to be a man. A father who could show me how to hammer a nail, swing a bat, repair a bicycle tire, and train a new puppy. I needed a dad to high-five me when I won, and put his strong arms around me when my world was falling apart. I needed him to teach me about the facts of life and get me sanely through puberty!

I needed a father I could rap with about man-to-man things, a father I could share life with over a cheeseburger, fries, and a Coke. Just hang out together sometimes. Growing up as buddies and best friends. Father and son.

For years, when people asked how I felt about my parents' divorce, I said I was all right. Things happen. I'm okay. I've adjusted well. Just look at my accomplishments. I've grown beyond it and it doesn't hurt anymore. That was my response for hiding the resentment and anger I had stuffed deep down in my heart.

As the Holy Spirit used God's Word and Zahn Martin to peel back the layers of hurt in my heart, we discovered that abandonment was the bedrock upon which my anger and arrogance were built. My fear of abandonment was two-fold. Emotionally, I had been left behind by my earthly father. It was a fact. Consequently, I felt rejected. Forsaken. Spiritually, I felt I had been left behind by my Heavenly Father. But that was a feeling, not a fact. As I tried to drift off to sleep night after night in that lonely hospital room, my heart ached and worried that I might be forsaken by my Father in heaven as I had been by my earthly father.

Hurdle #2: Anger

Anger is one letter short of danger! That blood-boiling, seeing-red emotion of rage we've all experienced is an unpredictable, explosive force that can be very destructive.

Anger affects, or should I say infects, everyone at one time or another. Some people deal with the wrath within by beating up on others. It's called assault and battery. Others handle anger by beating up on themselves. We call it depression.

While hospitalized, I realized I had a whole load of deep-seated, unresolved conflicts. My emotions had exploded as anger and depression because I'd surpressed my feelings for three decades.

I'd grown up angry. I wasn't mad all the time, but every so often, at certain junctures in my journey, anger erupted on the scene, seemingly coming from nowhere. I'd attributed it to my strong choleric personality and headstrong German heritage. But it wasn't my German heritage that had produced the anger. It was my heart.

Someone defined depression as "anger turned inward." It is

unacceptable in civilized society to express anger negatively. Outward expression of anger is out, so we turn it inward. On ourselves. We become the target of wrath's fury.

I didn't realize just how angry I was until I descended into the depths of depression. In that dismal pit of personal pain I came face to face with the fact that I was *angry*. I was *mad*. I was so mad I despaired of living, and sought to snuff out my very existence.

Emotions demand expression. God intended for us to deal with our feelings as they are experienced. It's easy to openly and positively express joy, happiness, excitement and feelings of fulfillment. We delight in sharing our emotional highs. These emotions are socially acceptable and elicit positive responses from those around us. Satisfaction comes from processing our feelings in a healthy manner.

But what about unhealthy emotions? The kind of feelings that produce pain — anger, bitterness, disgust, resentment, hatred. The ugly stuff we all experience. The emotional garbage we wish would be collected and carted away.

Expressing these feelings is taboo. The climate of what is acceptable changes dramatically when people express negative emotions. It's as though a cold front passes through the room. Permission to share is denied when these "demon emotions" surface. Our outlets for constructive expression are cut off. Yet these powerful emotions clamor to escape. Inner conflict now appears on center stage.

From earliest childhood, we're told "Don't get angry. You can't say that. Bite your tongue. Count to ten." (If very angry, "Count to one hundred.") We may feel these things but we can't express our true emotions. What would people think if we told them what we really feel?

Enter the stuffing process.

I love watching professional basketball. I'm awestruck with the athletic ability of the Air Jordans who fly through the air with the greatest of ease, making string-music as they jam the ball through the net. When I get to heaven, I'm going to ask the Lord if I can slam dunk! Just once.

I've always been teased because of my physical stature. A friend once wrote a jingle that went something like this: "Steve Roll will be ten feet tall when he gets to heaven. But everybody else will be eleven!" Get the picture?

I may be too short for dunking basketballs on this side of the Celestial City, but wait till I receive my glorified body! Move over Michael! Step aside Shaq!

In the NBA, the dramatic dunks that electrify the arena and the last-second buzzer-beaters from downtown that pull off an upset victory, make the sports highlights at ten. But there's another play that commands great respect.

A player makes a strong move to the basket, goes up to lay in a shot and boom! Out of nowhere comes a hand as big as King Kong's! Instead of the ball going in the net, the shooter eats the bouncing, orange sphere for lunch!

He has just been stuffed! The monster man in the middle gloats in his glory while the stuffing victim staggers down the court in shock and disbelief. He seriously wonders if he should ever try that move again in this millennium.

The Stuff. An awesome play in basketball. But an awful play in life. Hurtful emotions produced by painful experiences rise to the surface of our hearts, only to be stuffed. Rejected. Pushed down. Buried.

We can't deny how we feel. We hurt so bad; but we can't express it. It's forbidden. So we do what comes naturally in a society where honesty and integrity in relationships is at a minimum. We say, "Anger, get back in there. I can't let you out. I won't let you out. If others knew how angry I feel right now, they'd reject me. I can't take any more rejection."

So we slam the lid on our emotional trash cans. At all costs, we do everything we can to contain the negative emotions clamoring to be heard. We don't dare let the garbage in our hearts spill out. But there comes a time when a rubbish can that has been filled to capacity overflows.

You're probably like me the day before trash pick up: For some reason, our family has produced an unbelievable amount of rubbish in the last week. The "Herby-Curby" as we called them in Michigan, is so full that when the locking device is loosed, the lid falls off.

No problem. I become a human trash compactor. Placing one foot on the firewood pile and the other in the center of the trash can, doing my best to keep my balance, I slam, jam, and cram that last sack into an already bloated and bulging Herby.

When I've grunted and groaned long enough, sensing the

moment has arrived, I leap to the ground, grab the lid, and frantically fit it on top of this mountain of unruly refuse before it pops up like a Jack-in-the-box. As the lid snaps in place, I know I have succeeded in trapping the garbage. It can't escape. It has been signed, sealed, and waits to be delivered to the belly of a big, brown truck.

Stuffed.

Thanksgiving is one of my favorite holidays. I love the crisp, fall air and the brilliantly colored leaves blowing around the harvest landscape. It's a wonderful time for gathering together as family to give thanks to our Creator for the bounty of His blessings.

The celebration centers around a feast. It's turkey day. There's nothing quite like the hunger-arousing aroma that fills the house from a Butterball baking in the oven!

Personally, I've never cooked a turkey. Culinary skills are not my forte! But my wife cooks a great Tom turkey. They always turn out fabulously delicious!

My favorite part is the dark meat. My wife enjoys the stuffing. One evidence of modern cooking's grip on our household is that we use the stove top variety of stuffing. But the real pros, gourmets, literally stuff bread, seasonings, and who-knows-what-else into the belly of their bird. It cooks in there and comes out tasting mighty fine.

I have discovered an important principle about life. Turkeys, not people, are meant for stuffing. God never intended for us to stuff our feelings into the hollowness of our hearts. Our hearts are not emotional Herby-Curbys, either.

I was an emotion stuffer. I was good at it, too. We all know practice makes perfect. Some of us become pros at burying our true emotions. I had stuffed — slammed, jammed, and crammed — a lot of garbage in my heart over the years.

As the Lord began the cleansing process, I discovered I had stuffed my pain to the point that I could no longer keep the lid on. My heart overflowed, spewing forth unresolved feelings that for years had been stomped down into the deepest recesses of my soul.

Like most stuffers, I didn't know I was one. It took a crisis to jar the lid loose so I could reckon with my unmet emotional needs.

Healing requires unstuffing. Stuffers have to be unstuffed if they're to find emotional wholeness. In Ephesians 4:31-32 Paul wrote:

Let all bitterness, and wrath and anger and clamor and slander be put away from you, with all malice. And be kind to one another, tenderhearted, forgiving each other, just as God in Christ also has forgiven you.

There's an exchange here. It involves putting away or getting rid of some bad attributes and putting on or acquiring some good attributes. Cleansing means that all of the layers of bad emotions that have been pile-driven into the heart have to be unearthed.

We stuff things because we are afraid to be out of control. We stuff our anger because we are fearful that it will burst into rage. We stuff resentment and bitterness attempting to keep hatred under wraps. We stuff disappointment to keep disillusionment at bay. We stuff betrayal so we won't give in to vengeance. We even stuff love because we're fearful of the possibility of rejection.

Stuffing provides a false sense of security. If I bury that which is painful, I fool myself into thinking there's no pain. As I mentioned previously, for years I told people I was unharmed by my parents' divorce. That I felt no pain. That a broken home had not scarred my heart.

But I lied. Through my emotional crisis, I learned that the pain of my parents' dissolution as husband and wife affected me more profoundly than any other single event in my life. My whole foundation of love, acceptance, and approval crumbled when my parents decided to renege on their commitment to "till death do us part."

When I was six years old, my emotional world turned upside down . Insecurity vanquished security. Fear enthroned itself as the dominating force driving my emotions.

Throughout my life, I had been telling people I was one of the most secure people they had ever met. I carried myself in such a way that people thought I was a chip off the Rock of Gibraltar. I went to extremes to exude self-confidence and self-assurance. There wasn't anything I couldn't handle. In every situation I believed I was right and could prove it. I was convinced, and spent my adult life trying to persuade others, that I was secure, stable, and invincible.

But it was a facade. A false front. I was wearing a mask. Years of practice produced an accomplished actor. I played the starring role in a movie that could have been titled *What You See Is Not What I Really Be*. Deep inside, way down below the exterior of this tough, arrogant, self-assured, seemingly secure, got-it-all-together controller, was an insecure, love-starved little boy.

Whenever I heard his voice crying out, desperately trying to get my attention, attempting to introduce himself to me, I stuffed him. The things he wanted to deal with were too painful. I didn't want to open my heart to his agenda. Every time that guy tried to surface, I slam-dunked him. I put his cries out of mind, ignored his pleas for recognition, and fled from his invitation to slow down, stop and get in touch with my true self.

I would have never imagined that getting better could be so painful. It hurts to let go! The purging of the pain I had stuffed for years began when I said "uncle," and surrendered my weapons of survival to the One who knows me inside and out.

I recall well the day when a therapist asked me why I was so angry. She said my sad expression betrayed the anger in my heart. I didn't want to confess that I was angry. But her words unlocked the door to a closely guarded vault in my emotional house.

My rage had been locked behind that closed door. The anger had been stored up for so long I was afraid of the monstrous wrath that lurked in the darkness. If it ever escaped, somebody would be in trouble.

When Mt. Saint Helen blew it's top in Washington state, the eruption brought unbelievable devastation and created massive damage in the Pacific Northwest. For centuries, volcanic gases and ever-expanding layer upon layer of super-heated lava built up a nuclear-power pressure that could be contained no longer.

On that frightful day, the scenic mountain became a towering inferno. The explosion spawned fire-storms; spewed hot lava; and blasted volcanic ash, bringing death and destruction to everything and everyone within it's reach.

My heart had been like a volcano. Anger had built up beneath the surface for years. Occasionally, a small fissure would let off some steam. An angry outburst would erupt, a firestorm of displeasure. Someone would be burned by my intolerance or impatience.

The furious outbursts did concern me. I'd heard the saying that you can tell a lot about a person by how often they get angry, the relative importance of the things that make them mad and how long they stay that way. I got angry too often, over trivial things, and stayed upset. I had an anger problem.

The question was, why? Why did I get upset so easily and so suddenly?

I could get ticked off quickly. Over dumb stuff, too. I got angry when the men of the church stayed home to watch the Super Bowl instead of coming to hear my sermon. I became overly upset when nursery workers weren't at their posts on time. Stupid, little things made me irritable at home. I became inflexible and overbearing when the family didn't function the way I thought it should.

I had high expectations for everybody and everything. When life let me down, the disappointment incensed me. When people disagreed with me, and I perceived them as a hindrance or threat to my plans, I lashed out, sabotaging relationships and driving would-be friends away. A little lava here, a little lava there. Hints of a larger, future eruption loomed on the horizon.

Finally, the lid blew off. Resigning my position and thinking I had failed, ignited the anger, releasing a river of rage. Explosion after explosion ripped through my fury-filled soul, spewing unrestrained wrath on everything within reach of my memory. Flow after flow of molten fury poured forth from the crater in my soul.

There was no reason to hold the wrath back any longer. I had feared losing control before. But in the hospital I had nothing to lose. I had lost it all anyway. I was in a safe, protected place. I could let it fly. Let it fly I did.

One of Satan's wicked schemes for the demise of our church in Michigan was the spirit of strife. Unknowingly, I had contributed to that strife. The Bible says in Proverbs 29:22 that angry men stir up strife. They cause dissension among brethren because of the anger hidden in their own hearts. Their hot-tempered outbursts produce sinful actions that divide the brethren.

> "An angry man stirs up strife, and a hot-tempered man abounds in transgression."

I wasn't solely responsible for the spirit of strife that engulfed our fellowship. Satan was in the background, stirring the pot, using my unresolved anger to sow seeds of disunity.

My anger peaked in the hospital. As the river of rage roared unchecked from my heart, I couldn't believe I was so mad at so many people and so many things.

I was angry with those who had betrayed me. The Judases. Those who stabbed me in the back when I thought they would stand with me. Those who plotted with others in dark places to undermine and ultimately overthrow my ministry. People I had helped, who when pressured by the moment, were persuaded to hand me over to the self-righteous who sought my dismissal.

Betrayal wounds deeply. I was frustrated and angry because I couldn't understand how people I had loved could turn away from me in my hour of need. I understand better now how Judas's kiss on the cheek must have felt to Jesus.

I was angry with my superiors. I believe strongly in being submissive to my denominational supervisors. Loyalty to leaders has always been a strength of my character. I having always done my best to follow their counsel.

But I thought some poor decisions were made. I was mad because I believed my superiors had caved in to political pressure, that principle had bowed to personality, whoever screamed the loudest and longest carried the day. When push came to shove, I got pushed and shoved. I became a casualty in a system where tradition outweighed truth. Rules were more important than right relationships.

I looked to my elders for encouragement and guidance, but all I received was criticism and condemnation. Instead of counsel, I received chastisement. I was furious because they lacked the courage to take a bold stand for what was right. When I needed them most, they looked the other way leaving me alone to fight a battle I couldn't win without their support.

I resented being expendable. When I recalled the two public sessions where I was brought before the church to be criticized by anyone who chose to speak, my spirit swelled with rage. How could men of God, with years of biblical training and ministry experience, throw me to the sharks the way they had? They did nothing to protect my reputation. They just let me die in front of God, His church, and the community.

My anger knew no limits. I envied those who were successful and those who were making it in the ministry. It infuriated me to think that men of lesser talents (My arrogance caused me to judge.) were in their pulpits preaching while I paced the halls of a psychiatric hospital in search of myself.

I was angry with those who had paychecks and those who could take their wives out for a nice evening. I was mad at anybody that seemed to have it together while I self-destructed.

I was also angry at myself. I couldn't believe this had happened. How could I not have seen it coming? Why hadn't I done something differently? Why had I made this or that mistake? How could I have been so stupid to lose everything?

Sitting in the hospital trying to pick up the pieces of my shattered life made me feel like a nobody.

I turned the rage inside on myself. I beat up on myself with relentless fury, punishing myself for my failure.

Hour after agonizing hour, anger assaulted me and pounded my ego into the dirt. Negative self-talk tore my soul apart, tore me down. Angrily, I told myself how dumb I was; I was a loser, a worthless human being. I'd thought I was a good leader— but there I sat, out of the ministry, locked away in a hospital.

I beat myself with the stick of anger, then hung my head in shame. I could hardly face myself in the mirror. All I saw was a miserable failure, and that made me mad.

I was angry that I hadn't made better decisions; enraged with myself that I had let others walk all over me. I was furious that I hadn't triumphed over the forces of evil.

The anger that scared me most was my anger with my creator. I was mad at God.

When things had soured in the church, and I was on the way out, I'd thought certainly the Almighty would come to my rescue. How could He not? I'd loved Him and I was His servant. I'd lived for Him. I'd been a faithful preacher of the Good News. I'd won many souls for the Kingdom. I'd taken strong stands against evil. My convictions had been immovable. Ministries had grown under my leadership.

In the Bible, the Lord always delivered His servants from their enemies. He vindicated the righteous. He watched over his flock, ridding it of wolves in sheep's clothing.

So what had gone wrong in my situation? The forty acres behind the church building had been my prayer closet. I'd spent hundreds of hours on that piece of holy ground, pouring out my heart to God. In the heat of the battle, when the health of the church and the very survival of my ministry were on the line, I'd bombarded glory with fervent supplication. I'd hammered heaven for all I was worth, pleading with the Lord to come to my aid.

I'd trusted Him to take care of this mess. I'd fully expected Him to set everybody straight and secure my leadership position. I'd been looking to Him to deliver a smashing victory for my side.

But it hadn't happened. I'd lost. God appeared to have abandoned me in my hour of greatest need. Where had He gone? Why hadn't He delivered me? Why had He allowed those who opposed me to hang me out to dry?

One afternoon in the hospital courtyard I let God know how furious I was with Him for letting me down. With tears streaming down my face, fists clenched and thrust toward His heavenly throne, I cursed His name.

It's a frightening thing to be mad at God. Something inside tells you it isn't a good idea to be angry with the Almighty! Who are we to blast the Holy One with wrath?

My anger directed toward the Lord was driven by pain, but still, deep within I felt horribly guilty about being mad at my Maker. I believed it was sinful for me to express wrath toward Him. But it was there. In living color. Powerful, volatile, ugly things had erupted from the innermost regions of my soul and overflowed on my Father in Heaven.

A significant step forward in my healing process occurred when I realized that the Lord wasn't mad at me even though I was angry with Him. I'd had no doubt He would pour out His holy displeasure on me for striking the rock out of anger, as Moses had.

But He didn't! He loved and comforted me instead! He extended immeasurable loving kindness to me. In the maelstrom of my anger, His message to me was Mercy.

When I threw my spiritual temper tantrum, my Heavenly Father didn't condemn me. He consoled me. He put His big loving arms around me and calmed me down. Like toddlers initially resistant to their parents' holding them when they are throwing one of those fits before mom and dad, I tried to push away God's embrace. But He persisted in reaching out to me with His unconditional love.

The Lord knew how much I hurt. He had been with me every painful step of the way. He knew I really didn't want to be mad at Him.

In our discomfort, we forget that God knows pain. He came to earth in the person of Jesus Christ to experience our heartaches. As a suffering Savior, He could deliver us from the distress that sin brings.

When the only begotten Son of God died on the Cross, the Father knew better than anyone the piercing pain of rejection. Jesus came to His own, but they rejected Him (John 1:11) and cruelly nailed Him to a Cross. They hung Him in humiliation before the very world He loved and came to save (Luke 19:10).

I was relieved to know God wasn't mad at me. I wasn't going to hell for failing. When I threw fits (and I would throw some doozies down the road), He wrapped His arms around me. No one had ever done that before. When I fought, they walked out. But my Heavenly Father hung in there with me.

I was as bent out of shape as anyone could be. But God just kept loving me and began the process of restoring me to Himself.

Zahn knew my anger needed to be released in a non-destructive manner. He took me aside after a particularly heart wrenching group session that brought out a lot of anger, and suggested I become acquainted with an anger bat. I trusted my therapist, but wondered what in the world an anger bat was. We agreed to meet after lunch in a secluded conference room.

We met at the appointed time. In his hand Zahn held the infamous anger bat. A plastic stick with a thick foam covering, it looked like a chubby baseball bat.

He handed it to me and told me he wanted me to think about what made me angry and then strike the chair in front of me. It caught me off guard. Was this for real? A grown man was going to beat up a defenseless piece of furniture with a foam bat! I was embarrassed to say the least.

I hesitated, feeling rather stupid, but Zahn assured me no one would be joining us and I could trust him with this. He'd coach me. He would cheer me on as I attacked a chair and beat it senseless.

I decided to test my weapon. I gave the back of the chair a few good whacks. The bat didn't break. It didn't damage anything. I concluded this exercise wouldn't be hazardous to Zahn's or my health. I did advise Zahn to move back a little bit in case I became carried away! Then I gave him thumbs up and we began.

Zahn told me to start hitting the chair. It felt strange at first, but he supported me. He told me to hit the chair and hit it hard. He granted me permission to cut loose. I finally gave myself the okay to let that chair have it.

Zahn talked to me about some of the people who had angered me. As he talked, I whacked. The more he talked, the angrier I got and the more I whacked!

Rage welled up inside. My face flushed. I grew hot and began to sweat as I kept banging the bat on the chair. The blows became more intense. Zahn urged me to talk about my anger. As I voiced my wrath, I kept pounding. Blow after blow, I struck that poor chair with all my might. I beat it, and beat it, and beat it until I could barely stand.

As I hammered, that chair transformed into persons and situations in my mind. Tears poured out. I beat and wept. Wept and beat. I screamed at the top of my lungs. I tried my hardest to destroy that bat. But it refused to crumble. It withstood blow after blow.

The room echoed with my screams of anguish. For a while I lost touch with everything except that chair and bat. Rage took over.

I didn't realize one man could have so much anger bottled up inside. It poured out all over the place. When I became exhausted, Zahn cheered me on. "Hit it Steve. Hit it again. Harder. Get that poison out. Get the hurt out of your heart."

I obliged him. I beat the living daylights out of that chair. The nonstop blows drained my physical strength. Finally, after whacking that chair for more than an hour, I nailed it one more time. Then I hit the deck. Clothes drenched with perspiration, I lay on the floor totally exhausted, hoping and praying that the demon of anger had been exorcised.

Three more sessions were necessary before my rage was spent. The anger bat and I became good buddies. At each session, Zahn's coaching enabled me to disengage myself from the controlling anger that had held a death grip on my heart. In the days and months ahead, the Holy Spirit healed the wounds anger had inflicted.

As my therapy proceeded, I eventually uncovered the root of my anger. My sense of failure had brought me face to face with my folks divorce. For decades, I had suppressed my anger toward my parents.

I had become angry when dad walked out. I had wanted to tell my parents how much it hurt. I was angry that mom and dad didn't get back together.

I realized that I'd been waiting all those years for dad to come back.

Deep in my heart was a little boy who hoped and expected Daddy to ride home one day on a white horse and fix my broken heart. But he never did. He never returned to make everything all right.

Not knowing what else to do, I'd stayed angry.

Hurdle # 3: Arrogance

There's a story about a Texan who was visiting Niagara Falls. "I bet you haven't got anything like that in Texas," a local resident said, pointing to the falls. The Texan, scratching his head said, "No, but we have a plumber who can stop that leak!"

Positive pride can be a good thing. But negative pride (the Bible calls it arrogance) can be very destructive. Under the direction of the Holy spirit, the writer of wisdom penned the following words in Proverbs 16:18 about pride:

> Pride goes before destruction, And a haughty
> spirit before stumbling.

I had stumbled badly and nearly destroyed myself. My arrogance had tripped me up.

Solomon also writes in Proverbs 29:23a that "a man's pride will bring him low." How low a man goes depends on him. I fell to the bottom of the bottom because the controller in me was too proud to sincerely submit myself to others.

Anger gets many of us in trouble, and arrogance keeps us there. Proverbs 28:25 states:

> An arrogant man stirs up strife, but he who trusts
> in the Lord will prosper.

Proud people trust in themselves. The arrogance that dominates their attitudes and actions pushes people away. In any situation where two or more human beings have gathered, absence of humility will produce contention and strife.

Pride made me think I had all the answers. People don't respond positively to "know-it-alls." I was arrogant enough to believe I really did know what to do in every situation.

Pride is a subtle thing. I acted out of what I considered confidence. But in all honesty, sometimes, not every time, but often enough, it was cockiness. When arrogance rose to the forefront, I tuned out the suggestions of others and proceeded with great zeal and determination to persuade them my way was the right way.

I wouldn't budge when it was my will pitted against the wishes of another. I seldom compromised, rarely gave in. To me, middle ground was losing. Controllers have to win.

There were times concession would have been wisdom. People had good ideas. But mine were better. I was playing to win the game of gaining love, acceptance, and approval. I had to look good, perform well, and be in control. My pride did a great job of hiding the self-hatred that hid behind my arrogant exterior.

I recall battling with church members over the color of stationery, choice of logos, which new hymnal to order, and whether six or seven members should sit on the missions board. Pretty petty from a heavenly perspective. Those decisions wouldn't make much difference in the eternal scheme of thing. But arrogance drove me to prevail because I had to win every battle to feel secure.

Controllers regularly run over people and run them off. They ruin relationships because they aren't fully aware of what's driving them. Overly-domineering people are deceived by pride. They think they're loving people, when actually they're lording it over them.

Peter exhorted the elders of the church to conduct their ministry after Christ's example.

> *Therefore, I exhort the elders among you, as your fellow elder and witness of the sufferings of Christ, and a partaker also of the glory that is to be revealed. Shepherd the flock of God among you, exercising oversight, not under compulsion, but voluntarily, according to the will of God; not for sordid gain, but with eagerness. Nor yet as lording it over those allotted to your charge, but proving to be examples to the flock. And when the Chief Shepherd appears, you will receive the unfading crown of glory.*
>
> I Peter 5:1-4

Shepherds lead sheep; they don't drive them. Being driven by the controller within me, I unwittingly drove the people of our church, instead of leading them. I was guilty of "lording it over those allotted to my charge." Pride had stiffened my spirit, rendering me incapable of ministering to the flock with a humble servant's heart.

Pride drives people away. Humility draws them. Peter continues addressing the church body with instructions concerning humility. Verses five and six record these words:

You younger men likewise, be subject to your elders; and all of you, clothe yourselves with humility toward one another, for God is opposed to the proud, but gives grace to the humble. Humble yourselves, therefore, under the mighty hand of God, that He may exalt you at the proper time.

Note that humility is to be exercised by each member of Christ's body ("all of you"). Each person is to "clothe themselves" and "humble themselves."

We pray erroneously when we ask God to make us humble. His first choice is for us to willingly humble ourselves. We are to clothe ourselves, not others, with the coat of an humble attitude. If every Christian would put on the cloak of humility everyday, strife would be put out of the church in a hurry.

Peter makes it clear why we should humble ourselves before God and one another. He says that God opposes the proud. Do you realize how powerful that statement is?

Almighty God actively opposes those who operate out of arrogance. He fights against those who exalt themselves. From what I've observed, when God fights with someone, He wins! God isn't out to hurt our pride — He's out to kill it!

God's grace is given to the humble. The grace side of life is where God wants us to live. He wants to assist us, not oppose us.

I believe pride was the root cause of Peter's denial of Jesus after His arrest. Puffed-up in the Upper Room, he told everyone he would never turn his back on the Master! (Matthew 26:35) The humiliation of denying the Lord broke Peter's proud spirit, paving the way for humility's enthronement in his heart. The post-Pentecost Peter was much more humble than the pre-Pentecost version.

God calls us to be humble, but humility is our choice. The biblical principle is this: Humble yourself or be humbled! His highest Will is for us to voluntarily submit ourselves to Him. He promises to exalt us then with His mighty hand (much better than our puny hands!). He will put us where we need to be at the proper time. I have learned that "proper" or "due time" means His time, not mine!

The easiest way to receive God's grace is to humble ourselves. It's by far the best way to go. But there's another way, and it's hard. It's the way of humiliation. If we won't humble ourselves, God will humble us. He loves us so much that He will do almost anything to bring us to the end of ourselves and deliver us from arrogance.

I have a habit of learning things the hard way. In this case, many times the Spirit of the Lord had whispered "humble yourself Steve" in the secret chambers of my spirit. There had been opportunities for me to renounce pride and embrace humility. But in those crucial moments of choice, I wasn't contrite enough in spirit to step across the line from arrogance to humility.

Controllers don't have contrite hearts. A contrite heart is a repentant heart. Repentant hearts are necessary for God to do His cleansing and restoring work.

The sacrifices of God are a broken spirit; a broken and contrite heart; O God, Thou wilt not despise.
Psalm 51:17

Contrite hearts are prerequisites for revival. Isaiah 57:15 says:

For thus says the High and Exalted One, Who lives forever, whose name is holy; I dwell on a high and holy place; and also with the contrite and lowly of spirit; In order to revive the spirit of the lowly, and to revive the heart of the contrite.

I had to be broken to become contrite. The revival (renewal and restoration of heart) I desperately needed came through humiliation.

D. L. Moody said, "God sends no one away except those who are full of themselves." The Lord could do nothing but oppose my efforts while I was full of myself (arrogant). The humiliation of resigning broke me so that I could be emptied of myself.

The other half of Proverbs 29:23 says that "*a humble spirit will obtain honor.*" It was humbling for me step down from my pulpit. It was humbling to enter a psychiatric hospital. It was humbling to be out of control. It was humbling to spill my soul in a room full of women. It was humbling to be sedated because I was found crying uncontrollably on the bathroom floor. It was humbling to depend on others for finances. It was humbling to not have any answers. It was humbling to tell people I was a shepherd without any sheep.

Proverbs 22:4 says "*The reward of humility and the fear of the Lord are riches, honor and life.*" Broken, I was now in a position where I could learn the fear (reverential awe) of the Lord. He would show me the way of humility as I surrendered to Him and submitted to His reclamation plan for me. Riches, honor and life sounded wonderful! Humility before the Lord was the key to possessing these timeless treasures.

God, in His grace, allowed my life to get "out of control" so I could learn how to come "under His control." The Holy Spirit would work through the Word to remove the hurdles of abandonment, anger, and arrogance which had hindered my healing. Spirit-controlled, instead of Steve-controlled living was the reward waiting for me at the end of my restoration process.

Pastor to Pastor

1. Pastor, what are your motives for ministry? (Why do you do what you do?) Proverbs 16:2-3

2. Are there any unresolved emotional or spiritual conflicts in your life? (Get to them before they get to you.) Ecclesiastes 7:8-10

3. Have you worked through your personal disappointments in the ministry? (Remember: Turkeys, not pastors, are meant for stuffing!) II Corinthians 4:7-11

4. Any areas where pride is a problem? (If you're not sure — ask your wife. She'll tell you!) Proverbs 11:2

5. Are you secure in your personal relationship with God? (How do you really feel about your Heavenly Father?) Romans 8:14-17

Pastor to People

1. Pastors aren't perfect. (God is still working on them just as He's working on you.) Philippians 1:6

2. Give your pastor space to grow. (Let God make His minister.) II Peter 3:8

3. Love your leader in the low times. (Love your pastor when they're not so lovable). I Peter 4:8

4. Stay sensitive to your pastor's struggles. (Pray in secret for their victory.) II Corinthians 2:14

5. Affirm your pastor as a person often! (Let your leader know that you think they're a wonderful child of God). I Thessalonians 5:11

Chapter 6
Unholy Bride

For where jealousy and selfish ambition exist;
here is disorder and every evil thing.

James 3:16

Recently, I lunched with a man who had pastored churches for over twenty-five years before leaving the ministry the previous summer. As we talked shop, tears filled his eyes. He mentioned to me how much he missed being in the pulpit. He said he felt lost and didn't think he was of much value to God anymore.

I questioned him concerning the circumstances surrounding his situation. Fidgeting for a few moments, this gentle spirited man collected his courage and said, "I divorced the ministry. I should have left years ago, but I felt guilty that I was letting God down. I finally left because I couldn't handle the petty people and carnal behavior of the church body anymore."

Those words, "I divorced the ministry," rocked my pastor's heart. Across the table sat a spirit-broken servant of the Lord who had quit his calling. He hadn't really wanted to go. It had grieved him to leave. Ministry was the love of this brother's life. He'd given his best years in service to Christ and His church. But he grew weary and finally got fed up trying to deal with the unholy behavior of some members of Christ's bride.

Recent surveys indicate that anywhere from fifty to seventy percent of current ministers would seriously consider leaving the ministry if they could find a way outside of their current profession to adequately provide for the needs of their families. As it is, pastors are leaving the ministry today in record numbers. An exodus from the ranks of full-time ministry is in progress. With shocking statistics like this, the church has to ask herself why so many of her shepherds are contemplating looking for greener pastures.

The current mindset prevalent in America's churches assumes that when a pastor leaves a ministry, whether he is voted out or chooses to resign, it's because he did something wrong. The pastor is to blame. Everyone presumes he is the one who made it impossible for the relationship to continue because of scandal, sexual immorality, conduct unbecoming a minister, misappropriation of church funds, administrative differences, his inability to get along with the church organist, etc.

When I resigned my church, I hadn't slept with another man's wife, embezzled church moneys, committed any crimes, nor violated ministerial ethics in any way. I had provided good leadership commensurate with my gifts, style, training and experience. But when the church split, and I was forced out, Satan and certain church members did their best to convince me, and others, that I was singularly responsible for all that had transpired.

Part of the heavy spirit of shame and humiliation that hung over me during my depression was attributable to the sense of guilt I carried concerning how much I was personally responsible for when the church divided.

A big monkey jumped on my back when I walked out of that sanctuary for the last time. It rode me for months, mocking me and making me think that everything that went wrong was solely my fault. It kept whispering, "If only you'd treated so and so differently. If you'd let them have their way they wouldn't have opposed you. If you hadn't been so firm with them when they were out of line you'd still be pastor. Everything would be all right if you'd been more tolerant and had overlooked people's imperfections."

Satan tried to sell me a lie. He wanted me to believe that I was responsible for everyone's behavior. That no matter how unChristlike I was treated by others, I was somehow responsible.

But I found freedom, and my healing accelerated when the Holy Spirit showed me I wasn't responsible for everything that went on in the church; that individuals were responsible for their own behavior, not me; and that some of their behavior was directly responsible for the resulting heartbreak experienced by so many.

Some of you pastors who are reading these pages need to get this same monkey off your back. I feel deeply for you and empathize with your struggle. You've been beating up on yourself unfairly. You're bearing a burden of guilt that belongs on somebody else's shoulders.

Pastors fight two wars. The first war is holy. It's biblical and honorable. It's warfare with Satan, described in Ephesians 6:10-12 and II Corinthians 10:3-5. This warfare is spiritual (motivated by the Spirit). The entire church is to be united in this supreme effort to engage and defeat the enemy of men's souls. Winning this war pushes back the gates of hell and sets captives free!

The second war is unholy. It's non-biblical and disgraceful. It's warfare with the saints, described in I and II Corinthians. This warfare is carnal (motivated by the flesh). Instead of fighting Satan together, saints fight saints, creating disunity and division. The legions of hell prevail and gain ground from the church when she engages in unholy warfare. Disorder and every evil thing exists when saints battle one another.

As spiritual leader, the pastor gets caught on the front lines of both conflicts. He finds himself in a crossfire between Satan and carnally motivated saints.

Paul's letter to the Corinthians deals with just such problems. The letters to the Corinthians were corrective in nature. The Apostle Paul diagnosed the real issue behind this church's conduct when he wrote in I Corinthians 3:1-4:

> *And I, brethren, could not speak to you as spiritual men, but as to men of flesh (carnal), as to babes in Christ. I gave you milk to drink, not solid food; for you were not yet able to receive it. Indeed, even now you are not able, for you are still fleshly. For since there is jealousy and strife among you, are you not fleshly, and are you not walking like mere men? For when one says, "I am of Paul," and another, "I am of Apollos," are you not mere men?*

Paul wanted to address his brothers as "spiritual men," but he couldn't because they were still behaving like spiritual babies. As "babes in Christ," they were suppose to be maturing, becoming weaned from spiritual milk, moving on to "solid food." Instead, he found them unable to receive solid sustenance, so he gave them milk to drink.

Carnal desires dictated their conduct. Paul wrote that because of the "jealousy and strife among them," they were walking (living out their lives) in the same way natural men (men of the flesh) do. They were acting more like men of the world than men of the Kingdom.

The bulk of Paul's epistles to the Corinthians addresses everything from division over leaders, misuse of gifts, sexual immorality within the body, abuse of liberty, lawsuits between brothers, discipline and order in the church, to attacks on Paul's leadership.

The infighting within the fellowship over who was the better leader, Paul or Apollos, was no different than the political maneuvering that goes on outside the church.

The church of the 90's, with all of her high-tech sophistication and polished programs is still plagued with the same shameful conduct within her four walls. The reason: carnality.

Immaturity is one characteristic of carnality. Spiritual immaturity manifests itself in two forms. First, there are those newly born again. Recently saved, they still have one foot in the world. Fleshly influences direct much of their behavior. The discipleship process is designed to help them be transformed from the old life according to the world, to the new life of the Kingdom of God (Ephesians 4:17-24). Ideally, over time, and with training from God's Word, they should leave spiritual childhood behind and grow up into mature, spiritual men and women of God (Ephesians 4:13).

The other form of carnality involves those who have been "Christian" for some time, but who have never matured in Christ (Ephesians 4:15). These chronologically older believers are still immature and continue to operate out of the flesh. They equate maturity with longevity. Because they have been in the church for many years, they assume a mantle of maturity rests upon their religious shoulders.

They think they're spiritually-minded when in fact, their personal conduct reveals they're carnally-minded. Being self-centered and self-righteous, these church members bring the ways of the world into the body of Christ and operate out of the traditions of men.

Both types of carnality create conflict in the church. The pastor ends up being the one who is most affected by the fleshly behavior of believers. His primary role is to instruct believers in the faith and equip them for service (Ephesians 4:12). But he finds himself spending tremendous amounts of spiritual and emotional energy confronting childish conduct in his church. Pastors often "burnout" trying to put out the fires that fleshly behaviors ignite.

In Ephesians 5:22-33, Paul likens the marriage relationship between husband and wife to that of Christ and His church. In verses 25-27 we find these words concerning the nature of Christ's bride.

> *Husbands, love your wives, just as Christ also loved the church and gave Himself up for her, that He might sanctify her, having cleansed her by the washing of water with the word, that He might present to Himself the church in all her glory, having no spot or wrinkle or any such thing; but that she should be holy and blameless.*

I will never forget the day my bride walked down the aisle and captured my heart forever. She was absolutely beautiful. Set apart by the Lord for me. Pure, blameless, without wrinkle or spot. In a word, holy.

We pledged, before God and men, to conduct ourselves in purity and faithfulness till death should separate us. We were being joined in holy matrimony. Our love was based on a commitment to holiness.

The church is the bride of Christ. He loved her so much He laid down His life for her. He set her apart (sanctified) and cleansed her with His blood and the Word. His whole purpose was to present the church "in all of her glory." No spots or wrinkles. She should be holy and blameless. Hence, the church, is the holy bride of Christ.

As a young, idealistic pastor, I expected the church to conduct herself as the holy bride of the Lord Jesus. Christ had provided everything necessary for members of His bride to walk in holiness. But not everyone walks according to the Word. To my deep disappointment, the church behaved at times more like an unholy bride than a holy one.

Certain attitudes and actions of some church members create strife. Webster defines strife as "bitter, sometimes violent conflict or dissension; an act of contention; fight, struggle, discord; exertion or contention for superiority."

Strife is an ugly thing in the body of Christ. It's more common than we're willing to confess. We try to cover it up, pretending it doesn't really exist in our fellowship.

The Word of God is straightforward concerning strife. Paul grieved to the point of tears over the misconduct of the Corinthians. He was preparing to make a pastoral visit. In II Corinthians 12:20 he shared a fear he held in his heart:

> *For I am afraid that perhaps when I come I may*
> *find you to be not what I wish and may be found by*
> *you to be not what you wish; that perhaps there*
> *may be strife, jealousy, angry tempers, disputes,*
> *slanders gossip, arrogance, disturbances.*

Paul was hoping he wouldn't find these destructive practices among the Corinthian brothers. What pastor hasn't wished that these damaging behaviors might not be present in his church, only to find them fully operative in the lives of some of the sheep he tends.

Proverbs 6:16-18 minces no words regarding what God thinks about those who stir up strife in the body.

> *There are six things which the Lord hates, Yes,*
> *seven which are an abomination to Him: Haughty*
> *eyes, a lying tongue, And hands that shed innocent*
> *blood. A heart that devises wicked plans, Feet that*
> *run rapidly to evil, A false witness that utters lies,*
> *and one who spreads strife among brothers.*

What a list of dirty laundry! The Lord makes it plain; He hates these things. They're an abomination (something of extreme loathing, hatred, disgust) before the Holy One. Sadly, most of us have witnessed these disgusting behaviors in the body of Christ.

Clergy and layleaders alike find themselves targets of those who have nothing better to do than to spread discord. Part of my burnout was caused by those who spread strife in the church. At times, I all but pulled my hair out, wondering how to survive the assaults of those bent on carrying out their carnal plans for controlling the church.

Over many months of inner healing, I came to the conclusion that I had been up against what I call "unholy spirits." They lurked in the darkness behind the Sunday smiles, Christian lingo, and religious routine of some of the believers I served.

I initially felt disgraced by what I erringly thought was defeat. But the Lord showed me that I had battled well against forces of darkness beyond my control. Identifying the unholy spirits that drive strife-spreaders helped relieve the remorse and regret which had pounded me into the ground. With some, I'd fought a war that couldn't be won. God took me out of the church, sparing me further damage from those bent on their self-serving agendas.

Before we identify six unholy spirits that ruin relationships and divide churches, it's important to make some observations concerning those who spread strife.

- Satan plants some strife-spreaders in the sheepfold. They are "wolves in sheep's clothing" (Matthew 7:15 and Acts 20:29). They act like believers, but they aren't. Subtly and craftily, they deceive the sheep, sowing seeds of discord that ultimately create dissension and division among the brethren. Wolves need to be exposed and removed from the fellowship (Titus 3:10-11).
- Some strife-spreaders are believers. Intentionally, or unintentionally, they become "busybodies in other men's affairs" (I Peter 4:15, KJV). They're always stirring things up. They don't see themselves as sowers of discord. They're just "concerned Christians" watching out for the welfare of the church. Their sweet, sincere outward spirits attract innocent, immature followers. Strife-spreading saints can be longtime members or spiritual drifters from other fellowships. They're expert in forming underground factions that feed the fires of dissent. They need to be disciplined, restored to the fellowship, and taught to mind their own business (I Thessalonians 4:11).
- Saints who spread strife believe they're championing a holy cause. They really believe their course of action is correct. Ends justify the means when it comes to discharging their sacred trust to safeguard God's house. They're blinded by one or more of the following spirits.

The first unholy spirit could be called the spirit of rebellion. Resistance to authority is at the heart of this unholy spirit. "Who's in charge" is the issue.

Proud Lucifer (Satan) was kicked out of heaven because of his rebellious spirit (Isaiah 14:11-17). He wasn't happy being in heaven only a notch beneath God's throne. That wasn't good enough. He defiantly declared "I will make myself like the Most High" (verse 14). He wasn't satisfied with, nor submissive to, God's authority structure.

Adam and Eve rebelled against God's singular command to "not eat from the tree of knowledge of good and evil" (Genesis 2:16-

17, 3:6-24). They put their desires above His divine directive and it cost them the glory of the garden.

The children of Israel constantly rebelled against God's hand-selected servant. Time and time again, they "contended with Moses," "speaking against him," challenging his leadership (Numbers 11-14). Their contentious grumbling led to stumbling. Israel defied the Lord and His servant, and they ended up wandering in the wilderness for forty years under the disciplining hand of God.

God's messengers, the prophets, were ridiculed and rejected (Jeremiah 1:17-19).

The religious leaders of Christ's day, the scribes and Pharisees, contended with Jesus over His spiritual authority (Matthew 21:23).

The Apostle Paul had to defend his leadership because his authority was under attack by the Corinthians. (II Corinthians 11-13).

Pastor's have to deal with authority issues regularly in the life of the local church. Sinful natures, unchecked by the Holy Spirit, rebel against authority. It seems as though someone is always challenging who is in charge. It is amazing how the average congregation gives and takes away authority from its leaders.

When churches call a pastor to serve them as spiritual leader, they believe this is God's man of the hour. The pastor, hearing from the Lord, believes God has appointed him for this leadership role. So they agree to serve together.

The church warmly welcomes their new leader, applauding him as he goes to work. But when he begins to exercise his leadership role, some start questioning, "Who are you to tell me (us) what to do?"

Three months before I arrived in Michigan, I received a personal letter from one of the board members of my first church telling me that people were already taking sides regarding which pastor, the former one or pastor-to-be (me), they liked best. The letter also said that the board members were not "yes-men" and would think for themselves.

I was too naive to give much serious thought to the letter. I interpreted it as basically innocent. But it was far from harmless. It was a message that lines of authority were already being drawn.

Shortly after my arrival, a few longtime, influential church members visited my office to let me know what I could and could not do in their church. Less bold individuals mailed me their "do's and don'ts" lists. One man took me out for breakfast to help me understand "how things work around here."

I went about my business leading the church as God directed. My personal philosophy of ministry is to pray and obey. Pray and obey I did.

God blessed us with growth. Things were going very well. It looked as though we might have a marriage made in heaven. But when I started to make decisions that affected the direction of the church, rebellious spirits rose to challenge my right to lead. The honeymoon ended.

Without authority it is difficult, if not impossible, for pastors to lead effectively. Without respect and support for proper, biblical authority, a pastor is like a policeman who wears a badge but has no handcuffs, gun or jail. I have a friend who is a police officer in our city. One night when I rode with him on his beat, I asked him what frustrated him most about his job. He replied, "What really bugs me is arresting offenders, and then the system puts them back on the streets before I can finish the paperwork."

Because some of our religious systems undermine spiritual authority, many pastors feel frustrated trying to lead God's people. Feeling that their hands are tied generates frustration that fuels the fire of burnout.

God gives spiritual authority. The Apostle Paul makes it absolutely clear where a pastor's authority comes from.

In accordance with the authority, which the Lord gave me, for building up and not tearing down.
II Corinthians 13:10

Authority accompanies anointing. When God called Moses, He gave his servant authority to lead (Exodus 3). "I am who I am" (Exodus 3:14) appointed Moses to lead the nation out of Egypt. God didn't ask Israel whether they wanted Moses to lead or not. He didn't seek their approval, nor did He request that they grant His representative authority to carry out his mission.

Study of Scripture reveals that every time God's people acted independent of their leaders, they got themselves in trouble. For example, at Kadesh-Barnea the children of Israel sided with the majority report of the spies, even though it was a "bad report" (Numbers 13:32).

Joshua and Caleb implored Israel "not to rebel against the Lord" (Numbers 14:9). Refusing to "go up and take possession of the land and surely overcome it" (Numbers 13:30) under Caleb's and Joshua's courageous leadership proved deadly. The people incurred the wrath of God; and as a result, a whole generation died in the desert before they had another opportunity to obey the Lord and follow His leaders.

Jesus taught with authority (Matthew 7:29), cast out unclean spirits with authority (Luke 4:36), stilled the sea by His authority (Mark 1:41), healed the sick with authority (Matthew 8:1-13), forgave sins by His authority (Matthew 9:6) and performed signs and wonders with authority (Mark 11:15-28). All the good He did, flowed from His anointing (Acts 10:38).

The Pharisees openly challenged Christ's authority to do His ministry (Matthew 21:23). In rebelling against His authority, they were rejecting His anointing as the Messiah. They refused to acknowledge Jesus as God's Son. Their self-righteous, indignant rebellion lead to the place of the Skull where the Savior of the world was crucified.

David, while on the run from King Saul, had opportunity to personally avenge himself. But he understood God's authority structure. David declared, "The Lord forbid that I should stretch out my hand against the Lord's anointed" (I Samuel 26:11).

Saul was certainly wrong. He deserved correction. But David left it to the Lord. In verses 8-11, David told Abishai that the Lord would take care of Saul. David warned his servant that anyone who strikes the Lord's anointed "would not be without guilt."

Why is it that there are those in the church who don't think twice about "stretching out their hand against the Lord's anointed" and don't even blush when they bash the minister and his ministry?

The United States operates as a democracy. Our government functions fairly well under this system. The people have the right and freedom to vote their leaders in or out of office. Individuals and small groups can profoundly impact the course of our country by voicing their pleasure or displeasure and casting votes.

The Church of Jesus Christ, however, is a theocracy. Christ is the head (Ephesians 5:23). He's in charge. There are no political parties. The church operates under His headship through the leaders He calls and places in positions of spiritual authority (Ephesians 4:11). He anoints and appoints them as His representatives to equip the church to carry out His will on earth.

The biblical pattern for flow of authority in the church is different from that of a democracy. In simplest terms, it goes like this. God speaks. The leader obeys. The people follow. The church advances. Everyone rejoices!

Some church structures and denominational systems, however, function more like a democracy than a theocracy. Everyone gets a vote. A simple majority rules.

The intent of the framers of this church polity was noble and good. The idea was to provide members with an avenue to express their wishes. The systems constructed also provided some measure of checks and balances to insure accountability among church leaders.

But systems like these possess the potential for producing unhealthy churches. Individuals or groups with rebellious spirits exploit the church government systems to their advantage. Pastors become expendable. The underlying attitude can become "the people speak — the pastor jumps." If I don't like something the pastor does, then I'll just make some noise. Question his authority. Challenge his leadership. Recruit some allies. Do an end run. Share my "concerns" with his superiors. Vote against his proposals. Neutralize his effectiveness as spiritual leader.

Sheep need shepherds because sheep are followers. That's the way God designed it. Too many shepherds are being beaten up and are burning out because the sheep, who are supposed to be following, are trying to lead.

Is it any surprise then that clergy are confronted with rip-the-leader letter writing campaigns, public roasting, angry outbursts in meetings, insurrections, hostile takeovers, and character assassination?

God's antidote to the spirit of rebellion is submission to spiritual leaders. Hebrews 13:17 reads:

> *Obey your leaders and submit to them; for they keep watch over your souls, as those who will give an account. Let them do this with joy and not with grief, for this would be unprofitable for you.*

Church members are to obey and submit to their leaders. To submit means to voluntarily come under the authority of another.

Pastors provide a priceless spiritual service to believers. They watch over their souls. Pastors are instructed to do this soberly and seriously, remembering they will give an account of their shepherdship. The body of Christ is instructed to "let them do this (watch over their souls, lead) with joy and not with grief."

When the hand of the rebellious-in-spirit is stretched out to strike the Lord's anointed, joy departs the diligent, devoted pastor's heart. Joyless ministry is a major symptom of burnout. If spiritual leadership is conducted with grief, it is unprofitable for the pastor and body of Christ.

Bottom line: Obedience and submission to church leaders is advantageous to every believer. It is to their profit that their leaders be allowed to care for their spiritual needs with authority. Joyful and fruitful ministry will be the result.

The second unholy spirit is the spirit of criticism. Churches are composed of many different committees. But one group seems to be a standing committee in every church. It's the criticism committee.

This committee meets informally and irregularly. Much of it's business is conducted over the telephone, or in choir lofts, church parking lots, dimly lit hallways, and home group meetings. It's officers are sometimes known, but most of the committee members like to remain anonymous.

Criticism is a crippler of church unity. At the root of critical attitudes is a judgmental, fault-finding spirit. Faultfinders are always looking for what's wrong instead of what's right.

Jesus warned us against judging other people. In Matthew 7:1-4 He tells His followers not to judge for they will be judged in the same way they judge others. Jesus says we are to spend our time tending to the log in our own eye instead of focusing on the speck in our brother's eye.

Faultfinders Anonymous majors in overlooking logs and zeroing in on specks.

Criticism crushes a pastor's spirit more than anything else. Like the annoying drip of a faucet, after a while the constant criticism and complaining behind the leader's back wears him down. Gossip, backbiting, slander, murmuring, grumbling, and critical comments sap a pastor's energy and cool the fire in his heart.

For whatever reason, some people in the church believe criticism is their gift and complaining is their calling. They find fault with everything their leader does. He preaches too long; his sermons aren't long enough. He dresses too nice; he doesn't dress well enough to represent the congregation. He doesn't visit people in their homes often enough; he spends too much time with people and not enough time in his study. He pays too much attention to first-time visitors and neglects the regular attendees. His wife's hairstyle is too "poofy" and makes her look like she came out of Hollywood. His kids are too energetic at church. He doesn't love us like our previous pastor did.

On and on it goes. Where it stops, and if it stops, only God knows. The spirit of criticism is a close sister of the spirit of rebellion. Whenever you see people rebelling against the authority over them, criticism is not far off.

Jesus was the target of incessant criticism during his ministry. The religious people complained about what He did, how He did it, who He did it with, when He did it, and why He did it. The Lord never got a break from the faultfinders of His day. They even criticized Him as He hung on the Cross (Matthew 27:39-43).

Criticism erodes the pastor's confidence. Opposition comes with the territory when you choose to lead. Leaders can never please everyone. To try to will turn the best pastor into a wishy-washy wimp.

People with critical spirits have a way of getting under your skin. Because of the ever-present spirit of murmuring, pastors can find themselves taking a defensive posture as leader. Instead of boldly coming from the prayer closet and study armed with God's plan for the church, they sheepishly slide into board meetings, hoping to sell the people on God's Will. Being on the defensive, waiting for the next volley of complaint, is not the way to advance God's work.

God's antidote for the spirit of criticism is for brothers to build each other up through wholesome communication. The following Scriptures, when practiced by all, would help chase criticism from the church.

> *Let no unwholesome word proceed from your mouth,*
> *but only such a word as is good for edification,*
> *according to the need of the moment, that it may give*
> *grace to those who hear.*
>
> Ephesians 4:29

> *Remind them to be subject to rulers, to authorities, to*
> *be obedient, to be ready for every good deed, to*
> *malign no one, to be uncontentious, gentle, showing*
> *every consideration for all men."*
>
> Titus 3:1-2

He who goes about as a talebearer (gossip) reveals
secrets. But he who is trustworthy conceals a matter."
                                        Proverbs 11:13

He who goes about as a slanderer reveals secrets,
Therefore do not associate with a gossip.
                                        Proverbs 20:19

For lack of wood the fire goes out; And where there
is no whisperer, contention quiets down.
                                        Proverbs 26:20

Do not speak against one another, brethren. He
who speaks against a brother, or judges his brother,
speaks against the law, and judges the law; but if
you judge the law, you are not a doer of the law, but
a judge of it. There is only one Lawgiver and Judge,
the One who is able to save and destroy; but who
are you who judge your neighbor?
                                        James 4:11-12

Do not complain, brethren, against one another,
that you yourselves may not be judges; behold, the
Judge is standing right at the door."
                                        James 5:9

The third unholy spirit is the spirit of offense. The pastor
wondered why the usually-friendly board member's wife had
become evasive and distant. Upon inquiry, he discovered that a few
weeks earlier, he had passed by her in the crowded church lobby
between morning services without personally greeting her.

During stewardship month, as the preacher was teaching on
tithing, a couple got up and left the sanctuary. The pastor received
a letter later that week that read: "We will no longer be attending
your church because all you want is our money."

A choir member drops out because a person more gifted was
selected to sing the solo in the Christmas cantata. A ten-year
member pulls his church membership because his recommenda-
tions for the new facilities were not adopted.

People with a spirit of offense are some of the hardest people to deal with. Solomon must have been writing from personal experience when the Spirit penned these words through him:

> *A brother offended is harder to be won than a strong city! And contentions are like the bars of a castle.*
>
> Proverbs 18:19

Anyone who works with people knows the truth and sting of this statement. Jesus said in Luke 17:1-4 that offenses (stumbling blocks) will come, that they are unavoidable in life. But he gave stern warning to those who deliberately cause people to stumble. He then said unlimited forgiveness is the way to handle offenses.

The Lord Himself faced the spirit of offense in His own hometown. When he was teaching in the synagogue at Nazareth, the listeners were astonished and wondered, *"Where did this man get these things, and what is this wisdom given to Him, and such miracles as these performed by His hands? Is not this the carpenter, the son of Mary, and brother of James, and Joses, and Judas, and Simon? Are not His sisters with us? And they took offense at him."* (Mark 6:1-3)

They heard His wisdom and witnessed many miracles. But they were offended. Who was Jesus to be doing these things? Where did He get this power? (That they didn't have!) This was just the carpenter. Mary's boy. They all knew Him. Nothing special about Him.

Their spirit of offense caused them to doubt and disbelieve. Because of "their unbelief" (verse 6) Jesus could do no mighty miracle there (verse 5). He laid hands on a few sick people and healed them, but was hindered from doing what He might have done because they stumbled over who He was. They were offended that the power and wisdom of God came in a package called Jesus of Nazareth.

Pastors come in every size and shape. As the Lord's ministers of the Gospel, they often run into a spirit of offense in their hometown — the local church.

We live in a society permeated with an uptight, touchy spirit. We look for reasons to cry foul. — He or she offended me. Look what they said about me, or did to me. How dare they address me that way! Who are they to correct me? — We're an over-personalizing people who take the things that others say way too seriously. Offenses, according to the last half of Proverbs 18:19 should be spelled "of fences."

We build fences instead of bridges to people. Little Johnny comes home from school with a disciplinary note. We take offense with his teacher, a fence goes up. A driver cuts in front of us on the expressway without signaling, a fence shoots up. Republicans and Democrats insult each other, fences. Those "castle bars" keep our hearts apart and make it almost impossible to win the offended party over.

Three things are at the heart of a spirit of offense. First is unteachability.

Many people, even in churches, refuse to be taught. What spiritual leader, as he preaches, hasn't noticed the crossed arms, clenched teeth, and unopened Bible of the parishioner sitting near the back? The Pharisees were offended by and infuriated by Jesus because they were unteachable. Their traditions were more important than truth.

The Pharisees were also guilty of the second characteristic of offended spirits: unchangeability.

Jesus called the scribes and Pharisees to change from hypocrisy to holiness. Refusing to change, they took offense and got rid of Him.

Pastors run the risk of offense on a regular basis. Not because they try to, but because the very nature of their primary responsibility ("to declare the whole counsel of God" Acts 20:27) demands that people learn and change if they are to enjoy the blessings of the Kingdom. As an agent of change, the pastor delivers the message that has the power to transform lives into the image of Christ.

The Word of God is sharp and cuts right through the real issues we wrestle with in life (Hebrews 4:12-13). Biblical truth invites us to change. When we decide not to change, choosing instead to dig in our spiritual heels in resistance to the wooing of the Holy Spirit, offense raises it's ugly head.

The real object of our offense is God's message. But we can't deal with that. So we project our perceived "hurt" toward the pastor. The fence goes up between us and the messenger because we refuse to respond positively to the message.

Unwillingness to give the benefit of the doubt is the third characteristic of offense. People with the spirit of offense never hear "the rest of the story." They seldom seek facts before they pass judgment. Their ears only hear what they want to hear. It's as though they are looking for something to get upset about.

Offense-oriented people assume the worst about others. They think people are picking on them. Leaders are always near the top of their list of suspected offenders.

People with a spirit of offense seem to carry a chip on their shoulders. Somewhere back down the road of life, they stopped giving people the benefit of the doubt because someone hurt them. They stiffen up, always on the lookout for offenses. Building fences that keep people out.

Pastors have to walk on egg shells around these members. When present, a spirit of offense puts a cloud of tension in the air. I used to ask myself, "What's wrong with Mr. Smith? Why is he upset with me? I didn't do anything I know of that he should be offended about. What's the problem?" More often than not, the problem was with Mr. Smith, not me.

The spirit of offense can be very harmful in the body of Christ. It builds barriers. It holds back the supernatural power of God. Signs and wonders are scarce when offense abounds.

It violates the "bears all things, believes all things, hopes all things, endures all things" nature of love found in I Corinthians 13:7. The spirit of offense prevents believers from loving one another and going forward in unity to win their communities for Christ.

God's remedy for overcoming offense is love and forgiveness. Peter came to Jesus and asked the following question:

> *"Lord, how often shall my brother sin against me and I forgive him? Up to seven times?" Jesus said to him, "I do not say to you, up to seven times, but up to seventy times seven."*
> Matthew 18:21-22

Unlimited forgiveness is the key to overcoming the offenses that come our way repeatedly. Forgiveness is a decision of the will that we make if we want to love people like Jesus did.

I have made a personal commitment to not let myself be offended by anyone. With the help of the Holy Spirit, I choose to overlook offenses, take them to the Lord and leave them in His gracious hands. I will pray for the offender, forgive them, ask God to bless them, go out of my way to love them and then go on with the work the Lord has called me to do.

Pastors, you must lighten up on yourselves. Some people are plain old difficult. Love those who are oppressed with a spirit of offense. Forgive them. Don't allow their accusations to cause you to question your calling or to lose your passion for Jesus and the ministry.

The fourth unholy spirit is the spirit of bitterness. Bitterness. Just the way the word sounds sends cold shivers down my spine.

Bitter hearts are hard hearts. The issue behind hardness of heart is an unforgiving spirit. Satan is a master strategist when it comes to bitterness. He knows the essence of the Good News is forgiveness. Therefore, he works overtime to make life difficult so people will grow hard and become bitter toward God and their brothers.

Bitterness depresses the human spirit. Proverbs 14:10 says this about the bitter spirit.

The heart knows it's own bitterness, And a stranger does not share it's joy.

Job despaired of God's dealings with him. He struggled with understanding why his life had suddenly, and tragically, come unglued. You can almost feel his lament.

I loathe my own life; I will give full vent to my complaint; I will speak in the bitterness of my soul.
Job 10:1

Which of us has not known the poisonous bite of bitterness in our spirit at some time? Job was beside himself. He was hurting. Answers to his dilemma were shrouded in the mystery of faith. For a time, bitterness laid waste to his hope of better days.

Hurt visits our hearts, too. Life sours and we find ourselves speaking out of the bitterness of our soul. We don't want to be bitter, but deep down we know we are. We feel helpless as the roots of bitterness wrap themselves around our heart, strangling the love out of our life.

Bitterness destroys relationships. Bitter people are extremely difficult to deal with. The acid of resentment that eats away at their hearts alters them into spiteful, harsh, tough-talking, hate-walking antagonists. They hate life because, deep down, they hate somebody. Their venom of unresolved conflict with someone spews out, ruining all their relationships.

The deep, hardened furrows in her face from years of smileless days, and her steely-cold, look-right-through-you gaze instantly impressed me that this fifty-plus woman was not a happy camper. Time and experiences proved my initial impression more than right.

Donna was overly opinionated. She had something negative to say about everything and everybody.

She criticized everything I did as her pastor. It didn't matter what it was, she didn't like it. She didn't keep her views to herself either. Donna assembled other "negative Neds and Nellies" around her. She recruited more than a few bitter buddies. Her home doubled as Grand Central Station for the gossipers and grumblers in our church.

Donna's personal demeanor, her dress, the way she walked, and even her hairstyle sent the message: I'm bitter. I don't want to be. But I am. And you're going to know about it.

Everything about her was harsh. She talked tough. She prided herself on putting people down. She and her husband shared a stormy, love-starved relationship. Toughness, not tenderness, dominated their marriage.

Gentleness, kindness, and softness were foreign to Donna. Her adult children inherited their mom's stony-hearted disposition, making them miserable as they griped their way through life.

A number of years ago, a humorous article in *Readers Digest* gave the account of a woman who had been bitten by a dog and was advised by her physician to write her last wishes, as she might succumb to rabies. She spent such a long time with the pencil and paper that the doctor finally made a remark about the length of her will. "Will!" she snorted. "I'm writing a list of people I'm going to bite!"

Life makes some people better, and some people bitter.

Donna's life had been anything but rosy. A tragic automobile accident took her father's life when she was small and needed her daddy. As a young woman, she was sexually abused by a trusted uncle.

Because of the abuse, she never felt good about herself. Low self-esteem dominated her thinking and actions. Her poor-me attitude drove wedges between herself and the people she cared about.

Donna was angry with God, the uncle, and a long list of others (friends, employers, co-workers, pastors, authority figures) who she felt had crossed her. Claiming to know Christ, she made the religious rounds, trying desperately to uproot the resentment that had planted itself in the deep recesses of her heart.

In dealing with Donna, I frequently wanted to beat my head against a wall, wondering why this insecure, wanting-to-be- loved lady kept shunning the affection extended to her.

One day, as I was raking leaves in the yard, Donna pulled into our driveway. I walked over to her car. She was crying. I'd never seen this hard-shelled woman shed a tear. Through the tears, she shared with me that her husband was considering divorce. She said she couldn't handle that. I felt great compassion for Donna. I made a few suggestions and prayed for her. We agreed to meet for counseling.

During counseling, Donna came to a key crossroads. When she realized that she had been bitter for years and would only find freedom through forgiveness, she was faced with a choice: to forgive or not to forgive those who had hurt her.

Sad to say, she chose not to forgive. The crack in her defensive armor closed up. She stiffened up and became even more bitter. Her bitterness then poured out on me. She became a key player in my ouster as pastor.

The writer of Hebrews records these sobering words in chapter 12, verses 14-15:

> *Pursue peace with all men, and the holiness without which no one will see the Lord. See to it that no one comes short of the grace of God; that no root of bitterness springing up causes trouble, and by it, many be defiled.*

Bitterness is like a live vine that springs up and entangles every heart it touches. It causes trouble in marriages, families, churches, businesses, neighborhoods and nations. Bitterness defiles (contaminates, makes impure and unclean) many.

Bitterness, alone, in a few people can destroy the holy life of an entire congregation.

Bitter people fall short of the grace of God. Because they care and know what this verse says, pastors and lay leaders can find themselves running around with a holy ax, trying to chop this deadly vine out of the congregation. Inevitably, they become discouraged and disillusioned when they lose the battle to uproot bitterness from their parishioners and parish.

For pastors and parishoners alike, the biblical remedy to bitterness is to forgive. Note in the following passages the responsibility to forgive rests solely upon the shoulders of individual confessors of Christ.

*And whenever you stand praying, forgive, if you have
anything against anyone; so that you Father also
who is in heaven may forgive you your transgressions. But if you do not forgive, neither will your
Father who is in heaven forgive your transgressions.*

Mark 11:25-26

*And do not grieve the Holy Spirit of God, by whom
you were sealed for the day of redemption. Let all
bitterness and wrath and anger and clamor and
slander be put away from you, along with all
malice. be kind to one another, tenderhearted,
forgiving each other, just as God in Christ also has
forgiven you.*

Ephesians 4:30-32

The only way to root out bitterness is to personally forgive with the same loving spirit that Christ has forgiven us.

The fifth unholy spirit is the spirit of control. In chapter four, we dealt in depth with the controller's spirit. Our purpose here is to briefly cover some aspects of control not previously discussed.

Control is a colossal problem in the church. In his third letter, John the beloved wrote about a man named Diotrephes.

*I wrote something to the church; but Diotrephes,
who loves to be first among them, does not accept
what we say. For this reason, if I come, I will call
attention to his deeds which he does, unjustly
accusing with wicked words; and not satisfied with
this, neither does he himself receive the brethren,
and he forbids those who desire to do so, and puts
them out of the church.*

III John 9-10

Control is about power. Diotrephes was a power broker in the church. Loving to be first among the brothers (head honcho), he took it upon himself to decide what would be believed and who would be received. As leader of the Church, John called a spade a spade, and prepared to deal with this church controller.

The average pastor has witnessed enough politics and power

plays in the church to last him until Jesus comes back. Power. Influence. Manipulation. Conniving. Lobbying. Arm twisting. Control. Shameful behavior in the house of the Lord.

Whatever happened to servanthood? When James and John sought preferential positions in the coming Kingdom (being pressured by their opportunistic mother), Jesus responded with a word on leadership according to God.

> *Jesus called them to himself and said, You know that the rulers of the Gentiles lord it over them, and their great men exercise authority over them. It is not so among you; But whoever wishes to become great among you shall be your servant, and whoever wishes to be first among you shall be your slave; just as the Son of man did not come to be served, but to serve and to give his life a ransom for many.*
> Matthew 20:20-26

In a nutshell, the Master said this. The world is run by lords. Power is the name of the game. The Kingdom is lead by servants. Being great and wishing to be first is fine, as long as you understand that my followers serve and give —as I do.

A serious shortage of servant-givers in lay leadership positions exists within the local church today. Positions of influence attract people who are motivated by power. Some people pursue positions of power because they are used to being the decision makers and shot-callers out in the world. Others feel powerless and insignificant in the world, so they seek to carve out a power niche (place of importance and influence) for themselves in the family of God.

Power plays don't belong in holy places. The events during the last days of Jesus' life were the result of power struggles between the Pharisees and Pilate.

Jesus threatened the status quo. Alarmed that they might lose control over the people (Mark 11:18), the powers-that-be met late at night, conducted a kangaroo court behind closed doors, fabricating false charges that delivered a sinless Savior into the hands of power-intoxicated men to be destroyed.

Raw religious power. Nothing more than men in positions of influence, flexing political muscles in the name of spirituality.

Turf wars take place in the church all the time. Political fights occur over who should be the next church treasurer, what color to paint the pre-school classroom, or how much of a raise the pastor should get. So called "winners" of political tussles and tug-of-wars determine direction and hold tight the reins of the church machine.

A phrase pastors hear often during challenging leadership periods is "we're right behind you pastor." Pastors don't want to have some people behind them — those who are caught up in what we'll call "negative ownership."

Positive ownership declares that the church belongs to Christ, and that pastors and people are His servants who have the privilege of working together in unity to further the Gospel. The Holy Spirit is in control. Individual wills are set aside so God's will can be done.

Negative ownership is driven by the misguided notion that the church belongs to the members, that pastors and people are guardians who have the duty of making sure the status quo is maintained. The powerful are in control. Individual wills prevail.

Pastors are being forced out of churches today because of ill-defined concepts such as "administrative differences," "leadership styles," and the most familiar and popular excuse for releasing a leader from leading: "We're not being fed!" Actually, these are all smoke screens and cover-ups for political power plays.

Can anybody justify shouting sessions during business meetings; disgruntled members storming church buildings and pushing the lay leaders to the floor; mob scenes in foyers, demanding that pastors change their ways or there will be a change; closed-door meetings to pressure undecided board members to cast their votes a certain way, or plotting in the parking lot to advance personal agenda through the administrative councils? Can anyone explain how any of these scenarios have any business in the body of Christ? Unfortunately, pastors see scenes such as these all too often.

Is it any surprise that the Shekinah glory departs from our tents of meeting? In our pursuit to be powerful, we wind up powerless. Spiritually anemic. Unable to accomplish mighty things for God.

Let us not forget: the work of the Lord is advanced *"not by might, nor by power, but by my spirit says the Lord of hosts"* (Zechariah 4:6).

The final unholy spirit could be called spirit of envy, jealousy, and strife.

"We must be paying you a pretty good salary for you to be driving a shiny, new car, Pastor. I wish our family could afford an automobile like that."

Little did the author of that envy-laden pronouncement know that I couldn't have afforded a new car if it weren't for a generous gift from relatives for the down payment. We would also be making monthly installments to the local credit union for the next three years.

The spirits of envy, jealousy and strife are underlying factors of the previous five unholy spirits we have examined. James makes plain the nature of the jealous disposition and warns about its effect on the church body.

> Who among you is wise and understanding? Let him show by his good behavior his deeds in the gentleness of wisdom. But if you have bitter jealousy and selfish ambition in your heart, do not be arrogant and so lie against the truth. This wisdom is not that which comes down from above, but is earthly, natural, demonic. For where jealousy and selfish ambition exist, there is disorder and every evil thing.
>
> James 3:13-16

The "disorder" and "every evil thing" we have discussed are the unholy fruit of jealousy and selfish ambition. Carnality's root lies in self-centeredness. It manifests itself through jealous and envious activity in an effort to promote it's own selfish agenda.

James says believers who operate out of this supposed "wisdom" are living a lie. Their behavior is directly opposed to true wisdom. In their arrogance, they deceive themselves into thinking this is the way to go. But God's word says this wisdom that is fueled by "bitter jealousy and selfish ambition in your heart" is earthly, natural, and demonic.

Wow! Couldn't be clearer. Carnal behavior motivated by envy, jealousy, and selfish ambition is of the world and of the devil. There is nothing spiritual about it. It's the stuff of which hell is made.

People live in one of two tents: content or discontent. Discontent drives the spirit of jealousy. Writing to young pastor Timothy, Paul clarified the Christian's priority when it comes to ministry.

> But Godliness actually is a means of great gain, when accompanied by contentment. For we have brought nothing into the world, so we cannot take anything

out of it. And if we have food and covering, with these
we shall be content.

I Timothy 6:6

Note how he linked godliness with contentment. A mark of genuine, godly character is contentment.

Paul didn't speak theoretically. He spoke from personal experience. In Philippians 4:11-13, he testified that he had "learned to be content."

Satisfaction with life's constantly changing situations hadn't come naturally. Through thick or thin, meagerness or abundance, lean or fat, prosperity or poverty, in "any and every circumstance," he learned to be content (that means he consciously made the choice) with God's provision through Christ. There wasn't anything Jesus and Paul couldn't overcome! (verse 13)

So many discontent people in our churches disguise themselves as godly. What a charade. Two personal experiences serve as an example of what other pastors have shared with me.

One couple in our church served on a number of committees. They were highly visible and people looked up to them. They appeared very spiritual. But Sunday nights, after services, they drove by the parsonage to see whose car was parked on our driveway. Bitterly jealous of anyone who spent time with the pastor and his family, they reported their scouting results to the church gossips regularly. This created a lot of tension and dissension in the church body.

They could have fellowshipped with us in our home any time if they had just asked. But they never did. Eventually, their envy exploded and they left the church. But they left behind "disorder and every evil thing" that I, as pastor, had to deal with.

Another example is a woman in our congregation who came by the office one afternoon just as I had finished meeting with my administrative staff. She wasn't happy with the changes going on in the church.

Catching us in the hallway, our unscheduled visitor vented her personal discontent. Eyes flashing with anger, she pointed her finger at my secretary and shouted, "It's you new Christians who have ruined our church!" She went on and on, pouring out demonic, bitter jealousy from her envy-filled heart.

My secretary had been saved about a year previously. From the first day, she was on fire for the Lord. She had brought several family members and friends to our church. Most of them had made personal commitments to Christ. She was excited about her walk with Jesus and the vision of the church. The Lord called her to fill a staff position. She was doing a good job.

Can you imagine a Christian complaining that the newly born-again people are creating problems for the church? God help us. We're in big-time trouble when changes and growth which are result from sinners being converted to the Savior are unwelcome in our churches!

What's the solution to jealousy and selfish ambition? It is to have the attitude of Jesus.

> *Do nothing from selfishness or empty conceit, but with humility of mind let each of you regard one another as more important than himself; do not merely look out for your own persons interests, but also for the interests of others. Have this attitude in yourselves which was also in Christ Jesus, who, although He existed in the form of God, did not regard equality with God a thing to be grasped, but emptied himself, taking the form of a bond-servant...*
>
> Philippians 2:3-7a

Think what would happen if we started serving others instead of envying them. Imagine what might result if we decided to reside in the land of contentment and dedicated ourselves to pursuing and practicing godliness!

It's time for Christ's bride to turn from unholy and shameful practices to holy habits and blameless behavior. Considering the consequences of carnal conduct, can we afford to not change our ways? Count the cost if we don't clean up our act.

- Christ is dishonored. Our Savior's heart breaks when His children stumble. When the Spirit of the Lord is grieved, God cannot bless. Without His blessing, we can do nothing.
- Clergy are discouraged. Battling unholy behavior increases the risk of burnout. Wounded and weary, battered pastors might bail out of the ministry. What will happen to the church if she loses her leaders?
- Churches experience defeat. Division within the ranks

destroys dreams and strategies for carrying out a God-given, God-glorifying vision. Losing sight of her calling, the church wanders aimlessly while the Great Commission goes unfulfilled. Where will needy people go if the house of healing is a house that hurts?

- Children grow up disillusioned. Disrespect for pastors and disharmony between brothers teaches our kids that "anything goes" in God's house. Carnal conduct by parents disappoints children and can lead them to reject the church as a viable and desirable part of life. Where will our kids learn faith, love, and unity if it isn't at home and in the church?

- Communities stay spiritually dead. While the church fusses and feuds, Satan fills up hell with the precious souls for whom Christ died. If the church won't win the lost, the devil will.

Every individual believer in the body of Christ must choose to walk in the flesh or in the Spirit. Because choice determines course, and course dictates consequences, may each of us prayerfully consider our Christian conduct before God and men.

Now the deeds of the flesh are evident, which are: immorality, impurity, sensuality, idolatry, sorcery, enmities, strife, jealousy, outbursts of anger, disputes, dissensions, factions, envying, drunkenness, carousing, and things like these, of which I forewarn you just as I have forewarned you that those who practice such things shall not inherit the kingdom of God. But the fruit of the Spirit is love, joy, peace, patience, kindness, goodness, faithfulness, gentleness, self-control; against such there is no law. Now those who belong to Christ Jesus have crucified the flesh with its passions and desires. If we live by the spirit, let us also walk by the spirit.
Galatians 5:19-25

Revival will come when we forsake the deeds of the flesh and faithfully produce the fruit of the Spirit.

Chapter 7
There's Mercy in the Wilderness

I will open rivers on the bare heights, and springs in
the midst of the valleys; I will make the wilderness a
pool of water, and the dry land fountains of water.
Isaiah 41:18

Congratulations! You have just won an all expense paid vacation to either the Hawaiian Islands or the Sahara Desert. Please indicate your choice by checking the box in front of either Islands or Desert. Arrangements for your dream trip of a lifetime will be finalized as soon as we hear from you. Return your response card today!

Visions of swaying palm trees, hula dancers in grass skirts, surfers hanging ten in the blue-green waters of the Pacific and me sipping cool lemonade while catching some rays on the white sands of Waikiki win hands down over the Sahara. My choice is clear: Honolulu here I come!

I don't know about you, but I'm not into deserts. I don't do them very well. For one thing, deserts are hot. Oppressive heat makes me miserable. Deserts are also dry. H_2O is hard to come by. Lack of sufficient water makes the desert seem so lifeless. The desert is also a lonely place. No crowds and not a lot of fun things to do in the wide open spaces of the wilderness.

Burnout had dried up my spirit. I felt lifeless as I wandered in an emotional wilderness.

God knew I wouldn't check the box for desert; the Spirit of God led me to a place where He opened rivers, pools and fountains of waters to replenish my thirsty soul. This wouldn't be a dream vacation, but it would be the trip of my life.

There are times when God takes us into the wilderness. He always has a specific purpose in desert training: Men and women of

God are made there!

Moses, who had failed in his first attempt to free Israel, was forged into God's instrument of miraculous deliverance in the heat of the desert (Exodus 3-4). Paul, formerly called Saul, spent three years in Arabia unlearning religion and learning about a relationship with Jesus (Galatians 1:15-18).

Immediately following His baptism, Jesus "was led up by the Spirit into the wilderness to be tempted by the devil" (Matthew 4:1). The desert provided the proving ground where God's Son battled and beat the devil, preparing Him for success in His mission "to seek and save the lost" (Luke 19:10).

Israel spent forty years in the wilderness. Moses provided insight for the people as to why God had directed their path through the desert.

> *And you shall remember all the way which the Lord your God has led you in the wilderness these forty years, that he might humble you, testing you, to know what was in your heart, whether you would keep his commandments or not.*
>
> Deuteronomy 8:2

Humility…testing…what's really in the heart. The wilderness has a way of cutting through to the heart of the matter. Living is about walking with God and obeying His Word. The dynamics of the desert are unique and unrivaled in their potential for molding men and women into vessels God can use.

Pastors and laymen alike find deserts (spiritually dry times) less than desirable. We avoid them like the plague. Our flesh prefers the garden — lush surroundings, rushing streams, good times, prosperity, smooth sailing. But our spirits need the wilderness because there we learn lessons that aren't available in Eden.

The desert is not a destination. The wilderness is transition territory. It lies between Egypt and the Promised Land. Slavery under Pharaoh wasn't God's Will for His people; freedom under His Lordship was. Israel had to pass through the desert in order to enjoy liberty and the fruitful land of Canaan.

In a state of panic, the Israelites charged the Lord with ill intent in bringing them to the wilderness. In Exodus 14:12 the people cried out:

"For it would have been better for us to serve the Egyptians than to die in the wilderness."

The Israelites were filled with fear. But what a senseless statement. They voiced two errors in judgment. First, the people had quickly forgotten how awful slavery in Egypt was. Did they really want to return to the bondage of yesterday?

Second, they wrongfully assumed God had brought them to the desert to die. The Lord was delivering them from death, not taking them to their demise. The wilderness wasn't a graveyard — it was the gateway to abundant life on the other side of the shifting sand and howling wind.

Like Israel, we must pass through the wilderness to get to the Promised Land. God delivers us from sin through the new birth; then, somewhere along the way, a spiritual desert or deserts stand between us and the rich blessings He has promised us. There is no other way to Christian maturity except through the spiritual wilderness.

As with Israel (Exodus 13:18) and Jesus (Matthew 4:1), the Holy Spirit leads us through the desert. Time spent in the wilderness is not permanent. God doesn't exile us to the desert to perish. The Lord gently guides us through a temporary period (It really does end!) during which He polishes our character. The desert is part of His perfect plan for our lives.

The desert places teach us to depend on Him. God met the needs of His people while they were in the wilderness. Nehemiah, the rebuilder of Jerusalem, noted God's merciful care for Israel.

> *Thou, in thy great compassion, did not forsake them in the wilderness. Indeed, forty years Thou didst provide for them in the wilderness, and they were not in want.*
>
> Nehemiah 9:19, 21

The Lord led them, fed them, instructed them and strengthened them. They never lacked any good thing. The faith they would need in the future was formed in the crucible of the desert classroom. God provided the spiritual preparation necessary for Israel to conquer and occupy the Promised Land.

Wilderness time is not wasted time!

A pastor I highly respect met with me shortly after I entered my desert experience. He's a discerning, compassionate man. As I shared my heart, reciting some of my reservations about walking through the wilderness, this wise man of God leaned over and said, "Steve, the Lord must love you a lot to trust you with this time."

I was taken aback for a moment by his comment. I was looking at "this time" in the wilderness as something negative, an ordeal to be endured until something better came along. But his soothing, insightful words warmed my heart in a wonderful way. A light turned on in my mind! The Holy Spirit had spoken through this brother and revolutionized my perception of wilderness experiences.

God wasn't trying to make my life miserable. He was being merciful! This transition time was taking place because He loves me! God was leading me out of my personal Egypt to the Promised land I had always sought. Out of His great compassion, I was eventually led through the desert by a gracious hand that delivered me from the pain of yesterday, trained me to trust Him for today, and prepared me for the glorious tomorrows that lie ahead.

The desert is for our good. There is mercy in the wilderness! It's time that we, as God's people, stop badmouthing the low periods in our lives. They aren't foes to be fought. They're friends to be embraced.

It's a fact of life: Valleys produce fruit. Mountaintops don't grow orchards. Lofty summits are for regaining perspective and refocusing vision. We love the view from the top and live for the peak experiences. But if we want to pick fruit, we have to look somewhere else. The troughs between the peaks are where spiritual fruit is produced in God's Kingdom. Tough but tender, triumphant warriors are grown in the valleys of the wilderness.

Being set aside for awhile in the wilderness isn't banishment — it's a blessing! Sitting on the bench is still being part of the ballgame. We're still members of God's team. We're just set down for awhile so we'll be rested and ready to make the big play when the coach calls our number.

Did you know that God is God of the wilderness too? He's the Lord of transitions. I know this is true: God does not forsake his children in the wilderness! Hallelujah!

My desert stretched into three years before the Lord finished restoring me to Himself. During that divinely appointed time, I found Him to be more than faithful (I Thessalonians 5:23) as I traveled through the dry, dusty places and finally drank from springs of living water on the backside of the desert.

The Psalmist, who had spent more than his fair share of time in desert sands seeking the Lord's mercy, wrote about God's power to transform the wilderness into springs of water.

> *He changes a wilderness into a pool of water. And*
> *a dry land into springs of water.*
>
> Psalm 107:35

When our spirits are dry, God changes the wastelands of our hearts into refreshing pools of life-giving water. Isaiah echoes and amplifies the word from Psalm 107.

> *Behold, I will do something new, now it will spring*
> *forth, will you not be aware of it? I will even make*
> *a roadway in the wilderness, rivers in the desert.*
>
> Isaiah 43:19

The Lord, speaking through the prophet, announced that he would do something new! In the desert of my days, I certainly needed something new.

He went on to write that God makes a way in the wilderness. When you're lost in the desert and can't find your way, it is such a relief to know that He will make a way where there is no way! And when your soul thirsts and there is no water in sight, He makes rivers in the deserts!

The "something new" I needed came to me as I waited on God in the wilderness. Things happen in the desert that can occur nowhere else. Some special dynamics take place only in the "down times" of our spiritual walks. God works in mysterious ways in the wilderness because the desert is a place where:

1. Isolation forces intimacy with God.

Spiritual wildernesses are places of solitude. Stillness and quietness prevail. Distractions are minimal and privacy is maximal in the desert. Simply nobody's around to bother you or get in the way. Just you and God, face to face, up close and personal.

Psalm 46:10 exhorts us to "Be still and know that I am God" (KJV). The New American Standard translates this verse like this:

"Cease striving, (Let go and Relax!) and know that I am God." The writer encourages us to relax, sit still, get to know who God really is, and let Him do His thing! Talk about a simple prescription for beating burnout in today's super-stressed-out times!

Being still means we must stop wiggling. I don't know about you, but sitting still is hard for me. When I was a child, I was always one of the first to be found when the neighborhood kids played hide and seek. It was easy finding Steve. Just check out the noise. He was the one giggling, moving behind the drapes, or something! No matter how hard I tried, it was next to impossible for me to lay low and keep quiet.

Sitting still spiritually is especially difficult. We're constantly on the move, so busy with so many unimportant things that we underestimate the value of getting quiet before the Lord.

I'm amazed at God's patience level. He cordially invites us to meet with Him for intimate fellowship everyday. What do we do? We wiggle our way out of it. As seasoned spiritual squirmers, we find something "important" to do, ignoring the Lord's invitation. His call quiets and we end up forfeiting what we cannot afford to lose — time with God.

Spiritual strength and power flow from stillness. Isaiah 30:15 teaches us that "in quietness and confidence will be your strength." Winding down so we can listen for God's still small voice (see I Kings 19:12, KJV) puts us in a state where He can get through.

Let's be honest. We talk too much and listen too little. We make a lot of noise but produce few intelligible sounds. We tell God so much yet are willing to receive so little from Him. Why? We don't sit still long enough in His presence to hear Him out!

In the wilderness, there is nothing to do but watch for the Lord — and that is good!

When others let me down and left me in the desert, God picked me up. He and I went one on one. The loneliness of my heart forced me to seek the One who never leaves His children alone. He was there waiting to show me who He really is and what He can do.

My burnout was not of God's making, but He certainly used it to get my attention. For over a thousand days, when my desert drove me to my Savior's side, we developed a spiritual intimacy like I had never before known. Our hand-in-hand walk deepened my love for Him. Together, we worked through my hurt and walked toward my healing.

2. Inventory prepares the way for instruction.
When "normal life" has been disrupted, and we have been stripped of the externals that interfere with our intimacy with God, we can begin sincere soul searching. The solitude and stillness of the desert provides a private environment where we can examine our lives without embarrassment. David wrote in Psalm 26:2: *Examine me, O Lord, and try me. Test my mind and my heart.*

Our society is hooked on self-analysis and self-help. Self-examination is one thing, but spiritual-examination is another. Taking inventory of our lives is an excellent and effective exercise as long as we allow the Lord to share in the process.

David called on God to "test his mind and heart." He knew self-examination alone contained a serious shortcoming. If God is not involved, it's very tempting to take it easy on ourselves when we need to work on something . Like David, we need to submit ourselves to the Lord's examination because the Holy Spirit will keep us honest. Because He loves us and wants us to be healed, the Comforter won't cut us as much slack as we might cut ourselves!

Baring our souls before God is a prerequisite for becoming better. There is no room for games in the desert. What goes on in the wilderness is for keeps. The desert is about life and death. If we are to get better, we have to get down to the real issues.

My time out wasn't a time for sitting on a sofa, sucking my thumb, and wishing for things to work out. It was a period of intense, spiritual inventory, during which hundreds upon hundreds of hours were spent in serious study, prayer, fasting and seeking the Lord. As I searched the Word, the Spirit searched my heart.

Deserts are open spaces, exposing their inhabitants to the elements. Hiding places from the searing heat and wind-driven sandstorms are scarce. The desert of the heart is also an open place. There is nowhere to hide from the Lord. There are no secret places to shield us from His probing eye (Jeremiah 23:24).

God gave me a no-holds-barred examination. He didn't leave any area undisturbed. He thoroughly inspected every inch of my emotional/spiritual life, leaving no stone unturned. The writer of Hebrews captures well what I believe God was up to in my life. Chapter 12, verse 27 reads.

And this expression, yet once more, denotes the

removing of those things which can be shaken, as
of created things, in order that those things which
cannot be shaken may remain.

He shook me to the very foundations of my faith. Taking stock of my life opened my eyes to a lot of garbage that I had allowed to accumulate in my heart. I had to recognize and remove this rubbish before my spirit could be rebuilt.

When we honestly look at who we are, where we are at, what we have, and what we need, then the Holy Spirit can go to work.

Upon completion of inventory, God sent me to school. I was enrolled for a three-year course in the School of the Holy Spirit. Informal classes were conducted in our living room at home, out on the thirteen wooded acres behind our home, in local parks, and during early-morning and late-night prayer watches. Wherever I was, class was in session. Twenty-four hours a day, the Holy Spirit taught, and Steve the student soaked it up.

The Spirit had my undivided attention in the desert. My wilderness became the greatest learning experience of my life. The Holy Spirit instructed me and reminded me what Jesus said about life.

But the Helper, the Holy Spirit, whom the Father will
send in My name, He will teach you all things, and
bring to your remembrance all that I said to you.
                                            John 14:26

The Spirit's teaching brought a breath of fresh air. Talk about a personal spiritual tutor! Jesus' words consoled my heart and ignited hope in my spirit that there really was a "land flowing with milk and honey" (Numbers 13:27) awaiting me on the other side of the wilderness.

3.   Inspiration produces a renewed identity.

Our Lord Jesus was no stranger to the wilderness. The Gospels record many of His late-night and early-morning excursions to quiet, lonely places.

But He Himself would often slip away to the
wilderness to pray.
                                            Luke 5:16

Now when Jesus heard it, He withdrew from there
in a boat, to a lonely place by himself.
Matthew 14:13

And after He had sent the multitudes away, He
went up to the mountain by himself to pray; and
when it was evening, He was there alone.
Matthew 14:23

Jesus withdrew to the wilderness to wait on God. After ministering miracles and teaching truth all day, He would regularly steal away to be refreshed in the presence of His Father.

I believe His practice of "slipping away to the wilderness to pray" helped Him beat burnout. Can you imagine the stress load Jesus carried? Multitudes of people swarmed around Him day after day to hear words of eternal life and to receive His healing touch. He was an inspiration to many!

Those of us who inspire others and bring spiritual refreshment to their souls need to be inspired and refreshed ourselves. We know how ministering to people drains our emotional and spiritual batteries. That's why Jesus spoke the following words from Mark 6:31-32 to the ones who would be doing the ministry in the days ahead.

And He said to them, Come away by yourselves to
a lonely place and rest awhile. (For there were
many people coming and going, and they did not
even have time to eat). And they went away in the
boat to a lonely place by themselves.

Lonely places provide inspiration that busy places cannot. Jesus directed His disciples (That means us pastors and lay ministers too!) to get away to the desert places so the Spirit could breath into them His renewing power. Only then could they continue to carry the load of ministry and successfully fulfill their calling.

Wilderness time is time well spent. God directs every one of our steps — including the footprints we leave on the shifting desert sands.

But our pride resists being set aside. And Satan does his best to persuade us we don't need to wait on the Lord. Whether it's daily devotional time or extended periods of seeking spiritual renewal, the truth is — we do! We must if we are to minister effectively!

Burnout blurred my sense of who I was in Christ. During my

set-aside time, the Holy Spirit infused new life into my stressed-out spirit, inspiring me and renewing my identity as a victorious child of the Living God! Quiet walks. Tender talks. Wide-open sharing of my deepest desires. Pouring out my personal needs without being condemned. Emptying my fears and worries into the hands of my Heavenly Father. Receiving the help I needed. What an inspiring time the days in the desert were!

Releasing myself to God freed the Potter to lovingly and skillfully reshape the clay, so He could create a masterpiece.

In the dark shadows of an evening I will not soon forget, I surrendered, completely and unconditionally. That night's surrender started the process of death to self.

I lay on the floor, my face flat against the cold, hard tile in the bathroom of my hospital room. Extremely emotionally distraught, and physically ill, I felt as though my insides were going to come out. I was so upset I thought my heart would literally burst.

In a moment of utter anguish, as I screamed out to God for mercy, I heard Him whisper softly, "Surrender, Steve. Surrender."

Desperate for deliverance from the demon of despair that was tearing me apart, I hoisted the white flag over the castle of my heart, threw down my weapons, lowered the draw bridge, and voluntarily gave myself up to my conqueror. No more battles with God. Duels with my Maker were over.

Before God makes us in the desert, we have to die in the desert. Moses, Jesus and Paul all died spiritually in the wilderness. For them, spiritual death meant surrendering their wills to the will of the Father.

Moses died to his failure as a premature deliverer (Exodus 2:11-15). God raised him up in power through signs and wonders to be the real thing (Exodus 7:1-5).

Jesus died to Satan's temptations of world conquest and false worship by sticking with the Word (Matthew 4:1-11). The Father empowered His Son to stay on course to the Cross (Matthew 26:36-46).

Paul died to religious pedigree and legalistic tradition (Philippians 3:3-14). God raised him up with resurrection power to be the great apostle of grace (I Corinthians 15:10).

Spiritual death for these three pillars of the faith meant the surrender of their wills to the Will of the Father.

Death must always precede resurrection. We would prefer

resurrection without death. Unfortunately, it doesn't work that way in the Kingdom. The price of life is death. Jesus said so.

> *Truly, truly I say to you, unless a grain of wheat*
> *falls into the earth and dies, it remains by itself*
> *alone; but if it dies, it bears much fruit.*
> John 12:24

A grain of wheat dies when you put it in the dirt. Then, and only then, is the miracle of life unlocked. That tiny, seemingly lifeless seed bursts to the surface to multiply itself over and over and over again. It bears much fruit because life sprang forth from death.

That's what the Cross and empty tomb are all about. Men buried Jesus — but God raised Him from the dead! Out of Christ's death comes abundant and eternal life. Hallelujah!

The apostle Paul understood that if we were to live with Jesus we have to first die with Jesus (Romans 6:4-13). In Galatians 2:20 Paul identifies what we call "the exchanged life."

> *I have been crucified with Christ; and it is no longer*
> *I who live, but Christ who lives in me; and the life I*
> *now live in the flesh I live by faith in the Son of God,*
> *who loved me, and delivered Himself up for me.*

There's Christianity in a nutshell! Paul says that Paul is dead. He died on the cross with Jesus. Paul is history. He no longer lives. Jesus lives in Paul. Paul lives and walks by faith in Jesus, not by faith in Paul. His faith rests in the One who loved and sacrificed Himself for Paul.

Die to self, live for Jesus. That's the crucified life. I had preached it for years, but only in the desert did I come to the point where I buried Steve.

There is tremendous power in surrender and submission to God. For months I walked in the woods around our home and relinquished my rights to the Lord. Dying to self isn't easy. It's the toughest thing we will ever do. As a matter of fact, Paul said "I die daily" (I Corinthians 15:13). Dying to self is a daily process.

I didn't just roll over and die all at once. Bit by bit I crawled onto the Cross. I must confess I kicked and screamed a good part of the time too. But in those moments of protest, the Spirit would come and woo me to His side. Softened by His love, I bowed my head and knelt on the ground, lifted my hands to heaven, and said, "Not my will, but Your will be done."

One place in particular in those woods has been my "grave site." It's a raised mound of clay that used to house a colony of ants. The Spirit has led me time and time again to kneel on that spot in submission to Him. I can't explain it, but there's something very special about that piece of dirt.

Burnout is a by-product of trusting in ourselves instead of trusting in God. We say we have died to self and we live by faith in Him, but do we? It's vitally important that we settle the crucified life once and for all. If we depend on ourselves, we'll stress out. But if we depend on Him, we'll rise up and overcome!

Take it from a guy who knows. Dreams die. And the dreamers must die if they are to dream again! Death to self is the first step to new life in the Spirit. With new life comes new dreams and new beginnings!

My spirit had been restless for some time, hungering and thirsting for more of the Spirit-filled life. I'd preached once from Matthew 9:16-17, where Jesus talked about new wine and new wineskins. He warned that putting new wine into old wineskins, would cause the aged, non-elastic skins to burst. The wine would be lost on the ground and the wineskins ruined.

The proper way to handle the wine was to put new wine into fresh wineskins. Then "both would be preserved." It's obvious from this teaching that Jesus is interested in the preservation of the container as well as its contents.

God had been trying to pour new wine (the Holy Spirit) into me. But my old wineskin couldn't contain it. Burnout was the final bursting of my wineskin. When my spiritual life blew apart at the seams, the fresh anointing of the Spirit the Lord intended for me spilled on the ground, leaving me frustrated and fruitless.

Old wineskins wouldn't cut it anymore. I had to become a new container, a fresh wineskin in order to hold the renewing wine of the Spirit God was sending my way.

New Year's Day 1992, I felt compelled to go to the office to wait on the Lord. I told my family I would return when God and I were done doing business. I wasn't sure what He had in mind, but I knew I was supposed to spend some time with Him.

Arriving at my study, I opened the Bible to Isaiah 43:18-21. As

I read this passage, the Lord gave me a theme for the New Year: "Something New in '92" would be the watchword for my life and ministry the next twelve months. As I paced and prayed, praised the Lord and sought His face, a tingling sensation suddenly came over me. It was like a surge of power. It covered me from head to toe. Wave after wave of warmth flowed over and through my entire being. For a while it wouldn't let go. It just kept coming and coming and coming. I had never experienced anything quite like this before.

I felt as though I was being touched by a gentle, healing hand. I rejoiced and wept happy tears. I was overcome with joy that was indescribable. I felt like dancing!

I'm not a mystic, nor am I overly experience-oriented. I shy away from religious fads. No one could ever accuse me of being a spiritual space cadet! I do believe God works through visions, dreams, and emotional experiences as long as they are in keeping with Scripture. A touchy-feely person I am not, but there is no doubt in my mind that God anointed me with fresh oil that New Year's morning (Psalm 92:10).

John the Baptist said these words about Jesus and His main ministry to those who believe on His name.

> *As for me, I baptize you with water for repentance,*
> *but He who is coming after me is mightier than I,*
> *and I am not fit to remove His sandals. He will*
> *baptize you with the Holy Spirit and with fire.*
> Matthew 3:11

The soul-warming surge of power I experienced was the fire of God. Jesus baptized me with the Holy Spirit! Wonderfully and powerfully, the Lord immersed me in the living water of the Spirit of God!

The Holy Spirit would come many times in the days ahead to infuse me with resurrection power. While I drove my car, sat in my office studying Scripture, prayed in the woods, lay on my bed, even when I shopped at the mall , the Spirit would come and flow over me with a sweet anointing. Each time He visited, I felt that healing hand and sensed new strength had been imparted.

God was raising me from the dead! I was receiving new life in the Spirit. The Holy Spirit was pouring new wine into the fresh wineskin I was becoming. My wilderness became a renewing place.

Hiding in the shadow of His wings, God gently healed my hurt and restored me to Himself.

I went to the desert burned-out, broken, dried-up and ready to throw in the towel. I would leave revived, whole, overflowing with living water, and raring to go back to work for God!

Jesus exhorted spiritually thirsty people to come to Him and drink. Read again His incredible invitation.

> *Now on the last day, the great day of the feast, Jesus stood and cried out saying, "If any man is thirsty, let him come to me and drink. He who believes in Me, as the Scripture said, from his innermost being shall flow rivers of living water."*
> *But this He spoke of the Spirit whom those who believed in Him were to receive; for the Spirit was not yet given, because Jesus was not yet glorified.*
> John 7:37-39

Out of the depths of my belly, deep in my innermost being, from my spirit-man flowed "rivers of living water" when the Holy Spirit came over me. God said He would make "rivers in the desert" (Isaiah 43:19b), and He did!

My wilderness became an Eden. Isaiah's words in chapter 51, verse 3 profoundly describe what has happened in this man's heart.

> *"Indeed, the Lord will comfort Zion; He will comfort all her waste places. And her wilderness He will make like Eden, And her desert like the garden of the Lord; joy and gladness will be found in her, thanksgiving and the sound of a melody."*

He comforted all of my "waste places." My desert became His garden. Joy and gladness, thanksgiving and the sound of a melody have replaced depression's song of sorrow.

I am alive in Christ like never before! I am learning anew what it means for Christ to live in me. I can say with Paul that "the life which I now live, I live by faith in the Son of God, who loved me and delivered Himself up for me" (Galatians 2:20b). It has been a long time coming, but I am so glad it's here!

While I was searching in the desert for water to satisfy my

thirsty soul, the Lord brought Pastor Dan Beller, of Evangelistic Temple in Tulsa, into my life. He was gracious to meet with me on a number of occasions. Dan is a sympathetic listener with a shepherd's heart as big as the moon. He loves people like Jesus does. He has become a special friend.

Our discussions centered on the Spirit-controlled life. As I explained what I was experiencing and asked many questions, Pastor Dan smiled. With the wisdom that comes from personal experience, he told me that he was excited for me. He said I was entering a new dimension in my Christian life. As we talked about control he said, "Steve, the Spirit-controlled life is the most exciting and most scary thing there is. Being out of control and under His control is an adventure. It's what walking by faith is all about. Victorious Christian living is the fruit of being Spirit-filled and Spirit-controlled."

My spiritually seasoned advisor was right. My new life in the spirit is scary sometimes. But it's a good scary. There's nothing like it on earth. The Spirit-filled life is a wonderful way to live!

And it has been made possible for me because there is mercy in the wilderness. A father's love watched over a hurting son. He helped me die to self so I could live in the Spirit. Glory to God!

Hurting pastor, there is life in your desert. Rivers of living water run deep below the surface of your pain. Don't be afraid to let go and let God lead you to drink from His streams in the desert. Refreshment is just a step of surrender away. Die the death so you can live the life.

As the children of Israel who had been bitten by deadly serpents were healed and lived when they looked upon the bronze serpent on the standard (See Numbers 21:6-9.), look to Christ on the Cross and be healed from your hurt. You will receive mercy. Be assured that Jesus is close, waiting to pour new wine into a fresh wineskin.

Larnelle Harris wrote a powerful song called "Desert of My Days" that ministered healing to my heart while I trekked through the wilderness. As you read the words on the next page, ask the Holy Spirit to send a cooling rain to your thirsty soul.

> *I will be glad and rejoice in your mercy, for You have considered my trouble; You have known my soul in adversities.*
>
> Psalm 31:7

DESERT OF MY DAYS

In the desert of my days
There came no cooling rain
And the burning sun stalked me without mercy
And I cried out at the time
I must be paying for some crime
In my loneliness it seemed nobody heard me

The days were weeks, the weeks were months
The months seemed years
In the dust and sand a thirsty man
Battles fear
Praying help would appear

In the desert of my years
There fell no rain, only tears
As I struggled on with hope alone to cling to
The rugged hills all looked the same
Across the endless dry terrain
And to the silent skies I cried, "My God where are you?"

And the days were weeks, the weeks were months
The months seemed years
In the dust and sand a thirsty man
Battles fear
Praying help would appear

And then He came to me
In a cool and gentle breeze
And in a healing rain
I heard him say I love you

I've been here my child
Every weary mile
Though there must have been times
When it seemed like I'd forgotten you

And I've led you through
The barren desert to
The land of milk and honey now before you

Yes I led you through
The barren desert to
The land of milk and honey
The land of milk and honey
The land of milk and honey now before you

Chapter 8
Getting a Grip on God

The Lord appeared to him from afar, saying, I have
loved you with an everlasting love; Therefore, I
have drawn you with loving kindness. Again I will
build you, and you shall be rebuilt.
Jeremiah 31:3-4a

It was well into the night when I was startled from my slumber by the insistent ring of the doorbell. Not once, not twice, but over, and over, and over again it rang. Quickly collecting myself and clearing away the cobwebs from a sleepy head, I slipped out of bed and staggered downstairs, wondering who my midnight caller could be.

As I turned on the porch light, I recognized a familiar figure. It was my ten-year-old son, Adam who was supposed to be spending the night across the street at his friend Kevin's house . He appeared a little peaked as he leaned against the door. Dark circles underlined his eyes and he wore that unmistakable expression that says hurry up, I think I am going to be sick.

Opening the door, I asked Adam what was happening. He looked at me with pitiful puppy-dog eyes and weakly announced the obvious, "I'm sick dad."

I took his overnight bag and hugged him up real good. As we headed toward his bedroom, I asked him what he would have done if I hadn't heard the bell ringing and answered the door. Adam confidently replied, "I'd have just kept ringing the bell because I knew you'd come."

Love is all about being there for your loved ones when they need you. My son knew to come home and find his father. He knew deep down inside that his daddy would help him in his hour of need. That's what fathers are for.

When I had been heartsick, and in need of healing, I hoped my Heavenly Father would come to my aid. As a child and servant of God, I knew in my spirit that I had to cross the street of sorrow to receive my Heavenly Daddy's healing love. I pictured myself standing at heaven's door, desperately ringing the bell, attempting to get God's attention.

My life needed to be rebuilt. The rubble left behind by depression needed to be cleared away. My life would have to be reconstructed on the sturdy foundation of God's promises. Step by step, God would have to set me free from the emotional and spiritual captivity I had experienced.

Judah's captivity is recorded in the book of Jeremiah. God's people had lost everything. National dignity, material possessions, Jehovah's blessing — all gone. But many generations before, the Lord had made a covenant with their fathers. His promises to His children were based on His love for them. During their time of misery and mourning, God spoke a word of hope through the prophet Jeremiah. It was a promise of restoration. Look what God said to His people who had been knocking on heaven's door.

> *The Lord appeared to him from afar,* (God had not lost track of them in their captivity. He knew exactly where they were).
>
> *"I have loved you with an everlasting love"* (The Father had not stopped loving His erring children). *"Therefore, I have drawn you with lovingkindness."* (God wasn't finished with His people. He was drawing them to His side, his lovingkindness extending to them.)
>
> *"Again, I will build you, and you shall be rebuilt."* (Broken down Israel would be rebuilt! God promised that He Himself would build them up again.)

There would be a new day for God's chosen people. They would take up their tambourines, dance again, plant crops and enjoy the fruit of their labor. They would worship, sing and shout with gladness, and praise the Lord for bringing them out of bondage. They would be gathered to their homeland in large numbers. God would lead them. They would walk by streams of waters. They would walk on straight paths and not stumble. (Jeremiah 31:3-9)

All of these wonderful things would happen because God declared: "I am a father to Israel" (verse 9). Because of His great love, Father God would restore His children to His heart and help rebuild their lives.

Most of my life, I had struggled with God being my Heavenly Father. I knew the Bible said He was. I preached that He was. When reciting the Lord's prayer, it was easy to say "Our Father who is in heaven..." But when it came to confessing "My Father who is in heaven..." I spoke it, with reservations.

Maybe I subconsciously thought it was too good to be true. Maybe I didn't feel deserving. Whatever the reason, I questioned if God really was Steve Roll's Heavenly Father.

During a critical period a few months after I had been released from the hospital, my wife, who loves me very much said, "Steve, you've gotta get a grip on God. You have to decide once and for all whether or not you trust Him. Either He loves you, or He doesn't. Either He is who He says He is, or He isn't. You have to decide for yourself. No one can make the choice for you."

Talk about tough love! But God, in His wisdom, knew that I needed a blast to shake me loose from the paralysis of self-pity. After recovering from the initial shock of my wife's discerning diagnosis, I took my Bible and read through the entire book of Job in a couple of hours. I journeyed with this righteous man through every spiritual inch of his faith battle. I hurt as he lamented his loss. When he "argued his cause" with his Maker, I found myself standing on Job's side of the issue. I got irritated with his worthless comforters as they accused him of hidden sin.

Job's questions became my questions. I adopted his conclusions as he grasped at spiritual straws. I paid close attention in my spirit when God spoke to His servant, trying to penetrate his misunderstanding of the Creator's ways. Then I arrived at chapter 42, Job's confession. Let his immortal words sink deep into your spirit as they did mine.

> *Then Job answered the Lord and said, "I know that Thou canst do all things; and that no purpose of Thine can be thwarted. Who is this that hides counsel without knowledge?*
> *Therefore, I have declared that which I did not understand, things too wonderful for me, which I*

did not know. Hear now, and I will speak; I will ask
Thee, and do Thou instruct me.
I have heard of Thee by the hearing of the ear,
but now my eye sees Thee. Therefore, I retract, and
I repent in dust and ashes.

Job 42:1-6

Immersed in misery, I too had declared things that I did not understand. Things too wonderful for me. The things of God that He was working for my good in the midst of my greatest trial. I had grossly misunderstood. I had heard of Him — but in the days ahead I would come to "see Him with my eyes" like never before. For the next three years, I would spend every minute of my waking hours getting a grip on God.

My discovery of God as my loving Heavenly Father who has a great plan for my life, began when I retracted my rash conclusions regarding His activity (or seeming lack of activity) on my behalf. Like Job, I asked Him to instruct me. I would look directly to my Maker to teach me about Himself and our relationship.

Getting a grip on something you thought you already had a grip on isn't easy! I never knew re-learning could be so humbling. Gutting it out with God would require everything I could give.

Over time, I would find that the reward was worth the risk. A verse of Scripture spoken by Solomon kept me pursuing the process of spiritual rebuilding:

The end of a matter is better than it's beginning;
patience of spirit is better than haughtiness of
spirit.

Ecclesiastes 7:8

Patience does pay! Seven life-changing truths radically altered my relationship with God. A Heavenly Father came and met the needs of my hurting heart.

"God is a good God!" the preacher proclaimed enthusiastically. The attentive crowd jumped to their feet, shouting hallelujah's and clapping their hands in excited affirmation. I stood in silence, hands glued to my side. I wanted so badly to join in the chorus of praise, but I was having a difficult time reconciling depression and failure with the concept of a good God.

The devil loves to trick us into believing that God is bad, not good. Think about it. If you were Satan, wouldn't you want to try and persuade people that God was the big, bad guy in the sky? Why on earth would anyone want to trust their life to a bad God? If the devil can dupe us into deciding that God is malevolent instead of benevolent, we will reject Christ and remain in the evil one's camp.

Adverse circumstances can crush the good side of life right out of us if we aren't careful. So many "bad things" had happened, that I lost sight of God's goodness. Hurting doesn't feel good. Many days were "bad days" instead of "good days." But "bad things" and "bad days" don't make God a "bad God."

Pain tempts us to pay more attention to our feelings than our faith. When we don't feel good, we tend to focus on the bad things. Times of adversity cause us to point an accusing finger at God who is supposed to be a good guy in control of His universe. Listening to my feelings, I wrongfully concluded that the bad things had happened to me because maybe God is not good.

Getting a grip on God as a good God meant I had to look beyond my feelings and lay hold of faith. As the Lord gently walked me through His Word, I was relieved to find that God was indeed good. Scripture, not circumstance, convinced me of His goodness. The Bible has these things to say about God.

- God as a being is good. ("For thou, oh Lord, art good." Psalm 86:5)
- God's priority is good. ("Not knowing that the goodness of God leads you to repentance?" Romans 2:4) (See also John 3:16 and II Peter 3:9.)
- God's promises are good. ("Not one word has failed of all His good promise." I Kings 8:56)
- God's provision is good. ("For the lord your God is bringing you into a good land." Deuteronomy 8:7) and ("No good thing does he withhold from those who walk uprightly." Psalm 84:11)
- God's plan is good. ("That you may prove what the Will of God is, that which is good and acceptable and perfect." Romans 12:2)

- God's purpose is good. (*"And we know that God causes all things to work together for good for those who love God, to those who are called according to His purpose."* Romans 8:28)

What is God really like? Most of us would never think that television commercials could have any religious value, or that they could help us in our thinking about God. However, I heard of a Sunday school teacher who suggested to the children in her class that they take some phrases from commercials and see if they could make them applicable to God. She was amazed at the results, and I share in her amazement. Here is a new version of the faith of a child.

God is like — Bayer Aspirin. He works wonders.
God is like — Pan Am. He makes the going great.
God is like — Ford. He's got a better idea.
God is like — Dial Soap. He gives you round the clock
    protection.
God is like — Coke. He's the real thing.
God is like — Scope. He makes you feel fresh.
God is like — Imperial Margarine. He makes you feel like
    a king.
God is like — General Electric bulbs. He lights the way.
God is like — Pillsbury. He says it best.
God is like — Crest. He whitens and brightens.
God is like — Leggs. He never lets you down.
God is like — Milk. Everybody needs Him.
And how is this for a climax?
God is like — Hallmark Cards. He cared enough to send His
    very best!

According to Hebrews 1:3, God's Son is presented as "the radiance of His glory and the exact representation of His nature." Simply put, Jesus is the perfect picture of God. If we want to know what God is like, we look to Jesus. Doctor Luke's description of Jesus in Acts 10:38 was the crowning piece of biblical evidence that convinced me that God is good.

You know of Jesus of Nazareth, how God anointed Him with the Holy Spirit and with power, and how He

went about doing good, and healing all who were
oppressed by the devil, and God was with Him.

Jesus "went about doing good." A bad God doesn't go around doing good deeds. Christ's saving and healing power flowed from His goodness. To see good deeds is to see Jesus. To see Jesus is to see God. To see God is to see a God who is good!

Bad things had happened; but I started to heal when I allowed a good God to rebuild my life.

When my folks divorced, I wondered if my mom and dad loved me. When my college sweetheart broke up with me, I wondered if a woman would ever love me. When I lost my church, I wondered if God loved me.

Love, acceptance, and approval are powerful, driving forces in our life. Craving love, we do a lot of crazy things trying to capture the affection of our Creator and fellow creatures. People attempt to earn love, buy love, or take love. They will compromise for love, fight for love, even die for love.

When it comes to God's love, all we have to do is to receive it. The Bible says *"God so loved the world that He gave His only begotten Son, that whoever believes in Him should not perish, but have everlasting life"* (John 3:16). Jesus is God's free gift of love. Gifts are to be received and enjoyed. We receive salvation when we believe in the Son.

My journey to wholeness would require that I come to grips with receiving God's unconditional love.

For most of my life, I made love conditional. Love was an if-then proposition. If I get good grades, if I'm good looking, if I out produce others, then people will love me. If I preach powerful sermons, if I win souls to Christ, if I build a great church, then God will love me. That's how I thought love operated. It had to be earned. You had to prove yourself lovable.

I'm convinced my concept of conditional love
originated when my parents split up. Feeling re-
jected and unloved, I started down the path of
trying to prove to parents, peers, and Providence
that I was worth loving. What a lonely and disap-
pointing road conditional love turned out to be.

Augustine said, "God loves everyone as though there were but one of us to love!" During times of personal loss, distorted thinking tempts us to believe that God loves everybody in the world but us.

Thank God I matter to Him and He loves me no matter what! God's love is unchanging (Micah 7:18), unceasing (Jeremiah 31:3), unlimited (Romans 8:35-39), and unconditional (Romans 5:8). Nothing we can do will make God love us more. Nothing we can do will make Him love us less. The cross is God's proof of His unconditional love for each one of us.

The Lord knew how much I needed His love, acceptance, and approval. When I loved myself the least, His lovingkindness drew me to His side.

A little boy once defined lovingkindness as "when mom puts jam on the peanut butter!" Steve didn't love Steve, but God never stopped loving Steve. That's God's jelly. Hallelujah!

While I was in the hospital, I picked up the phone and called my dad. I told him I needed to hear him say he loved me. When my father said, "I love you son," something freed up inside. Years of wondering flew out the window of my soul.

My Heavenly Father met me regularly on the road to recovery. As we walked together, He too, spoke those spirit soothing words, "I love you, son."

If you're hurting and wondering if God loves you — He does! No matter where you are or what has happened, Jesus Christ loves you!

> *The Lord God is in your midst, a victorious warrior;*
> *He will exult over you with joy, He will quiet you in*
> *His love, He will rejoice over you with shouts of joy.*
> Zephaniah 3:17

I love being a father. It's music to my ears to hear my children call me dad. There's nothing like having your kids announce ecstatically, "Daddy's home!" — then take you down on the carpet and smother you with hugs and kisses. What dad's heart doesn't melt when his son or daughter reaches out to be held in his strong grasp.

Raising my children has taught me a lot about a father's love. I wonder if kids ever know how much their parents love them? Maybe they begin to understand just a little bit better when baby birds come to roost in their nests.

My children mean everything to me. I care about every detail of their lives. I'm involved in everything they do. It's my privilege to protect them from the big bad wolf, provide all the frosted flakes they can consume, put my arms around a tearful little leaguer when he strikes out at the plate, and pray for my boy and girl to grow up to be a godly man and woman. I get to pack their lunches, put love notes on their pillows, surprise them with unexpected presents, proudly applaud a pretty ballerina's program, and perform minor surgery on their owies! I teach them about life, help them pursue their dreams, guide them in making good decisions; and I correct their path when necessary.

I nurture them in the things of the Lord. I stand back and give them space as they stretch their wings, releasing them to God's care. Soon, I'll stay up worrying about what they're doing on their dates! What a great job being a dad is.

The Old and New Testaments present God as a Father who loves His spiritual kids. The father image appears again and again throughout Scripture. Seeing God as our Heavenly Father is key to a successful relationship with Him. I found it difficult relating to God as a Heavenly Father. Not having had my earthly dad around on a daily basis to nurture me and show me how to live right made me gun shy when trying to approach God as father. I just didn't know how to do it.

When I crashed, I needed a father's love. Out of desperation, I cried out to God as my father. Guess what He did? He loved me like a dad. He reassured me that I was His son and He was my Father.

Romans 8:14-15 gives us a glimpse into the heart of Paul. This Gospel-slinging, soul-winning, turning-the-world-upside-down spiritual John Wayne harbored warm feelings for God.

> *For all who are being led by the Spirit of God, these are the sons of God. For you have not received a spirit of slavery leading to fear again, but you have received a spirit of adoption as sons by which we cry out, "Abba! Father!"*

Paul is saying that when he was born again of the Spirit, he swapped slavery for sonship. No longer living in fear, and now walking in love as an adopted son in the family of God, he cries out with childlike affection, "Daddy! Daddy!" Paul relished the joy and rich rewards of knowing God as His Heavenly Father.

I had reverenced and known God as Lord, but when I started addressing Him as "Heavenly Daddy," rejoicing filled the void in my heart that had longed to know God as my Father. A whole new world of security and stability opened up to me when I got a grip on the fact that I was a child of God, a child who was loved by His father in heaven.

Elisha was hemmed in by trouble (II Kings 6:8-23), but you wouldn't know it by looking at him. An angry enemy army surrounded the city he was visiting. They were intent on capturing the prophet and making him pay for the words he had spoken against them. In the midst of overwhelming negative odds and a high probability of personal calamity, God's man remained cool, calm and collected.

His attendant was another story. He panicked as he watched the chariots circle the city. Despairing, he cried out to his master, "What shall we do?" (verse 15) Confidently, Elisha answered *"Do not fear, for those who are with us are more than those who are with them"* (verse 16).

Elisha saw something with the eye of faith that his servant didn't. He knew that God was for him and heaven's army outnumbered the Arameans! For the attendant's instructions and ours (He needed to chill out, and so do we!) Elisha prayed:

> *O Lord, I pray, open his eyes that he may see. And the Lord opened his eyes, and he saw; and behold, the mountain was full of horses and chariots of fire all around Elisha.* (verse 17)

Glory to God! What a powerful lesson for those of us who are prone to panic when life comes against us and we question if God is for us.

When the forces of hell overwhelmed me and everything that could go wrong did, like Elisha's spiritually blinded servant, I stood in fear of the circling chariots. But praise God—He answered somebody's prayers on my behalf, and opened my eyes. The Spirit showed me God had been on my side every step of the way. "Chariots of fire" stood guard over me as I battled through burnout. Blessing and victory would come because Almighty God was in my corner.

When we're hemmed in by distress and difficulty and think that no one is pulling for us, we need to think again. The Bible is clear that God is for us.

The Lord is for me, I will not fear; what can man do to me? The Lord is for me among those who help me; therefore I will look with satisfaction on those who hate me.

Psalm 118:6-7

What then shall we say to these things? If God be for us, who can be against us?

Romans 8:31

I heard a story about an election that was held in heaven. Steve Roll was being voted on as a candidate for salvation. God, Satan, and Steve were allowed one vote apiece. Ballots cast, the results were tabulated. God voted for me. The devil voted against me. I cast my vote with God, and we won two to one! Hallelujah!

During my depression, the devil worked overtime politicking to persuade me that God wasn't on my side. He cruelly pointed his crooked finger to circumstances that had crushed me. But the Holy Spirit compassionately pointed me to the Cross on Calvary. Christ's death and glorious resurrection had conquered sin, death, and the grave! (I Corinthians 15:54-57) More than enough eternal evidence that God is for me.

Of all those who help me, God is my biggest booster. My Heavenly Father is my greatest fan. He hangs over the banister of heaven, cheering me on to victory! He dispatches angelic helpers to battle on my behalf. Jesus Himself pulls for me by way of intercessory prayer at the right hand of the Father (Romans 8:34).

My confidence started resurfacing when I stubbornly refused to believe anything less than: God is for me. And if God be for me, everybody else might as well be!

After I had been admitted to the hospital and my wife had left, I felt so alone sitting on the bed in my room. I was tempted to ask the duty nurse if God made hospital calls anymore. I had always feared abandonment. Now, when the door to the outside world shut behind me, I was afraid the Lord had been locked out of my life too.

For the duration of my treatment, and for many months after, the question, "Is God with me or not?" racked my brain. I thought God had disembarked the train somewhere along the track while I was struggling to survive.

My feelings ran strong. All kinds of questions about God's presence plagued me. Does God take a hike when things get tough? Does His Almightiness head for the hills when His children stumble? Does Jesus bail out on His followers when things go bad?

The answer is No! Absolutely not. He never abandons His children under any circumstance.

On the contrary, the Bible affirms God's presence particularly in times of need. "The Lord is near to the brokenhearted" (Psalm 34:18). "I will be with him in trouble"(Psalm 91:15). My heart was broken and I was definitely in trouble. God said He was with me whether I thought so or not.

One of the very last things Jesus shared before He ascended to heaven was a word of guarantee concerning His presence in the lives of the faithful.

> *...and lo, I am with you always, even to the end of the age.*
>
> Matthew 28:20b

Always means always! No matter where I am; no matter what I've done; no matter what has happened; no matter how I feel — Jesus is with me.

The Psalmist asked, "Where can I go from Thy Spirit? Or where can I flee from Thy presence?" (Psalm 139:7) God's response — nowhere. Heaven, hell and everywhere in between finds God present and participating in the lives of the redeemed (verses 8-18).

Whether I was preaching from the pulpit or healing in a hospital, God was with me because He lives in me through the person of the Holy Spirit (Colossians 1:27). Circumstances, good or bad, don't change the fact that Jesus is alive and He lives in me! Where I go, He goes.

Settling once and for all that God is with me was crucial to my comeback. People who I had counted on in the past weren't with me anymore. They had walked. I needed to nail it down that my Savior would always walk with me, never away from me.

My faith is firmly established on the sure foundation of God's Word, but the Lord has also built my personal faith by speaking through signs in creation. Today, on the mantle in our formal living room sits an eye-catching ceramic figurine of a brilliantly-colored, red-feathered cardinal sitting on a tree branch. The incredibly, near perfect replica of this inspiring masterpiece of our Maker looks very real. This statue is a special gift from my wife.

Our home in Tulsa backs up to a greenbelt. Thirteen undeveloped acres provide our household with a private zoo. Raccoons, opossums, squirrels, turtles, birds of every kind, even a coyote regularly provide entertainment for the Rolls.

One morning I was sitting in the family room searching for a comforting word from my Bible. My spirit was still tender from the trauma of depression. I was now in the rebuilding phase, but I was weak, and every indication of God's presence was important.

A faint, tapping-type sound turned my attention toward one of the windows with a view to the backyard. My eyes followed the sound and to my surprise, a bright red male cardinal was banging his beak on the window, hopping up and down as he pecked on the glass! I froze — - tickled to be observing this feathered fellow's efforts to get somebody's attention. It was as if he was wanting to come in.

After a few moments, he flew away. Then I heard the familiar peck-peck in the front room. Following the sound, I found my little friend trying to get in the front door this time!

That cardinal came back every day for three weeks. For me, he was a special courier from the court of heaven. Each time I saw him or heard his sweet melodious song, the Lord said, "I am with you Steve." God got my attention and sent a very special personal message through a beautiful bird hanging around my house.

Since then, anytime I hear or see a cardinal, the Spirit whispers, "I am with you, Steve." Who says God isn't personal? Out of His love and mercy, He sent me a sign that helped me come to grips with the truth that God is with me.

Behind them, dust was flying from the wheels of Pharaoh's crack chariot corps. Before them, the Red Sea's current ran deep and strong, denying them a place to cross. The people of Israel, hotly pursued by their former cruel masters, were crying and having visions of dying. Moses, the deliverer, was trying his best to hold on to faith and obey his Boss. — Great stuff for a movie!

Exodus 14 reads like a disaster waiting to happen. Israel found itself between the proverbial rock and hard place. Pharaoh behind. Red Sea dead ahead. No exit signs or off ramps in sight. From a human standpoint, God's people were in trouble. Circumstances were clearly out of control.

Have you ever wondered if God is in control of your life? I have. You probably have, too. I'm sure many in Israel's camp wondered where God was that day when they felt the Egyptians breathing down their necks.

As we read "the rest of the story" we discover that Almighty God was definitely in control (Exodus 14:13-31). What a divine set-up. At God's command, the sea became a highway for Israel and a cemetery for Egypt. God's people were delivered, and Pharaoh's people were drowned. The Song of Moses, Exodus 15, extols the victory over Pharaoh that God wrought for Israel. What a song of celebration! A couple of verses in particular convince me that God was in control when it looked like everything was out of control.

> *I will sing to the Lord, for He is highly exalted; the horse and rider He has hurled into the sea. The Lord is my strength and my song, and He has become my salvation; this is my God, and I will praise Him; My father's God, and I will extol Him.*
>
> verses 1-2

> *Thy right hand, O Lord, is majestic in power, Thy right hand, O Lord, shatters the enemy. And in the greatness of Thine excellence, Thou dost overthrow those who rise up against Thee.*
>
> verses 6-7

> *Who is like Thee among the gods, O Lord? Who is like Thee, majestic in holiness, awesome in praises, working wonders?*
>
> verse 11

Although things may look as though they are out of control in the natural realm, it doesn't mean they are out of control in the spiritual realm. All hell can break loose on earth — but God is still on His throne in heaven.

Who is like Him, majestic in holiness, awesome in praises, working wonders? Nobody! No person or power in the universe is big enough, smart enough, or strong enough to overpower and overthrow Almighty God!

On Good Friday, the devil, demons, deluded religious leaders and power-driven Romans thought they had the situation under control when Jesus breathed His last and gave up the ghost on the Cross. Then came Sunday! When Jesus rose from the dead on Easter morning — He demonstrated once and for all that God is in control! It was frightening for me to be out of control. It was doubly scary to think God wasn't in control of my life either. Satan would like us to believe that adversity proves God is out to lunch.

Difficulties test the mettle of our faith to the max. Earlier, we took a look at Job. His situation was dismal at best. But God was in control every step of Job's trial. He literally told the devil what he could and could not do (Job 1:12, 2:6). God knew what He was doing, even though Job struggled to understand His ways.

Isaiah 55:8-9 helped me get a grip on God's being in control of my trials. The verses hang on the wall in my office where I can review them daily.

For My thoughts are not your thoughts, neither are your ways My ways, declares the Lord. For as the heavens are higher than the earth, so are My ways higher than your ways, and My thoughts than your thoughts.

When my life spun out of control, my puny thoughts were so far out of line my shortsighted thinking led me to believe the devil, the congregation, the denomination or some combination thereof was calling the shots. But it wasn't true. God's thoughts and ways were much higher than mine. I thought the issue was control, but the higher issue was trust. He was teaching me the greatest lesson of my life: that I can trust him because He is in control.

I don't need to be in control. I don't have to be in control. God never intended for me to be in control. His highest purpose for me is to rise above adversity through unshakable faith that knows that He is watching over me no matter what is going down around me.

When we hurt, we look for someone who or something that can heal us. After I checked into the hospital, I was administered the anti-depressant drug Prozac as part of my treatment plan. I was told it would help lift my mood. Bring me up a bit. Pull me out of the pit.

I believe God uses doctors and medicine in the healing process. I was not opposed to taking an anti-depressant. I knew there were some risks, but I was so out of it, I actually hoped the Prozac might contain some magic formula that would do for me what I couldn't do for myself: deliver me from depression. I asked the Lord to use the Prozac to assist me in my recovery. I viewed the medicine as a short term, temporary helper.

At first the Prozac seemed to work. It numbed my fears and neutralized my self-destructive thought process. My mood leveled out. I shifted into neutral and became more aware of my surroundings. But after three weeks on the medicine, I experienced disturbing side effects. Hot and cold flashes. Sudden agitation. Panicky feelings. One morning I woke up and felt like I was headed for the races. I was revved up on the inside. Wound up tight and ready to fly.

I reported to the nurse's station, where they checked my vital signs. The readings were within normal ranges, but something was driving me. When I attended my morning therapy session I could barely sit in my seat. I felt like I had to run. Where, I had no idea. Just run. Run, Steve, run. As fast as you can.

Before I realized what I was doing, I'd bolted from my chair and run out the door. I wound up on the floor at the end of the hall. I remember sitting there feeling like a sprinter on the starting line getting ready to run the 100 meter dash — I was in the blocks, hands just inside the chalk line, adrenaline pumping, awaiting the pop of the starter's pistol. But instead of a track, about twenty-five feet before me was a wall of glass windows. Something was urging me to run right through the glass barrier. It took all the resolve I could muster to hold myself back.

Just about the time I could resist no longer, Zahn Martin arrived on the scene and asked me what was going on. I told him that if someone didn't do something soon I was going to run right through the wall. Zahn prayed for me, asking the Holy Spirit to calm me down. He then called for my psychiatrist who, after assessing my situation, decided to take me off the Prozac.

It had helped stabilize me at first, he said. But then it worked against me, acting like a super-stimulant. A donkey might need help to get him moving, but how many race horses need to be pumped up to run for the roses? Even in my depressed state, this mood-elevator was too much for a high energy guy like me.

The drug of choice had contained no magic. Anti-depressants wouldn't deliver me from depression. So, pills weren't the answer. Deep in my heart I knew the power of God through His Son Jesus was the solution. I didn't need chemicals as much as I needed Christ.

Even though for a time the Lord seemed to me to be light years from Louisiana, He would be My healer. Exodus 15:26 declares "For I, the lord, am your healer." The psalmist in Psalm 107:20 says, "He sent his word and healed them, and delivered them from their destructions."

My recovery process began in earnest when I looked beyond men and medicine to God and His Word for the healing of my hurt. What a prescription Doctor Jesus had for me! He would do for me what I could not do for myself.

Getting a grip on God for me meant taking a new trip with God. It involved shedding my pride as a pastor and getting in touch with Him in ways I had always dreamed about. The following illustration may help you to understand my joy in discovering what a great God you and I are privileged to serve.

I looked forward to our physical activity times at the hospital. Taking brisk walks around the jogging trail that wound it's way through the grounds lightened the load for a few moments each day. Included in the recreational courtyard was a play area for children. Swings, a teeter-totter, monkey bars, and a shiny, silver slide stood calling adventurous, fun-seeking young patients to come and play.

As I did the adult thing and walked the trail, I watched with envy as free-spirited little ones climbed, crawled, jumped, slid and shouted their pleasure with uninhibited joy. They were innocent and having so much fun! Too soon for the kids, the monitor blew the whistle signaling playtime was over. I stared at the play equipment while the children hurried into the building.

Then the strangest thing happened. The swing set called me, beckoning me to come and have some fun. I felt a pleasant, irresistible force urging me to hurry over there and play. I thought, "Now I know you're crazy. When a fully-grown man wants to go and play on the playground, surely a screw is loose somewhere! I mean, let's get real. Swings and slides are for kids." But I really wanted to give it a whirl.

I would have to ask our attendant for permission. How embarrassing. I was certain he'd think I'd flown over the cuckoo's nest.

As we walked away from the jungle gym, my heart pounded. I wanted to be a kid again. Finding the necessary courage, I asked if it would be all right if I went over to the swing and swung for a while. The attendant never hesitated. Maybe he'd received this request before. With the attendant's "yes you can" echoing in my ears, and fellow patients cheering me on, I hustled over to the playground. Before I knew it, a little boy in a thirty-seven-year old body was zipping down the slide and climbing all over monkey bars. I mounted a swing and pushed skyward. I kicked and kicked and kicked. It felt great. I went as high as I could, swinging through the air, laughing, and loving it! I was having fun. Life had become hard. So serious, it wasn't fun anymore.

Having swung myself out, I returned to the ward. That evening I realized that someone was awakening inside. The kid I never knew was coming alive. I'd been out of touch with a significant portion of my life: a child's innocence and joy. The pure, uncomplicated enjoyment of the good life God has given.

In the midst of my crisis, the Holy Spirit called me to come and enjoy God. To sit before Him and have some fun. To lighten up our relationship, loosen up and let His love fill and thrill my heart.

As that swing restored me to the lost joys of childhood, God's grace would restore me to the innocent and joyful walk with Him that had been lost somewhere along the way.

In thy presence is fullness of joy.

Psalm 16:11

Chapter 9
Bouncing Back From Burnout

Thou hast turned for me my mourning into danc-ing; Thou hast loosed my sackcloth and girded me with gladness; that my soul may sing praise to Thee, and not be silent. O Lord my God, I will give thanks to thee forever.

Psalm 30:11-12

One of my hobbies is refinishing furniture. I'm particularly fond of restoring antique pieces to their original glory. By no stretch of the imagination am I a pro; but I have become a pretty fair do-it-yourself amateur.

My fancy for reclaiming and renewing furniture started in graduate school. A gentleman in Wilmore, Kentucky purchased antiques from auctions and estate sales. He was one of those guys who could, in two seconds flat, sniff out a bargain in a cob-web covered corner of a broken-down barn! He crammed his basement with the precious relics he rescued, and then made them available to college and seminary students at reasonable rates.

Our first piece was a buffet that had once graced someone's home in the 1930's. We paid the thirty-five dollar asking price, put our treasure in a pickup, discussed it's potential as we transported it home, and then positioned it under the light in the center of our garage floor as we prepared it for cosmetic surgery.

I didn't know a lot about the refinishing process in those early days, but I knew just enough to be dangerous.

Excited about our restoration project sitting in the garage, I snuck over to Sears and bought sandpaper, stripping compound, rubber gloves, stain, varnish and funny little foam brushes that were guaranteed to produce a streakless finish. Then I took the step that showed I was serious about this refinishing business. I purchased our first power tools.

Imagine the look on Jo Ann's face a few days later when she opened her birthday presents and found a Craftsman power drill and sander.

I can still see "the look" — my beloved's exasperated expression which communicated unmistakably that smart husbands who want to stay married a long time don't buy their wives power tools for their birthdays! It didn't take long after that for me to shop at the softer side of Sears!

We still chuckle about Jo Ann's power tool birthday — at least, I do!

We kept the tools and I tackled my unsuspecting victim with the zeal and ignorance of a novice. I slopped stripper all over the buffet, the garage, me, and anything that got within twenty feet of my brush. I scraped and sanded cross grain, scarring the soft wood, adding scratches, dings and dents that weren't there before.

I was in too much of a hurry, and applied the stain and varnish when it was hot and humid. The two ran together, resulting in a dark-chocolate, milky-looking finish that was plain old ugly! I ended up redoing the buffet two more times before it was presentable enough to be displayed in our dining room.

To this day, it looks all right. But it could look a lot better if I had understood then what I know now about the essentials of refinishing furniture.

My refinishing pride and joy is an oak dresser that sits in our guest bedroom. We were looking for some baby furniture when we came across this piece among a number of items some friends were leaving behind when they moved.

We liked the looks of this dresser, even though it was painted lime green! Using a nail, I scratched through the hideous color and concluded that the real dresser, underneath layers of paint, was waiting to be delivered from the cruel covering that was concealing its natural beauty.

I took my time with this project. Properly and painstakingly removing coat after coat of lime green, pink, then white paint, I finally found the wood. What a discovery! It's a sin that such splendid, tiger-striped oak would be buried under common house paint. I gently sanded (with the grain this time) every square inch of that dresser's resurrected surface. I handled it with kid gloves, treating it like a newborn child.

Making sure the temperature and humidity factors were just right, I hand-rubbed a carefully chosen stain into the gorgeous wood's thirsty pores. Then came the polyurethane. Each semi-clear coat was applied with loving care, allowed to dry thoroughly and then lightly buffed with superfine steel wool.

The result is a magnificent masterpiece, if I do say so myself. Everyone whose sees my dresser's restored glory stands back and says "Wow!" When I tell them what it used to look like, they can't believe it. When I think about it, neither can I. What a difference restoration makes.

Marty is my insurance agent. We met when I came to Tulsa. I had been out of the hospital about six months. We formed a business relationship and also shared our hearts as brothers in Christ. He, too, had experienced some hurt in the church.

About two years after our first meeting, we were enjoying lunch together. As I shared the new things God was doing in my life, Marty interrupted. "Steve, you're not the same man I met two years ago. You're different—so alive and on fire. Something's happened to you."

Inside I shouted a hearty Hallelujah! I spent the next hour talking about my spiritual renewal. How God had healed my hurt and raised me from the dead. How my life had been restored and I was rejoicing. Psalm 19:7-8 describes what had happened in my heart.

> *The law of the Lord is perfect, restoring the soul; the testimony of the Lord is sure, making wise the simple. The precepts of the Lord are right, rejoicing the heart; the commandment of the Lord is pure, enlightening the eyes.*

The Lord's law is perfect. His testimony is sure. His precepts are right. His commandments are pure. I bounced back from burnout because His Word enlightened my eyes, made me wise, and restored my soul.

Burnout had left me like my old 1930's buffet and lime green dresser — out of service and in need of restoration. I needed a spiritual refinishing job. Not a surface fix, but a deep, thorough, complete overhaul. Layer after layer of pain had buried the spiritual beauty of my redeemed soul.

I had tried on my own at various times to renew my heart. I'd scrubbed and scraped and sanded on my soul. I'd covered my pain with different shades of stain, sealed my spirit with a protective coat of shiny optimism. But I'd always ended up like the buffet — all right, but not a magnificent masterpiece that glorified God.

So the Master restorer went to work on reclaiming and refinishing me. Jesus knew how to renew me after His image.

Healing the heart is like refinishing a painted oak dresser. Coats and coats of lime green paint must be removed- one coat at a time. Cruddy, old, emotional material has to be exposed and discarded. Then comes the sanding. The Holy Spirit makes the rough places smooth. He skillfully wields the Word of God on those places where we need to be spiritually refreshed. Then the Cross draws us to the Savior. The blood from His wounds restains us and reminds us that we have been bought with a price. Finally the protective finish is applied. God seals us with His love.

The result: A restored and rejoicing child of God! A bounce back, comeback kid for Christ, so changed that people stand back and say, "Wow, look what God has done!"

The oak dresser that I brought back to life looks as good as or better than it did when it was first made. Without question the Steve Roll that God brought back to life is better than ever! I feel as though I've been born again, again! That may not be theologically correct, but it's the only way I know how to describe the rejoicing in my heart!

Nothing compares with coming back from the depths! Depression beat me up and left me for dead on the side of the road of life. But Jesus, the Good Samaritan, came upon me, had compassion, bandaged up my wounds, took me to a safe place, and ministered to my needs. (See Luke 10:30-37.)

God's refinishing process produced four powerful results.

First, He rebuilt my heart.

Proverbs 13:12 reads *"Hope deferred makes the heart sick; but desire fulfilled is a tree of life."* Verse 19a states that *"desire realized is sweet to the soul."*

My heart was broken and needed rebuilding. It was sick because my hopes were dashed. My desire was that someone could fix my hurting heart. Like Humpty Dumpty who sat on the wall and had a great fall, and all the king's horses and all the king's men couldn't put Humpty Dumpty together again, neither could any man put my shattered heart back together.

But the One who made me could. If He can make us, He can remake us. That's why the much loved twenty-third Psalm reads in verse 3 "*He restores my soul.*" God is the one who rebuilds His children's broken hearts.

For a time, I really thought my heart was beyond repair. I couldn't see how the gaping holes could be closed and the fragmented pieces put back together. But when the Great Physician arrived, spiritual surgery commenced. He opened up my heart and operated on my wounds. He actually made my "spiritual ticker" stronger than it had been before I burned out. I rejoice in an overhaul job that has left me solid, stable, and strong in the Lord.

Second, He renewed my vision.

Satan knows that "*where there is no vision, the people perish*" (Proverbs 29:18). Through depression, he did his best to destroy my vision. He knew I would perish if I lost sight of the dream God had given me.

It was a painful process parting and plowing through the dark clouds that dimmed my view of God's plan for my life. But I am so glad that behind the darkness the vision still burned bright.

To enable me to dream again, God first reminded me of the day as a young believer when I knelt by my bed to say yes to His call to preach the Gospel. He also called to mind another time, in the Oregon woods, when He gave me a vision for revival in America.

He showed me meetings I had preached when people came forward to receive Christ. He brought to mind the faces of those whose lives my ministry had profoundly influenced.

During my prayer time on December the 8th, 1993, He gave me ten goals for my new ministry. Rejoicing as I wrote them down, I realized that it would take the rest of my life to accomplish this list.

God wasn't done with Steve Roll! The vision was alive and well! It was the one I had carried in my spirit for two decades, but there was something new — the man needed to carry out the mission was now ready to do it God's way.

Third, He revived my spirit.

My heart has always been consumed with revival. Like the psalmist, I have called out to God many times the request of Psalm 85:6.

*"Wilt Thou not Thyself revive us again That Thy
people may rejoice in Thee?"*

I have prayed for the world, America, the church and people to
be revived by the Spirit of God. My burnout brought me to the point
of needing to seek revival for myself. My spirit, once vibrant with
the fire of God, was now gasping for breath, in need of resuscitation.

God answers those who pray for revival. He, Himself, revived
me. I was able to bounce back from burnout because the Holy Spirit
breathed new life into my lethargic spirit. Spiritual power energized
me for dreaming again and believing that God has a great future in
store for me in the ministry.

I rejoice in Him for reviving me. That bounce I had lost from my
step is back! I'm stepping high and moving boldly ahead to be a
spark of revival for others who need spiritual renewal.

Fourth, He restored my joy.

A few years ago a Christian man came to me for counseling. He
said he wasn't happy. Life wasn't fun anymore; he was losing his
joy. Difficult times had gotten him down. I told him to not let
anything or anyone steal his joy, that it was important for us to keep
our focus on the source of joy because if we can hold on to joy, we
can ride out the storms of life.

In the depths of depression, I needed to heed my own advice.
Crushing circumstances had caused me to lose focus. Satan stole my
joy for a while because I forgot the source of joy. Scripture tells us:
"The joy of the Lord is our strength" (Nehemiah 8:10). *"In his
presence is fullness of joy"* (Psalm 16:11). And *"the Kingdom of
God is not eating and drinking but righteousness, peace, and joy in
the Holy Spirit"* (Romans 14:17).

When King David called on God to "create in me a clean heart, O
God, and renew a steadfast spirit within me," he also asked the Lord to
"restore the joy of thy salvation" (Psalm 51:10. 12). Note that he desired
that the joy of thy salvation (not my salvation) be restored. Having
suffered great losses because of his sin and disobedience, David now
knew that true joy is found in one place: God's salvation.

The Lord turned my mourning into dancing when I refocused
my attention on my source of joy — Him. I traded in the sackcloth
and ashes and girded myself with gladness when I remembered that

Jesus is my joy! Salvation is the most important thing in my life. Joy returned in even greater degrees when I again saw Jesus as my precious Savior and Redeemer. I had looked to life, the ministry and people to provide joy. They didn't because they couldn't. Only the Lord brings the kind of joy that men and demons can't touch.

I'm so excited now about my walk with God, I feel like a child at Christmas. When my children were a little younger they could hardly wait for Christmas morning. Thoughts of Santa coming down the chimney and visions of a Cabbage Patch doll or a radio controlled car waiting under the tree made it impossible for them to sleep.

I remember one year vividly. Both kids were wide awake at four a.m. They were bouncing off the walls in their bedrooms. We told them they had to stay in their beds until five o'clock. Yeah, right. Talk about a parental blunder. They were so full of anticipation they were about to explode. When we realized there was no way on earth that they could cool their jets and wait another hour, we gave them the signal to head downstairs.

They literally flew down the staircase. I'm sure those tiny feet never touched the carpet. The trail I followed was one of excited talking and happy screaming as they burst into the living room to inspect the goodies under the tree. When they unwrapped the present that contained the gift they wanted most, they erupted with pure, uninhibited, unadulterated joy. Their eyes sparkled and danced with fire.

My Christian life is like Christmas morning. I look forward to each day. I'm full of anticipation as to what the Lord has around the next corner. Life and ministry are an adventure once again. I'm enjoying the journey. No more destination disease. Every moment is special because I journey with the joy of my life — Jesus Christ.

God has restored me and I'm rejoicing! I'm becoming the man I have always wanted to be. I will give thanks to Him forever.

Pastors, your joy should not be in your ministry. It should be in the One who called you to the ministry. Joy is not found in people, it is found in a Person. Joy has nothing whatsoever to do with circumstances. It has everything to do with Christ. Don't let anyone or anything rob you of your joy. If you have lost your focus, look to Jesus and joy will return. You can come back from your setback!

A friend of mine from the hills of Kentucky grew up in a family of good old country boys. While working together one day, Troy and I had a deep discussion about life's trials and adversities. Troy summed up our experience on earth with these simple words of homespun wisdom. "Sure enough, it's always something, ain't it?" I chuckled in agreement.

Setbacks are part of life. How we handle the "it's always something, ain't it" stuff is often the difference between failure or success. When life delivers a blow that knocks us backwards, that setback becomes a test. It tests our resolve to comeback or stay back. Many people who experience a setback, stay back — and regret it the rest of their life.

The devil specializes in using life's little difficulties to trip us up and take us out. He's always scheming and strategizing as to how to set God's people back (Ephesians 6:11).

Satan hates it when the righteous go forward. He knows that when we go ahead, we leave him behind. So He works overtime to push God's people back. Once the devil sets us back, he cleverly erects strongholds (spiritual barriers) to keep us there.

Paul describes these strongholds and how to tear them down in his second letter to the Corinthians.

> *"For though we walk in the flesh, we do not war according to the flesh, for the weapons of our warfare are not of the flesh but divinely powerful for the destruction of fortresses. (strongholds). We are destroying speculations and every lofty thing raised up against the knowledge of God, and we are taking every thought captive to the obedience of Christ."*
> II Corinthians 10:3-5

As a believer who has had his share of setbacks, and will no doubt experience more, I love phrases like "divinely powerful" "destruction of fortresses" and "destroying speculations." Those are fighting words! And if you've been set back, you know it's a fight to come back.

The good news is — the fight is the Lord's! (I Samuel 17:47) Our weapons of war aren't humanly powerful but "divinely powerful." God wields the sword against Satan. He destroys the enemy's strongholds in our lives through His power, not ours.

Heartbreak in the ministry set me back. Satan erected strongholds of failure, depression, fear and a lack of confidence to keep me back. But God's will is for us to comeback from setbacks!

God and I leveled the strongholds. I took every one of my thoughts and made them "captive to the obedience of Christ." With the help of the Holy Spirit, I made a series of decisions, and took certain actions, based on His Word, that put me on the comeback trail. Then God responded with power.

I am a comeback kid! Glory be to God! I'm not pouting; I'm shouting! I'm not looking back; I'm looking ahead. All because I chose to come back and not stay back because of a setback.

Let me share some simple concepts that helped me along the comeback trail. I don't have all the solutions to your situation, but I believe that if you'll work on these ten things, your setback will turn into a comeback.

1. Stop beating yourself up. Start building yourself up!

Put the rod away. You aren't a worthless worm! Give yourself a break. Quit tearing yourself apart with negative self-talk. "Dummy" isn't befitting a child of God! Jesus didn't give His life for you to limp around like a loser!

Resist every impulse to speak bad things about yourself. We all make mistakes. Every person who has tried to do anything great for God has a flops, failures, and fumbles list!

Focus on the good things about yourself. Think about and verbalize what is good about you, what makes you special. Rehearse your successes. Pump yourself up by thinking on the things Paul recommended in Philippians 4:8.

> *Finally, brethren, whatever is true, whatever is honorable whatever is right, whatever is pure, whatever is lovely, whatever is of good repute, if there is any excellence and if anything worthy of praise, let your mind dwell on these things.*

Make the effort to fix your mind on this list of excellent things. Dwell on what is true, honorable, pure, right, lovely and of good repute, and you will drive the devil's lies away! Praise, instead of pain, will fill your heart.

You are somebody very special! Please be kind to yourself. Cut yourself some slack. Pat yourself on the back once in a while — it sure beats pounding on it!

2. Pay the price to wait on God

My life's verse is found in Isaiah 40:31. My mother shared it with me when I was first born again. I underlined it in my Living Bible and wrote it on the tablet of my heart.

> *But they that wait upon the Lord will renew their strength; they will mount up with wings as eagles, they will run and not be weary, they will walk and not faint.*

Comebacks require courage. There is a cost to conquering setbacks. Waiting on the Lord is the price we must pay if we're to soar on eagle's wings high above our heartaches.

Waiting on Him takes time. If you have been beaten up, the only way you'll get better is to make the sacrifices necessary to receive His healing touch. That means saying "yes" to time in personal devotions, prayer, fasting, and listening to the Spirit. It also means saying "no" to everything that tries to tempt you away from the secret place.

It takes courage to say "no," and commitment to say "yes." It's not cool in most ministry circles to take time off, but if you're committed to wholeness, you will muster up the courage to say "yes" and "no" where appropriate.

We hinder our healing by neglecting to make the tough calls. The right call might mean a few weeks off. Possibly a sabbatical. Maybe a year or more out of active ministry to regroup. Those decisions come with a price tag. When we want something really badly, we find a way to pay for it. Waiting on the Lord to be renewed in His strength is the one thing we can't afford not to pay the price for.

3. Let go and let God love you.

I love it when I come home and my children drop whatever they're doing to love on their daddy. We hug or cuddle up on the couch for a few minutes to soak up nothing but loving. It's the best medicine in the world!

Weary warrior, drop your weapons and reach out to love your Heavenly Father. Let go of your inhibitions. It's perfectly natural for a child to run and jump into the outstretched arms of his daddy. Your Father is waiting. Let God hug you up!

You know you want to feel His arms wrapped securely around you. It's okay. Be a child again. Leap into Daddy's lap. Love Him and let Him love you back.

You need a lot of love when you're coming back from a setback. Tons of it. The way to get it is to go to the One who is love (I John 4:7-21). Don't let anything keep you from the Father's embrace, for "love never fails" (I Corinthians 13:8).

4. Surrender so the Spirit can set you free!

"Now the Lord is the Spirit, and where the Spirit is, there is freedom" (II Corinthians 3:17). Nothing is like being spiritually free! The Spirit of the Lord liberates us to experience the fullness of the Father's love when we surrender.

Are you bound up? Tied up by tradition? Roped in to a routine of lifeless religion? Does what people think about your religious experience and performance matter more to you than the free operation of the Holy Spirit? Is there something stirring within you that you want to let loose, but you're afraid to? If you answered "yes" to any or all of these questions, you need to be set free.

The "holy ground" where I pray behind our home contains many precious memories. I'll always cherish the afternoon of a lovely spring day when I first tasted freedom. I was walking along a line of tall trees, praising God, singing, making melody in my heart to the Lord. I was completely caught up in enjoying His presence. As I rounded the end of the row of trees, I was overcome with joy and rejoicing. My spirit was so full, before I knew it, I leaped into the air, waved my hands toward heaven and shouted at the top of my lungs, "Yes!" As I landed, I exclaimed "I'm free. I'm free. Hallelujah, I'm free!"

Freedom in the Spirit is essential to coming back. The key to liberty is full surrender to the Holy Spirit. Let go of your hang-ups. Give the Holy Spirit unrestricted access to your heart and unconditional permission to do a fresh work.

Do you really want to be a comeback kid? Are you sure? If you answer "yes," surrender and the Spirit will set you free. Like Nike says, "Just do it!" You'll be glad you did!

5. God has forgiven you — forgive yourself.

The day had not started well. Hurtful memories from my resignation haunted me as I tried to work on the next Sunday's sermon for the church I was pastoring in Tulsa. I instructed my secretary to hold my calls and I scooted out of the office.

Standing at the back of the sanctuary, I felt frustrated as I prayed. Something seemed to be impeding my intimacy with the Father. Turning to leave, I was drawn to look back to the cross hanging on the front wall. As soon as I did, Jesus's presence filled the room. I did not literally see Him, but I sensed that He was standing in front of the altar, reaching out to me.

I asked, "Lord, what's wrong? Why do I still feel like I'm a failure?"

Speaking softly to my spirit, Jesus said "This cross means I have forgiven you. You're not a failure in My eyes. I love you. But you're a failure in your eyes because you don't love yourself. You're holding things against yourself. You need to do one thing to set yourself free. Forgive Steve.

Tears streaming down my face, I ran down to the front, knelt before the Cross, and spoke the simple words that unlocked the hurt in my heart, "Steve, I forgive you."

That moment changed the direction of my journey. As Jesus stood over me, assuring me of His love, the Holy Spirit filled me with "the peace of God that passes all understanding" (Philippians 4:7). Comeback could now become reality because Steve no longer crucified Steve.

Not forgiving ourselves is a comeback-blocking tactic of the enemy. We pastors are the worst offenders when it comes to this self-forgiveness business. We receive the Lord's forgiveness. We accept forgiveness from others. We forgive others. But we balk at forgiving ourselves.

I have shared with so many ministers who wouldn't forgive themselves. And in all honesty, the issue is not couldn't, but wouldn't.

In Mark chapter 11, Jesus preceded His monumental passage about mountain moving faith with a word about the absolute necessity of forgiveness. In verse 25 we read:

> *And whenever you stand praying, forgive, if you*
> *have anything against anyone; so that your Father*
> *in heaven may forgive your transgressions.*

Anyone. That includes yourself.

As part of my healing process, I had released, through forgiveness, everyone I had anything against, except one. Myself.

You can't heal until you forgive yourself. Why not do it right now? Go ahead. Do what you know you need to do. Release yourself. Say these words out loud. "Jesus, I forgive (your name)."

The Father's healing love can now flow freely through you because Jesus and you have forgiven you. Glory to God!

6. Choose to be better; refuse to be bitter.

Do not let bitterness take root in your heart. No matter what has happened to you, make the conscious choice to be better, not bitter.

You will never know the glory of coming back if you become bitter. Remember — bitter or better is up to you!

Early on during my recovery process I battled bitterness daily. I would see someone who I thought had done me dirty, or I would remember an event, or I might see someone in another city that reminded me of "that person" and boom — bitterness raised it's heinous head. All kinds of devilish thoughts poisoned my spirit. Major ugliness rose up in me.

Choice time. I could let bitterness fester, or I could forgive the object of my displeasure (Matthew 5:43-48). Sometimes it took every ounce of spiritual energy I could summon, but I decided that I wouldn't let anyone make me bitter. No one, ever.

If you want to stay back in your set back, be bitter. It's guaranteed to destroy any hope of comeback.

In Ephesians 4:31-32, Paul, who had reasons to be bitter, told us how to beat bitterness.

> *Let all bitterness, and wrath and anger and clamor and slander be put away from you, along with all malice. And be kind to one another, tenderhearted, forgiving each other, just as God in Christ also has forgiven you.*

Bitterness is deadly baggage that will only hold back your comeback. Put it away. Bury it in the blood of Jesus.

I take great personal satisfaction in the fact that I've come out of this better, not bitter. I rejoice and give thanks to my Savior who has taught me to forgive and bless those who make life difficult.

7. Learn to laugh again!

How long has it been since you laughed? Can you remember the last time you let loose with a belly-busting, side-splitting roar of laughter? There was a time when I wondered if I would ever smile again, let alone laugh.

Life can get heavy. Laughter is God's good medicine that lightens the load. Proverbs 17:22 says *"A joyful heart is good medicine."*

The burden of burnout wiped the smile off my face and silenced my laughter. Joy and laughter also vanished from our family life. We used to laugh a lot. We had fun in our home. When depression's black cloud descended, laughter ceased, and our spirits dried up.

I knew we were healing, individually and as a family, when we started laughing again. Ecclesiastes 3:4 states that "there is a time to laugh." The time to laugh is when you are enduring hard times. Part of surviving a setback is learning to laugh again.

I can't pinpoint exactly when, but there was a day when laughter returned to our home. The heavy atmosphere hovering over our home evaporated. We started noticing the funny things in life again, and laughed. Silly little things set off the giggles that put us, as my grandma used to say, in stitches. We laughed so hard that we cried, and happy crying is a good sign that you're on your way back!

Start laughing again. Read the comics. Let "The Far Side" lighten up your day. Tune in to the clean, classic sitcoms like "The Dick Van Dyke," "Bob Newhart," and "I Love Lucy." Rent a video like the "Out of Towners" with Jack Lemmon or "What About Bob" with Bill Murray and Richard Dreyfuss. Everyone in the ministry should watch "What About Bob?" at least twice a year. It will help you stay sane.

Whatever it takes, laugh! It's healthy. It's an important ingredient in the cleansing process. You'll feel great when you re-enter the lighter side of life.

8.   Take back stolen territory.

In Joel 2:25 the prophet says that *"The Lord will make up to you for the years that the swarming locust has eaten, the creeping locust, the stripping locust, and the gnawing locust."*

I have known all of those locusts. Creeping things have swarmed, stripped and gnawed on me! Thank God for His promise to make up to us what has been taken. What we think we lost, He will restore, even better than before!

The Lord taught me something about my part in the "making it up to you" process. He told me to practice the principle of taking back what is mine. As His child, certain things belong to me. Satan has no right to anything that God's Word says is mine!

When the devil picks my pockets, I immediately confront him in the name of the Lord and take back whatever he took. For example, one day he ripped off my peace. So I got on my bike, took a prayer ride through the neighborhood, quoted Scripture, rebuked the devil and took back my peace.

When five kings overran Sodom, abducted Lot and his family, and stole their possessions, uncle Abraham knew exactly what to do. He went after the wayward kings, defeated them, and brought back his relatives and all their goods and possessions. (See Genesis 14:12-16.)

No matter what you have lost during your setback, go get it back! Be bold. Take authority. Don't be pushed around by the loser of the universe any more!

I don't like being ripped off, and neither do you. It's time to start raiding the enemy's camp. You will experience healing power when you reclaim what is yours.

9. *Release yesterday — reach for tomorrow.*

Comeback kids walk in the present, dream about the future, and forget the past.

Alexander Graham Bell gave us some great advice regarding the future. He said, "When one door closes, another opens, but we often look so long and so regretfully upon the closed door that we do not see the one which has opened up before us."

Yesterday is a done deal. The door is shut. Stop trying to open what God has closed. There is a door marked Comeback waiting for you to enter. But it's in front of you, not behind. You can push it open and walk towards tomorrow as soon as you release your grip on yesterday.

10. *Begin rejoicing and keep on rejoicing!*

In the midst of our crisis, a man of God spoke comforting words of encouragement over our lives. Prophesying that God was doing His work in Jo Ann and I, he said "If I were you, I would just rejoice."

Another man of God, named Paul, said something very similar. In I Thessalonians 5:16 he declares "Rejoice always." He also says in Philippians 4:4 "Rejoice in the Lord always; again, I will say rejoice."

A popular praise chorus from Isaiah 61:3 exhorts us to "put on the garment of praise for the spirit of heaviness" (KJV). Praise paves the way from setback to comeback. If you want to leave the spirit of heaviness behind, start praising God and rejoicing in the Lord.

Then keep doing it. Everyday, every way, and in every thing, give Him thanks and rejoice always.

Rubber meets the road in our Christian life when we can sincerely rejoice always. The edge in overcoming adversity and defeating setback is praise!

How's your praise life? If you're struggling — start rejoicing. Enter His gates with thanksgiving and into His courts with praise. Bless His name. Lift your hands in praise, and worship the Lord. Rejoice and give thanks for every benefit He has bestowed upon you.

You want to see the dark clouds disappear? Rejoice and keep on rejoicing!

Start your comeback today !

One day when my son and I were browsing in a sporting goods store, we came across a great T-shirt. It showed a baseball infield. A base runner, eyes looking toward second, had his foot firmly planted on first. The caption read: "You can't steal second with your foot on first!"

It's true in baseball, and it's true in life: You can't move ahead if you won't leave where you are. You can't have a comeback if you keep your heart stuck in your setback.

God is in the business of making comeback kids. Pastors and laymen, take the risk. Steal second. Put these principles into practice. You might be surprised at how fast you can get to second once you decide to take your foot off first.

Chapter 10
Overcoming Fear With Faith

*The Lord has taken away His judgments against
you, He has cleared away your enemies. The King
of Israel, the Lord, is in your midst; you will fear
disaster no more.*

Zephaniah 3:15

Sorrow looks back. Fear looks around. Faith looks up.

Fear is an awesome foe that we must face and overcome as we travel the comeback trail. Fear is a powerful paralyzer. If you've ever been held in it's disabling grip, you know how fear works to prevent you from taking steps of faith that will propel you forward.

As I ascended from depression's depths, fear also surfaced and stood at my side. Apprehension and anxiety, fueled by fear, became my constant companions and caused me nothing but grief every time I attempted to go ahead with God's new direction for my life. Fear of disaster stalked and stymied my resurging spirit each step of the way.

One Sunday morning in Tulsa, before church services, the Lord gave me Zephaniah 3:12-20, a tremendous passage dealing with the restoration of God's remnant Israel. These verses contain an encouraging and forward-looking word for people who are being harassed by fear.

Because "the Lord is in your midst," the prophet matter-of-factly announces to the people, "you will fear disaster no more."

I remember praying with the worship team and telling them that God's word for the day was this: There is no reason for any of us to fear disaster in our lives or for our hands to hang limp because the Lord, who is a "victorious warrior" (verse 17), is always with us.

God knew I needed that word as much or more than anybody in that prayer room. My hands were hanging limp by my side. That's not where a man of God's hands are supposed to be. Limp hands are a sign of dread, discouragement, and defeat. Zephaniah strongly exhorted the people "Do not let your hands fall limp" (verse 16).

According to the Bible, a believer's hands are to be raised in praise to God (Psalm 134:2). Holy hands are to be lifted up in prayer (I Timothy 2:8). Trusting hands are to be lifted toward God's holy sanctuary when we need help (Psalm 28:2). We are to clap our hands as we shout to God with the voice of joy (Psalm 47:1). Our hands are to be working hands, energetically doing God's business (Ecclesiastes 9:1). A Christian's hands are to be reaching out to raise up needy people in the name of Jesus (Acts 3:7).

Hands that are hanging limp are heavy with fear. Hands that are lifted up are full of faith. My hands needed to move from "limp" to "lifted up." My faith had to overcome my fear for my victory to become complete.

Before burnout becomes blessing, fears must be conquered. Without exception, every hurting pastor and layman I have ever counseled has shared issues with me that "scare them to death," things that terrify them, Fears, real or imagined, that cause them to tremble, literally immobilizing them from taking steps toward healing.

The beginning point for beating fear is to identify its source. The Bible is unmistakably clear concerning fear's source.

> *For God has not given us the spirit of fear; but of*
> *power, and of love, and of a sound mind.*
> II Timothy 1:7

Fear doesn't come from God. Love, power, and a sound mind do. Your heavenly father is not the source of your dread. Satan is. The deceiver sends fear for the purpose of paralyzing and rendering ineffective the spirits of power, love, and a sound mind.

What flies out the window first when we're gripped by fear? Power, love and a sound mind. We feel powerless, lose sight of God's love, and think we're going insane! Clever, isn't he!

Overcoming fear is a spiritual battle. We can fight effectively when we know that fear is neither of God, nor of our own making, but is of the devil. The evil one and the fear he inspires can be decisively defeated by faith.

One aspect of fear that particularly disturbed me was that Satan tried to con me into believing that I was the only person on earth who was scared. Has he ever pulled that one on you? Ever hear a subtle suggestion that sounds something like this? Hey, look around. Nobody else is fearful. No one else is afraid like you. There must be something really wrong with you because you're so frightened.

You might be suffering under that same demonic delusion right now. If you're wondering whether anybody else has ever felt the fears you do, let me review for you some of the fears that terrorized me. I share them so you will realize you aren't the only one in their grip and so you can rise above them just as I have.

1. Fear of being forgotten

Many times during my restoration process I wondered if God or anybody remembered me. Did anyone recall the good deeds I'd done in the ministry? What about the help I was giving to others while I was healing? Did it matter to anybody, or did out of sight really mean out of mind?

I feared that being out of circulation in the ministry meant that Steve Roll might be out of business as a minister. Two years of isolation had me questioning if anyone out there knew my address. How would anyone know about me and my abilities? How could I ever start over again if nobody knew I existed?

The Lord calmed this security-shaking fear with Hebrews 6:10 and Isaiah 49:14-16.

> *For God is not unjust so as to forget your work and the love which you have shown toward his name, in having ministered and in still ministering to the saints.*
>
> Hebrews 6:10

> *But Zion said, "The Lord has forsaken me, and the Lord has forgotten me." Can a woman forget her nursing child? And have no compassion on the son of her womb? Even these may forget, but I will not forget you. Behold, I have inscribed you on the palms of My hands; Your walls are continually before Me.*
>
> Isaiah 49:14-16

God says He does not forget our work or love for Him. Others may, but He will never forget us. Our names are written on the palms of Almighty God's hands! Every time He looks at His palm, He sees your name and mine. That's remembering!

2. *Fear of what others think*

We care very much about the opinions of others. Too often, our self-esteem is greatly affected by how others assess us as persons. Appraisal by others can be healthy. It can also be unhealthy. Overvaluing the opinions of others can lead to, among other things, worry and fear. The devil did a real number on me in this area.

He had me in stark terror worrying about what others would think of my bout with depression. What would people say? How would they treat me when they learned I'd been hospitalized and had struggled with suicidal thoughts? Surely no one would be interested in calling me to pastor their church.

I was petrified with fright when I thought what people might think of me when they heard my story. Satan pushed me into a negative thought pattern that was accusative and condemnatory. He pulled out all the stops in his attempt to cement me in my setback and silence any thought of a comeback. I battled fiercely and furiously, trying to fight off the torturous fear that I was finished in the eyes of men.

Then I found Proverbs 29:25. "The *fear of man brings a snare, but he who trusts in the Lord will be exalted.*" It set me free from the fear of men's opinions.

I realized that two opinions are all that matter in life. God's and mine. What He thinks about me and what I think about me are what count in the long run. Now my priority is to be faithful to the One who called me, and to walk in His favor. Man's favor is a bonus.

3. *Fear of the depression returning*

If you've survived a heart attack, it's human nature to fear another one. If you've had a business go belly up, you might live in fear of going bankrupt when you start over again.

I remember too well a number of times when I felt "blue" after I had started recovering from depression. Fear swept over me, causing me to wonder if I was going to slide in to the pit of deep despair again. It was as though an icy hand grabbed me and sent a chill through my whole being. It really scared me to think of even the possibility of descending into depression ever again.

Satan had a heyday with this one. Demons of fear jumped all over me, taunting, jeering, and chiding me I wasn't cured; I would always be depressive; I would never be even-keel emotionally again; I might as well get used to living in the dark shadows of despair.

What a frightening prospect! In reality, it was a big lie designed by the devil to keep me from taking steps to higher ground. A phrase in Isaiah 60:20 gave me hope that my fear of staying depressed was unfounded: "And the days of your mourning will be finished."

The Spirit of the Lord delivered me from depression. He showed me how to stay delivered and how to defeat despair's dark advances. The day would come when I would say, "The days of my mourning are finished!"

4. Fear of reentering the ministry

Someone once said that if an ocean liner could think and feel, it would never leave it's dock because it would be afraid of the thousands of huge waves it would encounter. It would fear all of it's dangers at once, even though it had to meet them only one wave at a time.

One wave at a time or not, it terrified me to think of stepping back into the ministry. All I could envision were ghosts and goblins hiding in the bushes, poised to pounce on this shell-shocked pastor.

I was afraid of the pressures and responsibilities. I wondered if I could cope with the demands of ministry life once again. Would I have confidence to lead God's people to fulfill a dream? How would I handle conflict with parishioners in the future? Would I be emotionally strong enough to endure the spiritual attacks that come with ministry?

The evil one pounded me over and over again with his answers. "Of course you won't make it. You'll fall flat on your face in disgrace." My heart filled with fear when I listened to his lies.

But the devil didn't count on Christ rebuilding my confidence. Christ-confidence readied me for a fearless reentry to the ministry God had prepared.

5. Fear of financial ruin

This fear sounds pretty earthly and secular compared to the other ones, but it was a fear I faced daily for two years. I went without a predictable, regular paycheck for twenty-five months.

Bills take on a whole new character when you are wondering how you'll pay them! When you have a paycheck, at worst, bills bug you. So you gripe a little, pay them, and then give God thanks for His gracious provision.

Without income, bills can get under your skin. They have a way of belittling you and bashing away at your ego. My fragile, male, you-gotta-be-providing-for-your-family ego really took a licking. Each "please pay this amount" was a not-so-subtle reminder that I didn't have a "real job." Fear of running out of money ruined many potentially good days.

Near the end of his life, the Psalmist wrote this word of testimony.

> I have been young, and now I am old; yet I have not seen the righteous forsaken or his descendants begging bread.
>
> Psalm 37:25

I'm still young but I've witnessed first hand God's provision of our every need. He performed financial miracle after miracle after miracle! Every bill and obligation was met on time and in full! Hallelujah! I give God all the glory for sustaining my family.

That's an all the more notable miracle in light of the fact that financial analysts report that the average American family is just a step away from bankruptcy if it misses two paychecks!

6. Fear of the church family

My deepest wounds had come at the hands of church people. Those I had counted on had let me down. Some I had trusted turned betrayer. I found myself developing a suspicious spirit. A number of times I told myself I would never trust anyone in the family of God again.

Fear of being hurt was the force driving this distrust. I was truly afraid of opening my heart to God's people. What if some of them broke it again? How would I deal with the next Judas? Would I be able to give my brothers and sisters the benefit of the doubt and not be suspicious of them?

It's difficult ministering to people if you're questioning what they're really up to. First John 4:18a says, "There is no fear in love; but perfect love casts out fear." Fear temporarily overshadowed my love for God's sheep. Fears can be dealt with in different ways. This fear would have to be "cast out" by a renewed love for the body of Christ.

7. Fear of getting excited again

An acquaintance once told me I could sell anything to anybody because my excitement and enthusiasm for life was contagious. He said that if I believed in a product or service, my zeal would easily convince a customer to sign the dotted line.

Mr. Enthusiasm found himself full of fear. I was terrified to dream again and believe God for great things. I was afraid to allow my hopes to be raised very high because someone might dash them again. My balloon of high expectations had burst before.

I felt like a child who wants very much to play ball on the little league team, but who's so scared that he might not be chosen, he doesn't even want to try out.

I believe my enthusiasm for God and His work is a gift. The Lord has favored me with personal charisma and infectious zeal which He has used to touch many lives. No wonder the devil threw up a roadblock of fear to try and stop the spread of my renewed enthusiasm.

The word *enthusiasm* comes from two Greek words: *En Theos*, meaning *"in God."* Enthusiasm literally has it's roots in God! The source of genuine enthusiasm is the Almighty.

Makes sense doesn't it. Our Creator is excited about what He has done for His creation. So should we be. Knowing that we're redeemed by God's only Son should put a shout in our souls that makes a dramatic ninth-inning, game-winning homerun pale in insignificance!

En Theos overruled and overpowered the fear that Satan used to try to permanently snuff out the fire of God that burned in my soul. Satan's strategy backfired. Out of God's cannon would come a man of faith more fired up than ever!

8. Fear of nightmares

Fear manifests itself in many ways. Psalm 91:5 states, *"You shall not be afraid of the terror by night, or the arrow that flies by day."* I believe whole-heartedly in this scripture. I'm convinced the Lord protects His trusting children from the situations mentioned.

During my depression, I came to understand in a very personal way what some of that "terror by night" is. One way that the prince of darkness attacked me was through nightmares.

Nightmares are unwelcome and uninvited. They sneak up on our subconscious when we're defenseless. Bad dreams invade our minds and play on our insecurities and fears. I experienced nightmares for over three years. They began in Michigan, before I was forced to resign my pastorate.

One theme dominated my dreams: fear. I was absolutely terrified by the nightmares. I have never been so frightened in all of my life.

Typically the dreams consisted of a dark, shadowy figure trying to come through the door or window of the house.

I began screaming in the night — blood-curdling screams that startled my wife from her sleep. She would reach over to awaken me from my torment, and comfort me. In a state of sheer terror, my heart would pound so fast that I was certain it was going to burst through my chest.

I remember one night in particular when the intruder, dressed in black, had succeeded in pushing his tentacle-like arms through the front door. As he reached for me, I could see his face. His eyes had the look of a wild animal intent on capturing and killing its prey. Even more disturbing to me was that he resembled one of the men who had been orchestrating my ouster from the church.

As he reached for me, I kicked and struggled in a desperate attempt to escape the clutches of his evil grasp. But I couldn't elude him. Darkness hemmed me in. When my personal night stalker finally grabbed my feet and started to take me away, I screamed from the deepest part of my soul. As I thrashed and groaned by her side, Jo Ann gently shook me, arousing me from my terror.

As I awakened, the intruder relinquished his vice-like grip, and vanished. But the dream left me in a state of paralyzing panic. Pulse racing, sweating profusely, I was unable to move, frozen to the bed. I was even scared to go to the bathroom, fearing my tormentor might be lurking around the corner.

The nightmares came and went. I had no control over my intruder's calendar. But the pattern was the same. A dark, mysterious figure chased me down and dragged me away.

Sometimes my stalker reminded me of someone who was harassing me. Other times his identity remained secret. He crashed through doors, shattered windows, and broke through every barrier in his relentless pursuit of me.

When the nightmares came, I felt helpless. Defenseless. No one else was ever present in these dreams. Just me, all alone, pitted against this frightening creature from the depths of darkness. I was in a fight for survival. I cried out for help, but there were no rescuers.

No one to come to my aid. Just him and me. Battling for my soul.
The nightmares continued to haunt me in the hospital. They
became super scary as the medications I was receiving enhanced the
vividness of the intrusions. The darkness darkened and my stalker
became more violent. The dreams became so intense and so
frightening that I feared falling asleep at night. My hospital room
became a horrifying place when the dark one came because my wife
wasn't there to cuddle and comfort me.

The horrific dreams followed me to Tulsa. For a short while
they were less frequent. I hoped they were diminishing as I was
progressing in the healing process. But just about the time I thought
they were history, my fear-producing foe would reappear.

I felt set back. It scared me that they weren't gone. What was
wrong with me if they were still showing up? I prayed. I asked God
to protect me. I believed he did. But my evil-minded intruder
managed to slip through the lines of angelic defense and take
another shot at me.

One night I had the nightmare of all nightmares. This time I was
suspended over a black hole. My adversary was pulling me into the
lightless abyss.

Terrified of falling into this bottomless pit, I asked my tormentor
who he was. I'd asked before, but he had never responded. This time
he did. In a deep, soul-chilling voice, he answered, "I am death."

I screamed like I have never screamed before. Upon waking up, I
told Jo Ann the intruder had come and identified himself as death. The
unrelenting adversary who had violated my emotional space even in
the night was seeking my life. Death was trying to destroy me.

Identifying the adversary proved significant. The dreams were
about my destruction. Satan had played on my deep-seated fears of
rejection, abandonment and failure. The evil one kept coming to me
with the same threatening message: I'm going to take your life
Steve. I'm coming for you. You're going to die a disgrace and
failure. Destroy your own life. You can't escape.

Zephaniah 3:17 says "The Lord your God is in your midst, a
victorious warrior!" At the height of my fear, the fearless one
stepped in to deliver me and defeat my tormentor. He fortified my
faith by reminding me that He was with me and He had already won
the victory over death!

I did more than escape Satan's death grip. I triumphed over him in Jesus's name! Faith overcame fear! My fears turned into cheers as I focused on my deliverer Jesus Christ.

I no longer fear nightmares. Not long ago, I had one. I woke up, submitted to God, rebuked the devil, and he fled (James 4:7). I rejoiced in the Lord, assured Jo Ann I was all right, rolled over, and slept like a baby. Praise the Lord!

In my battle with fear, I discovered four simple things that help me defeat fear. I call them fear busters.

1.   Face your fears.

Don't turn your back. Don't try to flee from what you fear. Stand up to it. Stare it down. Recently I faced a fear head on. Guess what? Standing up to it and refusing to back down broke it's hold over me. It retreated like a whipped dog! Talk about feeling good. If you want to walk tall, face your fears in the name of Jesus. When He shows up, your fears have to flee!

2.   Don't feed your fears.

Quit dwelling on them. Don't give them attention. Refuse to acknowledge them. Starve them. If you don't feed them, they can't grow. Do a little weed and feed — weed your fears and feed your faith!

3.   Fight your fears.

It was Emerson who said, "Do the thing you fear, and the death of fear is certain." Never surrender to your fears. Don't lie down and let fear triumph over you. Put on your armor. Stand behind the shield of faith, charge what you fear and conquer it with the sword of the Spirit. Plant the flag of the King of Kings and Lord of Lords over your conquered foe!

4.   Focus on faith.

Psalm 56:3 says, "Whenever I am afraid, I will trust in you." Faith negates fear. Therefore, when fear comes, look to Jesus. Let faith rise up in your spirit. Take your fears to God, trust Him, and watch your fear disappear.

Heavy hands become light hands when we hand our fears over to God. The Bible is filled with commands to be courageous. Someone once counted the "fear nots" in the Bible and discovered that there are 365 verses with this divine command — one for every day of the year!

One of the most frequently spoken phrases of Jesus was, "Fear not." The Savior knew that fear makes life burdensome, so He lovingly exhorted His followers to put their faith in God, not fear. As a new believer over twenty years ago, I came across John 14:27:

> *Peace I leave with you; my peace, I give to you; not as the world gives, do I give to you. Let not your heart be troubled nor let it be fearful.*

Jesus wants our hearts to be free of trouble and fear. He provides a peace that the world cannot give.

We live in a fear-filled world. Faith lifts us above the fear around us. When we take our eyes off the troublesome things surrounding us and fix our eyes on Jesus, He fills our hearts with peace.

In II Chronicles 20 we find the account of how Jehoshaphat overcame fear with faith. Judah was surrounded by three armies (described in verse two as "a great multitude that had come to make war. In his humanity, the king became fearful. But note how he handled his fear.

> *And Jehoshaphat was afraid and turned his attention to seek the lord and proclaimed a fast throughout all Judah. So Judah gathered together to seek help from the Lord; they even came from all the cities of Judah to seek the Lord."*
>
> verses 3-4

Jehoshaphat turned his attention from the invading armies (fear) to seek the Lord (faith). Then he acted on his faith.

I like to call this inspiring incident "What To Do When You Don't Know What To Do!" Jehoshaphat ordered a fast and prayed to the Lord (verses 6-11). Look how this man of God prays in verse 12.

> *O our God, wilt Thou not judge them? For we are powerless against this great multitude who are coming against us, nor do we know what to do, but our eyes are on you.*

I love his honesty ("we are powerless and do not know what to do") and his humble faith ("our eyes are on you"). In actuality, he did know what to do. He looked to God for help.

God answered his prayer through a prophet. In verse 15, the Lord said to Jehoshaphat .

> *"Do not fear or be dismayed because of this great multitude, for the battle is not yours, but God's."*

The prophet told him to go down against them (face their fear). They wouldn't have to fight because the Lord was with them and would fight for them (verse 16-17).

The king responded by worshipping and leading the people in praising the Lord (don't feed your fear) (verses 18-19). Then he obeyed the Lord's instructions (Fight your fear). They placed the praise singers out front and shouted the glory of God.

When they sang and praised the Lord, God ambushed the enemy, causing them to destroy themselves. Jehoshaphat and the people watched the Lord wipe out their adversary (remove their fear) and then they spent three joyful days collecting the spoil! (reward for their faith) (verses 20-25). In verses 26-30 we find their celebration of God's great victory over their enemies.

I believe one of the keys to Judah's victory over their fear is found in verse 20. Jehoshaphat stood and said, *"Listen to me, O Judah and inhabitants of Jerusalem, put your trust in the Lord and you will be established."*

Jehoshaphat encouraged them to turn from their fear and focus on their faith. When they "put their trust in the Lord their God" He did for them what they could not do for themselves.

Overcoming fear requires that we turn to God and trust Him to deliver us from those things that frighten us.

The Lord has helped me overcome my fears. I did what the psalmist did to find freedom from fear.

> *I sought the Lord and He answered me and delivered me from all my fears.*
>
> Psalm 34:4

Out in the quiet places of prayer the Lord heard my cries for help. He heard me out as I shared my fears. Then He showed me step by step how to build my faith.

Fear can't get a foothold where faith is strong. I discovered some things in the wilderness that have been instrumental in rebuilding my faith. If you want to have a faith that drives away fear, consider putting into practice the following.

- Study the heroes of faith (Hebrews 11).
  Be inspired by their examples. Let their faith stimulate yours.
- Saturate your spirit with faith messages.
  Listen to preachers/teachers who build your faith with well- balanced, biblical messages on trusting God.
- Surround yourself with friends who have strong faith.
  The most important lessons in life are more often caught than taught. Spend your time with believing-believers. Shun doubters. Hang out with brothers and sisters who will stretch your faith. Remember, iron sharpens iron.
- Speak faith.
  Develop the habit of positive confession. Say with your mouth what you are trusting God for. Faith grows when we speak what we believe!
- Step out and walk by faith, not by sight (II Corinthians 5:7).
  Show your faith. Demonstrate in daily life that your trust is in the Lord. Put into practice what you say you believe.
- Seek the Lord to increase your faith.
  As the disciples did, ask Jesus to increase your faith. (See Luke 17:5.) Call upon the Holy Spirit to give you a greater measure of faith. Receive what He sends.
- Most important of all, sit at Jesus's feet and soak up faith from the One who is faithful and true. (Revelation 19:11.)

If we really want to learn how to walk by faith, we need to look to the Lord daily.

> *Fixing our eyes on Jesus, the author and finisher of faith, who for the joy set before Him, endured the Cross, despising the shame, and has sat down at the right hand of God.*
>
> Hebrews 12:2

Faith overcomes fear because Jesus is at the right hand of the Father in heaven!

I slipped into a seat on the second row in the rapidly-filling sanctuary. I knew in my heart that I should attend the special meetings I saw advertised on the church marquee.

From the time the first praise chorus was sung my spirit was tender. I sensed that God wanted to do something. I bowed my head and opened my heart to whatever the Lord had in store for me.

The pastor's words grabbed my attention. They described me to a T. I was ready to dream again, but I was still afraid of the church. I sat on the edge of my spiritual seat the whole message. When the preacher gave the invitation to come forward, I was the first one to the altar. It was time for me to be delivered from my fear of God's house and the body of Christ.

No one laid hands on me. I wasn't prayed over. I don't even recall the evangelist's exhortation. I do remember the Holy Spirit touching my heart and lifting my fear.

Lifting my hands toward the Cross, I told the Lord I loved Him, that I would always serve Him, and that I didn't want to be afraid of loving the church anymore. Tears streamed down my cheeks as I released my fear and received the comfort of the Holy Spirit.

After the benediction, I went to the back of the sanctuary. As people filed out to go home, I stayed for awhile. Over the next hour, the Lord assured me that everything would be all right. That I could trust the bride again. That the church was my family, not my foe.

While the ushers were dimming the lights and closing up the building, the Holy Spirit restored a servant of God to the body of Christ.

> *Do not fear, for I am with you; do not anxiously*
> *look about you for I am your God. I will strengthen*
> *you, surely I will help you, surely I will uphold you*
> *with My righteous right hand.*
> Isaiah 41:10

Chapter 11

Confidence That Conquers

*For the Lord will be your confidence, and will keep
your foot from being caught.*

Proverbs 3:26

I had not preached publicly for over eighteen months when I was asked to speak at a high school chapel on a Christian campus. The opportunity thrilled, yet terrified me.

I love to preach. Communicating God's Word comes easily and naturally for me. But something strange was happening. I found myself hesitant and seriously wondering if I still had what it takes to proclaim the Good News.

My wife couldn't understand why I didn't share her excitement about speaking again. Imagine her surprise when I told her I wasn't sure I knew how to preach anymore. I shared my fears of failing in front of the students. I even expressed that I was seriously considering declining the invitation. Her concerned gaze searched mine as she tried to understand the problem.

The problem had nothing to do with anointing, gifts or sermon content. It was about confidence. I wasn't sure I could communicate effectively anymore. The once-self-assured servant of God found himself in the grip of a crippling confidence crisis.

My battle with self confidence began back in Baton Rouge a few days after I had been discharged from the hospital. I was sitting in the dining room working on my resume. While reviewing my ministry qualifications and accomplishments, wave after wave of panic-producing anxiety washed over me. My insides literally shook as an inner voice suggested that I would never serve in the ministry again.

That day I started doubting myself. The depression that had

crashed in on my life left in its destructive wake an emotionally
shell-shocked survivor with shattered self-confidence.

Lacking confidence in who you are and what you can do,
cripples a comeback more than anything else. You have to believe
you can come back before you come back. Without confidence you
can't conquer the thing that set you back.

Tough times in the past had rattled, but never shattered my
confidence. I had always known where I was headed and what I
could handle. Confidence had been my middle name. But things
were different now. Burnout had blown away the bedrock of my
self-assurance. The seemingly unshakable person who had never
feared trying was now nowhere to be found. He'd simply blipped off
the screen of life.

Suddenly I was in no man's land. The man I had been was gone.
The man I hoped to be had not yet shown up. God was working on
a new model that would be a great improvement over the previous
version. But while He was working, I was questioning everything
about myself. The guy who'd encouraged himself with "yes you
can," now chided himself with "no you can't!"

A twelve-year-old boy on my son's baseball team has the ability
to be a good power hitter. He makes consistent contact with the ball,
and drives it deeper into the outfield than any of his teammates.
When he gets in the groove, his natural swing kicks in and he
pulverizes the baseball. During practice he has slammed numerous
homeruns over the fence.

But in a live ballgame it's a different story. This potential
slugger strikes out eighty percent of the time! He chops at pitches,
strokes at balls over his head, swings way late. More often than not,
with two strikes against him, he doesn't even lift the bat off his
shoulder; he just stands there and takes a third strike call. When the
umpire calls him out, he looks shocked. Then he hangs his head in
shame, shuffles back to the dugout and manufactures some excuse
to justify his poor showing at the plate.

What accounts for a player who's a longball hitter in practice
turning into a strikeout king on the playing field? Lack of confidence. He doesn't believe he can hit the pitch. It's all mental. He
psyches himself out. He's convinced that his adversary on the
mound will overpower him.

Many of God's children struggle with hitting the ball when they step back up to the plate. Fastballs freeze them in their tracks. Curve balls and change-ups confuse them. Sliders sneak across the strike zone. Swinging without assurance and authority sets them up to strike out. "Strike three, you're out" sends them to the bench wondering why they can't put the ball in play.

Satan loves it when Christians lose their confidence. He'll do everything within his power to crush our confidence in ourselves. He knows that if we lose our assurance and doubt our destiny as children of God, he can stop us dead in our spiritual tracks. Christians who lack confidence make no dent in the devil's territory.

A number of "confidence crushers" contribute to striking out in the game of life. I've struggled with all of them. Maybe you have too.

1. Poor past performance

The camera zooms in on a middle-aged man eating lunch in a crowded city plaza. While munching on a hamburger, he flashes back to a moment forever etched in his memory. He replays standing at the plate, bat in hand, as a little leaguer. At a big moment in a big game, he struck out. The commercial takes off from there, promoting it's product that makes us feel like a winner even if we have lost in life.

Past failures can affect present performance if we allow them to crush our confidence. After Peter denied the Lord, he might never have been heard of again. Talk about a confidence crisis!

He'd said he wouldn't deny the Lord. Then he did. Having failed so miserably, how could he be confident he would ever be a faithful follower of Jesus Christ in the future? Restoration to the Lord (John 21:12-17), being filled with the Spirit (Acts 2:1-13), and preaching at Pentecost (stepping up to the plate to swing the bat again) (Acts 2:1-36) turned Peter into a homerun hitter for God's team! (Acts 2:37-47).

The devil will do his best to remind you of your strike-outs, errors, and poor play in the field. He will also work hard to get you to forget your hits, RBI's, and game saving defensive plays. That's the kind of dirty dog he is.

We beat the devil when we get back in the game. But you'll never hit the ball if you don't swing the bat. I've found the best way to rebuild crushed confidence is to step boldly to the plate, swing the bat, and make some new memories by smacking the ball all over the yard in Jesus' name!

2. Negative people

We've had to teach our young ballplayers to tune out the negative comments from the stands. There are always a few bleacher creatures who don't want you to hit. So they let you know. They razz and ridicule everything from your stance to your swing. They egg you on, telling you that you can't hit. "Hey batter, you're no hitter. My dead grandma could hit better than you." When you fan the ball, they cheer.

If you listen to the negative nerds in the stands you'll start doubting yourself. It's important for Christians who are coming back from a setback to surround themselves with positive voices. We can't afford to let the negative crowd break our confidence. We need to seek out positive people who will boost our belief in our abilities.

The Lord did a very special thing for me during my healing process. The devil and his demons, voices from the past, some insensitive people around me, and at times my own spirit kept telling me my homerun-hitting days were history. So God sent some heavenly little ladies to take me under their angelic wings and help rebuild my confidence. These ten ladies (average age seventy) have become my personal cheerleading squad. When we first met and formed a Bible study group, they had no idea that my confidence was shot to pieces.

Every Tuesday we meet is a spiritual shot in the arm for this reemerging man of God. Their sincere love for me has helped me love myself. Their belief in me has me believing in myself again. They've prayed for me when I wasn't sure how to pray. They call me up just to say hello and share a word from the Lord. They drop notes of timely encouragement in the mail. They send me on my way with homemade goodies that make me and my family feel very special.

We have been blessed by their sweet fellowship. Until we cross over to glory, they will never know how important their support has been in restoring me to God and His plan for my life.

If you want to hit safely and successfully again, surround yourself with people who tell you, "You're a hitter. Step up and drive that ball. You can do it." It won't be long and you, too, will be believing you can hit it!

3. Compete and compare

"How many did you have in services Sunday?" a pastor asked his colleague at the ministers' monthly fellowship luncheon. When he heard that his friend's church attendance exceeded his own and that their offerings were up, he became discouraged.

Sound familiar? Pastors do it all the time. Lay people do too. I call it compete and compare.

In America, competition and comparison is the name of the game. We compare our children's looks, height, clothes, grades, how fast they run and how well they spell to the other kids on the block. We compare our car and house to the Jones' across the street. Physical appearance, material possessions, positions, talents, and accomplishments — all subject to comparison.

Then we do the competition thing. The goal is to best our neighbors. Long hours at work, living beyond our means, and emphasizing appearance above character becomes the norm.

There's a reason why we succumb to this maddening game. It's rather simple. Being ahead of somebody else boosts our self-esteem and self-confidence. Being the head and not the tail makes us feel better about ourselves — so we think.

Comparison and competition do have value. Healthy, properly motivated competition brings out the best in people and stretches them to maximize their potential. Comparing ourselves to others for the sake of self-improvement is commendable.

But there are some inherent dangers in the compete and compare game. Somebody is always a little bigger, stronger, prettier, thinner, faster, smarter, or richer than us. Therefore, competition and comparison can become twin killers of self-esteem. Rather than build confidence, they can crush it.

We must careful about comparing ourselves to those behind or below us. It can lead to cockiness. The temptation to look down on those whose status doesn't measure up to our own can adversely affect our service to them.

If we're blessed to be near the top in a given situation, we must be on guard against misplacing our confidence. Placing confidence in our abilities alone can lead to some rude awakenings. Situations will spring up in which what we can accomplish solely by our own strength is not enough.

An equally deadly danger, if not more so, is comparing ourselves to those we consider being ahead of us. In this case, cockiness is not an issue. Crushed confidence is.

There are always pastors somewhere with more members, bigger budgets, finer facilities and faster growing churches than ours. When we fall into the trap of competing with our brothers instead of cheering them on and thanking God for their success, we run the risk of losing confidence in our own abilities — especially if our ministries don't grow like theirs do.

I've been there. When my confidence was rooted in what Steve could do, I was always disappointed and disheartened. Why? Because even when I did my best, someone else was always doing better. Always.

The devil would point his finger and mock me. "Sure, you had five hundred in church today, but so-and-so had five thousand. Why didn't you have five thousand? What kind of a pastor are you?" You know what happened to my confidence. It went right down the tubes.

Competing and comparing are potentially lethal confidence cripplers for clergy. Participating in these games contributes greatly to burnout because we pour too much energy and effort into bettering our brothers instead of bettering ourselves.

Paul made a conscience-freeing, confidence-building confession that has helped me in coming to terms with being confident and content about who I am in Christ.

> *But by the grace of God, I am what I am, and His grace toward me did not prove vain; but I labored even more than all of them, yet not I, but the grace of God with me.*
>
> I Corinthians 15:10

God's grace makes each of us uniquely special. I'm just as important as you, and you're just as important as me in the Kingdom. My ministry and your ministry are both vital to the success of God's redemptive plan.

Glory to God! I'm not you and you aren't me. Your gifts aren't mine and my gifts aren't yours. I haven't done anything exceptional and neither have you. There isn't anything that we are or have that we have not received (I Corinthians 4:7).

Do you know that the Lord isn't into cloning pastors? Too many of us strive in vain to be like this or that "super pastor." We need to stop that right now! It isn't His will for us to stress ourselves out trying to be like some other servant of God who appears to be doing more than we are.

Did you know that He is into cloning little Christ's? (Romans 8:29) God's goal is Christlike servants who place their confidence in Him. If you want to conquer your confidence crisis, be yourself and be confident in the grace of God that's at work in your life. Amen.

4. Misplaced confidence

Confidence erodes when we rely on the wrong things. The following three areas produce false confidence that crumbles under pressure: Works, Self, People.

Works

Many people put their confidence in religious works instead of a relationship with Christ. They believe that if they diligently do the things that please God, they can have confidence that He will come through for them. I call it legalistic confidence.

It works like this: "I went to church three times this week. I put an extra hundred dollars in the offering plate. I fasted all day Friday. I prayed three hours instead of two on Saturday morning. I signed up to volunteer two hours of my time to help with the church garage sale next month. Because I have done these good deeds, surely God will be with me."

For pastors it goes something like this: "I worked up four messages this week. Last Monday I stayed up all night in intensive care with Mrs. Smith's daughter. We raised $7,000 above our missions goal. Our worship attendance is 225 more than this time last year. I was named minister of the month in my denominational district. I'm a dedicated, hardworking pastor. I know God will help me out because I'm such a good shepherd of His sheep."

All of these benevolent deeds are beneficial and bring blessings to others and ourselves. But confidence based on works is shaky. What happens to our confidence base if we're unable to do anything for God? What if we fall $7,000 short of our missions goal and our attendance is down 225 from last year. What then?

Self

Self-confidence is part of healthy self-esteem. We must believe in ourselves to accomplish anything in life. People with no self-confidence seldom amount to anything.

But self-confidence can be carried too far. When we look to ourselves as the one and only source of ability, know-how, power, and strength, trouble is just around the corner.

In II Corinthians 3, Paul addressed his role as a minister of the new covenant. He spoke of the source of the confidence through which he personally stood and preached to others. Note in verses four and five not only where Paul said his confidence (adequacy) was, but also where it was not!

> *And such confidence we have through Christ toward God. Not that we are adequate in ourselves to consider anything as coming from ourselves, but our adequacy is from God.*

Paul knew that outside of Christ man is flawed and limited. In Christ, a redeemed man is adequate for any task because the source of his confidence and adequacy is God.

People

It's natural for us to place our trust in humans. But experience testifies to the fact that people disappoint people. We have all let someone down who put their confidence in us. We have all been let down by someone we placed our confidence in.

People aren't our best bet as our source of confidence because they're no different than us. They have no power greater than we do. They can only do what we or any other human being can do.

Confidence that conquers must be founded upon something that goes beyond mere human ability.

Out of my burnout and brokenness came many blessings. Most of them were hidden from me at first. The Holy Spirit revealed them one at a time as my heart healed. Without question, a major blessing I received had to do with my source of confidence. God taught me that confidence in Christ, not confidence in Steve, is the key to victorious Christian living.

My life fell apart because I trusted too much in myself and other men. I didn't really rely on Jesus like I should have. I put my confidence in my ability instead of in His. I don't know how many hundreds of times over twenty years I'd quoted Paul's famous words in Philippians 4:13 *"I can do all things through Christ who gives me strength."*

I believed it but I didn't live it. Steve was always showing up trying to get a piece of the action. I thought I could do all things through Christ and myself. Hard times helped me realize that nothing good would happen through me, but everything good would happen through Him. With God's help I handed my confidence from Steve to Jesus.

A wonderful transformation has taken place in my life since then. A heavy burden fell off my back when I transferred my confidence from Steve to Jesus. I have been set free from the pressure of thinking everything depends on me. Hallelujah!

I don't have to try and pull off anything anymore because the Lord is my confidence. He keeps my foot from being caught (Proverbs 3:26). I don't have to rely on me because *"He is able to do exceeding abundantly beyond all that we ask or think, according to the power that works within us"* (Ephesians 3:20).

My confidence is now firmly based in Him. When the children of Israel stood at the bank of the Red Sea, their leader Moses knew where to put his confidence as Pharaoh's chariots bore down on the defenseless people of God. While others cried, he confidently told the people not to fear, but to go forward, for the Lord would fight for them (Exodus 14:13-15). Moses had confidence in God!

Moses' confidence in God meant the great deliverer of Israel understood his part and God's part. Note the division of responsibilities outlined in verses 16 and 17:

> *And as for you* (Moses), *lift up your staff and stretch out your hand over the sea and divide it, and the sons of Israel shall go through the midst of the sea on dry land.*

And as for me (God), behold, I will harden the hearts of the Egyptians so that they will go in after them; and I will be honored through Pharaoh and all his army, through his chariots and horsemen.

Moses' part was to lift his staff and divide the sea. God's part was to harden the enemies' hearts so they would chase after Israel. Then Moses would close the sea and God would drown them! What a great team victory for the Lord's side!

Faith and confidence in God moved Moses to hold his staff over the impassable sea and divide it. He was certain that God would do what He said He would do: defeat Pharaoh for His honor and glory!

Our part in this faith walk is to trust in the Lord, to put our complete confidence in Him. God's part is to take care of us by performing His promises.

My wife's life verse is Psalm 27:1-3. I love what it says about being confident in life.

> *The Lord is my light and my salvation; Whom shall I fear? The Lord is the defense of my life; Whom shall I dread? When evildoers came upon me to devour my flesh, My adversaries and my enemies stumbled and fell. Though a host encamp against me, I will not fear. Though war rise against me, in spite of this, I shall be confident.*

The writer is saying that no matter what calamity comes against me, through Christ I can confidently conquer any crisis!

While I was attending seminary, we lived in a little house on a quiet street a few blocks from campus. We had a nice yard with lots of trees and bushes. It provided a pleasant setting where two busy people could catch their breath and relax.

Spring fever bit me every year. I dug up some ground and planted a small flower and vegetable garden. During study breaks I could be found pulling weeds, picking petunias and fertilizing tomato plants. As I puttered in the vegetable patch, I kept my eye on the neighborhood. I particularly took note of the pets that roamed freely while their people were at work. Diagonally across from our house lived the homeliest dog I have ever seen.

He was older, and walked with a noticeable limp. He sported a "coat of many colors." Wiry black, gray, white and tan hair stuck out in all directions. He always looked like he needed a shampoo and a comb. One of his eyes was cocked off center. His tail was crooked and bent. — a furry zigzag that looked as though it had been caught in a car door one too many times!

He looked so pitiful. I don't know what his owners named him, but he was so ugly that I just referred to him as Old Ugly.

Old Ugly thought he was king of the hill on our block. He made sure to strut his stuff when any other animals encroached on his space. Poor Old Ugly would charge off the front steps with that twisted tail swaying behind him. As he lumbered across the yard in pursuit of his prey, he uttered a hoarse, raspy-sounding bark that, in all honesty, wouldn't scare a flea. Observing Old Ugly patrol and protect his turf provided great entertainment.

One afternoon while I was planting some flowers in the front yard, our next door neighbor's cat strayed into Old Ugly's territory. I almost died laughing watching this poor excuse for a dog trying to catch the sleek, fleet-footed feline.

They disappeared around the corner of my neighbor's house. As I peered through the bushes trying to see what was happening, Old Ugly raced by me, contorted tail tucked tightly between his legs. He yipped and yelped all the way across the street before hiding out somewhere in his self-proclaimed kingdom.

Something had certainly rattled Old Ugly's cage. Curiosity drove me to check it out. As I rounded the corner of the house, I saw a sight I will never forget. My neighbor's cat was calmly sitting directly under the heaving chest of a jet-black, perfectly-built one-hundred-fifty-pound Doberman Pincher named Alex.

That cat had nothing to fear from Old Ugly. She put her confidence in Alex. She didn't have to handle Old Ugly because she knew Alex could do a better job.

Confidence that conquers is found in the shadow of Christ's cross. When we take our stand under His banner, we need not fear anything the Old Ugly's of life try to do to us.

As dugout coach for my son's little league team, I'm the team motivater. My role is to keep the boys in the right batting order, and to boost their confidence. I believe in the boys and their abilities to be good ballplayers. When their confidence sags, I pump it up by reminding them who they are and what they know they can do. It's gratifying seeing them "fire up" because someone took the time to boost their confidence.

If we play in a tough league, we may not win as many games as we'd like. But I know this, the boys are learning some great lessons about confidence. They're experiencing some things that will stay with them for life.

The writer to the Hebrews talks about holding on to our confidence in Christ.

> *Therefore, do not throw away your confidence,*
> *which has a great reward. For you have need of*
> *endurance, so that when you have done the will of*
> *God, you may receive what was promised.*
>   Hebrews 10:35-36

Note how confidence, endurance and receiving are linked together. To receive we must endure. To endure we must have confidence.

Doing the Will of God requires that we have utmost confidence in the One who called us. Confidence in Christ has a great reward indeed — we receive all that our father has promised! No wonder we're exhorted to hold on and not lose our confidence.

I want to share ten lessons I have learned that build confidence.

1. I can "let go and let God" because He knows what He is doing. (Revelation 22:13; Genesis 18:25)

2. My success is God's problem, not mine. (I Thessalonians 5:23)

3. When we do what we can, God will do what we can't. (II Chronicles 20)

4. The Holy Spirit is my Helper and constant companion. (John 14:16-17)

5. I don't have to know it all. I do need to know Him. (Philippians 3:10-11)

6. My part is to sow the seed. His part is to grow the seed. (Mark 4:26-29)

7. God will never disappoint me. (Romans 10:13)

8. Things run a lot smoother when I make it easy on myself and hard on God. (Jeremiah 32:27)

9. Life has not passed me by. It's all in front of me. (Jeremiah 31:17)

10. The Lord is still working on me. He isn't finished with me yet.

For I am confident of this very thing, that He who began a good work in you will perfect it until the day of Christ Jesus.

Philippians 1:6

Because He is still investing in me, I have confidence to follow Him and become all that He has ordained for me to be. Confidence in Christ has me looking forward to the future!

Chapter 12
How to Beat Burnout
Before It Beats You

*Seek the Lord and His strength, Seek His face
continually.*

Psalm 105:4

As a little boy I loved to go to the circus. When Ringling
Brothers Barnum and Bailey rolled into town, I begged to go see the
"greatest show on earth."

The big top housed an exciting world of breathtaking entertainment. Sights, sounds and smells unique to the circus setting
bombarded my senses with simple pleasures that somehow linger
in my memory today. When I was a child, the circus was still a tent
show. I remember what it was like to be an innocent, wide-eyed
child at the circus.

Creaky, wooden stands corralled a sea of human commotion
and ceaseless chatter. Concessionaires' voices bellowed as they
peddled popcorn, peanuts and soda pop. Eyes of young and old
alike sparkled with expectation while waiting eagerly for the
performance to begin.

When the circus band struck up a rousing, attention arresting
tune, the arena darkened as the house lights dimmed. Previously
swirling spotlights now focused on the center of the ring. A tall,
handsome, handlebar-mustached master of ceremonies stepped
into the circle of light, enthusiastically welcoming the ladies,
gentlemen and starry-eyed children to an enchanted evening they
would never forget.

Commanding the eager crowd's attention with his booming
stage voice, he directed our gazes to ring number one. All eyes
fastened on a fearless animal tamer who bravely placed his head in

the gaping mouth of a ferocious lion. In ring number two, majestic, powerfully built tigers jumped gracefully through hoops of flaming fire. While in ring number three, pretty girls rode glittering, painted elephants which performed amazing stunts that animals of their size aren't supposed to be able to do.

With the tangy taste of mustard from grease-soaked corn dogs lingering on my lips, I laughed hysterically as comically clad, red-nosed, frizzy-haired clowns ran around the arena performing their crazy antics and silly shenanigans. I did my best to wipe away tears of joy with fingers cemented together by sticky cotton candy!

Dancing bears, high stepping horses, mischievous monkeys, fire-eating magicians, and mind boggling jugglers set the stage for the headline attractions — the trapeze artists and tightrope walkers.

My heart pounded with anticipation as the "daring young men and women of the flying trapeze" climbed to their precarious perches high above the admiring crowd. Back and forth, my eyes followed every rhythmic swing of the trapeze bar.

I listened intently as the ringmaster introduced the death-defying routines that increased in difficulty. Throws, exchanges, somersaults and flips thrilled the entire audience, keeping everyone on the edge of their seats. I gasped with relief each time the free-flying acrobats were safely caught and secured in the grasp of their muscle-bound catchers.

Then came the act that always captured my fascination: the high wire artists. Walking across a thin wire suspended in the air seems so incredibly impossible. I can barely walk along a sidewalk curb without falling off! These gutsy guys stepped, bounced, jumped, ran, skipped rope, juggled, stood on chairs, hoisted partners on their shoulders and rolled balls with their feet across that skinny cable. And the really good ones did their thing without a net!

I always wondered how they stayed on that wire. Obviously, they were talented, skilled, strong, had practiced a lot, and were not afraid of heights!

But the key to successfully tiptoeing along that tightrope and not falling to the floor below was balance. Highwire specialists understand the principle of balance. Their very lives depend on this law of life. Whether they use a long pole, shift body weight or work natural forces to their advantage, they know that to be out of balance can be disastrous. Shifting to some extreme position without counterbalancing can lead to a deadly fall.

Life is a balancing act. Many people burn out because their lives are out of balance. Have you ever tried to drive on tires that are out of balance? The car shakes and may not respond properly to the road underneath it.

When our lives get out of balance, life can be pretty bumpy.

The Bible is a book about balance. In His Book, God has recorded everything we need in order to stay on top of the tightrope of life. If I could have sixty seconds to send a message to every person in this stress-filled society, I would say this as loud and clear as possible: Get back to the basics. Go to the Bible. Learn about balance. Live out daily the lifestyle of wholeness that Jesus modeled for us in God's Word.

God's Will is for each of us to experience a long, satisfying life (Psalm 91:14-16). Burnout robs us of the opportunity to live full, satisfying days every day of our lives.

We're all familiar with the old adage "an ounce of prevention is worth a pound of cure." Some very simple things will help us keep our lives balanced so that we can beat burnout. It doesn't have to beat us.

Satan is an opportunist. Some people work too much; others don't work enough. Some worry too much; others aren't serious enough about life. Some play too much; others don't play at all.

Americans have evolved into an extremist lifestyle. We pour our energy and effort into a few select areas while neglecting other things that are vital contributors to wholeness.

Balance is the key to staying on top. Many lives are broken and ineffective quite simply because they are out of balance.

The basis of much abusive behavior in life, whether directed at self or others, is the absence of balance. When we lean too far one way or the other, Satan takes advantage of our extreme position and uses it against us. We wear out and end up collapsing under the heavy burden of unbalanced living.

Jesus Christ was the most balanced human being the world has ever seen. The Son of God knew when to work (John 9:4) and when to rest (Mark 5:31). The Savior knew when to preach (Mark 1:14-15) and when to pray (Mark 1:35). He knew when to feast (Matthew 9:10-15) and when to fast (Mark 9:29). He knew when to speak (Matthew 23) and when to remain silent (Matthew 27:12-14). He knew what to live for (John 4:34) and what to die for (Matthew 20:28). His was the heaviest, hardest life anyone could ever live. Yet we never see Him

burning out! Even as He hung dying on the cross, He was in control of
His destiny (Luke 23:14).

I burned out because some areas of my life were out of balance.
I don't want to ever again experience what I did. I don't want
anybody else to either. I've learned some things that have helped
me. I believe they'll help you keep burnout at bay.

I'm certain that if you'll honestly and prayerfully evaluate your
life in light of these burnout beaters, the power of God will assist you
in preventing burnout. All of the suggestions are essential to a
balanced lifestyle.

Have some fun with this. Don't be too hard, or too soft, on
yourself in any area. If you aren't sure about an issue, ask someone
close to you what they think. Remember — Christian living is all
about wholeness, and wholeness is all about balance!

1.   *Maintain a consistent devotional life.*

At the core of wholeness is a daily relationship with God where
we draw near to Him to receive spiritual nourishment. Neglecting
to set aside regular time to personally worship, adore, praise and
receive direction from our Savior opens the door to burnout.

Ministry, by it's very nature, is demanding. It drains energy and
depletes emotional resources. Caregivers who are constantly giving
will give out unless they make time to take in. A dry well can't
quench anybody's thirst. Many ministers live on the ragged edge of
burnout because they have allowed people to drink their well dry.
The solution is to drink daily at God's well. Shepherds spiritually
refreshed by "living water" (John 7:37-39) can effectively water
and feed God's sheep.

Spiritual leaders must be doubly on guard against the temptation to skip quiet times. We reason that because we're doing
spiritual work all the time anyway, we can skip our personal
devotions. Busy ministers often substitute sermon preparation time
for waiting on God. But studying and reflecting on the Bible in order
to work up a message is not the same as waiting on the Master for
the pure joy of sitting at His feet to love Him.

When ministering to Christians who are emotionally and spiritually burned out, I have found that nearly 100 per cent of the time,
somewhere along the line they stopped praying and reading the Word
of God regularly. When we stop meeting with the Lord it doesn't take

long for our lives to get out of whack. Devotions, like multiple vitamins, need to be taken daily if we're to stay spiritually healthy.

The Holy Spirit, as Comforter and Helper, will keep us balanced. The only way to receive our Father's instruction for the day, and the power and wisdom to carry it out successfully, is to check in regularly with Him. Unhurried, uninterrupted, uninhibited devotional time with Jesus will keep us spiritually strong.

> *My soul, wait in silence for God only, for my hope*
> *is from Him. He only is my rock and my salvation,*
> *my stronghold, and I shall not be shaken.*
> Psalm 62:5-6

2. Stay emotionally healthy.

Feelings are fickle. They change with the wind and aren't to be trusted. Though the way we feel isn't always a reliable reflector of reality, balance requires that we stay in touch with our feelings. We need to know who we are emotionally.

As doctors and nurses who work with the physically ill must keep themselves physically healthy, so too, pastors and lay ministers must keep themselves emotionally well since they serve primarily emotionally/spiritually disabled people. Another person's troubles can create problems for pastors who aren't secure and stable emotionally.

I care very much for caregivers, especially God's choice servants who have answered His call to bring Christ's love and hope to hurting people. Everyone knows that pastors care. But caring for people can be a double-edged sword. I cared so much for others that I forgot to take care of myself.

Emotional collapse awaits those (I was one of them) who labor passionately to rescue and save others but allow their own emotional house to get out of order.

Ask yourself a few questions. Why are you in the ministry? What motivates you to help others? What pushes your emotional hot buttons? Do you find yourself angry, frustrated, or unfulfilled in your work? Are there any emotional conflicts in your heart that you haven't resolved?

Have you successfully worked through your folks' divorce or your own divorce? Have you faced and conquered the physical or sexual abuse forced upon you while you were growing up? How do you really feel about having been an only child? Have you properly dealt with that disappointing setback that blew you away a few years ago? How have you handled the put-downs you experienced in childhood that make you feel so insecure as an adult?

These hard, heart-probing questions elicit emotion. These strong feelings underlie who we are, and influence (positively and negatively) what we do. Most of the personal insecurity and frustration I experienced with life was due to the fact that I hadn't resolved the anger I felt toward my parents for getting divorced. Anger tipped my emotional scale out of balance for over thirty years.

What does Steve Roll's unresolved anger have to do with you? Specifically, probably nothing. But to stay balanced and beat burnout, you must be certain your emotions are healthy and in order.

Identify your strongest feelings. What are they? Examine them. Why are they so powerful? What triggers them? Why do they keep surfacing?

Don't be afraid to face your feelings. Understand your personality type's strengths and weaknesses. Having put your finger on sensitive areas, talk them out with a trusted confidant. Work through your pain. Receive the Holy Spirit's healing for any damaged emotions you have experienced.

Regularly check your emotions. What have you been feeling lately? Why do you think you have expressed this emotion? Is it healthy or unhealthy? Are any adjustments needed? God made us emotional creatures, but balance is always His standard. Rejoice that you have feelings. Channel them to be used for the glory of God and the good of men.

3. Laugh a lot!

The lighter side is a great balancer of the serious side of life. If you don't think God intended for us to laugh a lot, open your eyes to creation. What a menagerie of goofy creatures (including you and me!) God put on this earth. If you take time to notice, animals and people are hilarious! Have you ever noticed how dog owners and their canines resemble each other? It's rather comical. The other day I saw a lady walking her poodle down our street. Their curly white hair looked so fooh-fooh. I thought for sure they had both just returned from a perm at the beauty shop!

I love watching people at malls, airports and garage sales. They do some of the craziest things. Just sit somewhere and observe. Occasionally I chauffeur my wife on the garage sale circuit in our city. What an education. It's truly amazing how one man's junk becomes another man's treasure.

One Saturday I laughed myself silly watching a considerably overweight gentleman demonstrate for his pencil thin wife how to hula a hula hoop. Flesh seemed to fly everywhere as the fluorescent orange sphere orbited his rotating torso. He laughed and laughed and laughed as the hoop picked up speed around the curves. Onlookers were cracking up, too. But it didn't matter. This jolly giant was having the time of his life being a carefree kid again!

Battle burnout with laughter. Laugh at life. Laugh at your situation. Laugh at the ministry. Laugh at yourself. Laugh. You'll live longer and enjoy life more!

4. Enjoy the little things of life.

Life is made up of little things. Simple things bring real satisfaction. Pleasure can be found in seemingly insignificant events right at our fingertips. In our pursuit to own the garden, I'm afraid we forget to smell the roses!

Feel out of balance? Burnout nipping at your heels? Hold your spouse's hand and take a leisurely stroll through the park. Watch the squirrels frolic in the trees. Drive out of town and stop for home-made apple pie and fresh brewed coffee at a hole-in-the-wall, mom and pop restaurant. Walk through a nursery and enjoy the fabulous colors and sweet fragrances of God's garden flowers.

Play monopoly with the kids — and let them win. Celebrate their victory with a big bowl of vanilla ice cream covered with chocolate syrup. And don't forget a half-dozen or so Oreo cookies on the side!

Snuggle up in front of the fireplace with a good book. Pet a puppy. If you're a morning person, welcome the new day by catching the glorious rays of first light at sunrise. If you're a night owl, walk under the twinkling stars and marvel at the grandeur of a harvest moon.

Make a snowman. Bake homemade cookies. Soak in a hot tub. Swing on the porch. Cradle a baby in your arms and rock it to sleep. Row a boat. Pop popcorn. Play catch in the backyard with your son. Stage a puppet show with your daughter. Paint a picture. Shoot some hoops and listen for the swoosh of the net as you sink a jump shot. Soak up a sunset. Make some hot cocoa with marshmallows. Take a nap.

Are you getting the picture busy pastor? Step away from the big, eternal things for a moment and enjoy the blessings of everyday life. Don't miss the special treasures God has tucked away in the little things along the way.

5. Listen to your wife!

Scripture poses the question *"An excellent wife who can find? For her worth is far above jewels."* (Proverbs 31:10) I want to go on record stating that I have found an excellent wife. Jo Ann is more valuable to me than any jewels. I love her with all my heart — and I have learned to listen to her.

God gave me my marriage partner to provide balance in my life. She has gifts I need to receive if I am to stay healthy and productive.

Men usually balk at listening to their wives. But it's not macho at all to turn a deaf ear to your mate. It's a stupid mistake. There are three important reasons why you'll be much better off if you pay attention to your wife's counsel.

First, our wives will let us know when our lives are tipping out of balance. They'll tell us when we're putting in too many hours at the office, neglecting the family, and not taking time out to enjoy those "little things."

Second, our spouses have built in radar that senses when we're on the verge of burnout. They zero in on our mood swings, crankiness, and irritability. They have a sixth sense that knows when we're pushing the limits and teetering on the edge of physical, emotional or spiritual exhaustion. They warn us because they love us.

Third, they'll suggest what we need to do to rebalance our lives and back away from burnout. They're very wise and discerning. A woman's intuition is given by God for her family's benefit. They're more sensitive to solutions than we realize.

My wife has saved my skin more than once. I've learned not to resent, but to respect her advice. Next to Jesus, she loves me like nobody else on earth. She's pulling for me, not against me. Jo Ann is God's gift to help Steve keep on track.

Burnout won't catch up to you if you'll heed the voice of your precious wife. You'll be spared a lot of grief if you'll just listen to her. (And all the wives said Amen!)

6. Get a life outside of the ministry.

As a young pastor, I filled every waking moment with "The

Ministry." My wife will tell you how hardheaded I was when it came to time off. I was so consumed with the Lord's work that I even tried to avoid vacation because I was certain the church couldn't make it without me.

Ministry is part of life, not life itself. That may sound sacrilegious and even border on being blasphemous in some clergy circles, nevertheless it's true. All ministry and no play makes a dull pastor. Pastors who have no interests outside the parish walls are high-risk candidates for burnout.

Holy work needs to be balanced with a hobby. Healthy diversions from the seriousness of our calling help us return refreshed for the next round of sacred battle.

How about it? Can you name a hobby or two that you regularly participate in? Does gardening, painting, athletics, antique cars, scuba diving, carpentry, playing a musical instrument, collecting rare books, flying model airplanes, or whatever is of personal interest to you have a spot regularly reserved in your daytimer?

By now you know that for the past three years, I have been an assistant coach for my son's little league baseball team. It's a delightful distraction from the ministry. I love helping the boys develop their skills as ballplayers. The boy in me likes wearing a pinstriped Yankee jersey with "Coach" on the back, too!

It's never too late to take up a hobby. Go do that thing you've always wanted to do for fun. Don't hesitate any longer. There really is life outside the ministry!

7. Stay in good physical shape.

I Timothy 4:6-16 discusses a good minister's discipline. Even though there is a phrase in verse 8 that says "for bodily discipline is only of little profit," I believe being in good shape physically is another vital component in preventing burnout.

Regular exercise and good nutrition are essential for combating exhaustion. Christian leaders should set the example in keeping God's temple holy and healthy. A healthy body is a happy body. And a happy body will help you do your ministry better and longer.

I know someone in the ministry who is heading for the grave in a hurry. Why? Because he neglects taking care of his body. Mild exertion leaves him breathless. His blood pressure is dangerously high. His physician has told him he's headed for a heart attack if he doesn't watch his weight and get some aerobic activity regularly.

I don't always like the thought of working up a sweat or saying no to that second piece of cake, but I do like the results. Bicycling, sit ups and pumping light weights three or four times a week keeps me fit and trim. I feel sharp and energized. I also like what I see in the mirror!

Vigorous exercise also stimulates endorphins — those happy hormones that keep the blues away. Workouts really help keep depression at bay.

Schedule workouts and keep those appointments. Learn to enjoy exercise. If you're into jogging, jog. Racquetball, hit the courts. Go to the gym with a friend who will help keep you motivated.

You're only helping yourself and your ministry by staying fit!

8. Keep your heart pure.

The veteran Apostle Paul exhorted young Timothy to "keep yourself pure" (I Timothy 5:22). If we don't keep ourselves free from sin, we become susceptible to burnout.

In the past few years we have witnessed a number of shameful falls of prominent pastors from the ranks of the ministry. Some of them crashed and burned because they were living a double life. Lust, greed, selfish ambition, and other sordid sins hid in their hearts.

Sin always finds us out. Over time, events exposed the real condition of their souls.

An impure heart is a vicious battleground where energy intended for ministry is consumed trying to stave off an enemy within. Fighting within ourselves wears down our resistance to the devil's attacks and the strength draining demands of ministry.

If you're wrestling with impurity of thought or deed, get help immediately. Don't wait. The Holy Spirit has told you what to do. Brother or sister in Christ, go do whatever you need to do to keep yourself pure.

9. Keep the home fires burning.

According to the Bible, a pastor's priorities are God first, family second, and ministry third. God is usually a solid number one with most clergy. The scramble for second is the stress producer.

Too many pastors succumb to the pressures of ministry and place it ahead of their families. Not a few ministers find themselves burning out because they have their priorities out of order.

An unbeatable buffer against burnout is a solid, satisfying family life. Homes is to be a secure, happy haven from the stresses and strains of this world we live and labor in. We have to work — but we get to go home! Strong relationships with our wives and children are a must for balanced living. Thoughts of family should warm our hearts like nothing else.

Keep romance burning in your marriage (Proverbs 5:15- 19). Mutually satisfying emotional and sexual intimacy between marital partners relieves stress and reinforces the "two shall become one flesh" bond. This sacred union is nearly impossible to break when tenderly nurtured. Burnout preys on couples who have lost the fire in their relationship. A good, growing sex life is holy and healthy. Happy marriage beds help husbands and wives hang in there together through tough times.

Spending meaningful time with our kids keeps us young and energetic. My children want Daddy to be with them more than anything else. My journey is much richer because of the blessing two red-haired youngsters bring to my life.

How's your family life, pastor? Does your wife still have the privilege and power to interrupt you on the spur of the moment and steal you away for a romantic interlude? Do you have the courage to drop your work to share a once-in-a-lifetime experience with those precious little people who call you dad?

If the home fires are burning bright, burnout can knock on your door, but it won't get past the threshold. Families united in love can withstand any storm that blows their way.

10. Know your limits and respect them.

Everyone has limits. Contrary to the hype coming out of Hollywood, there are no bionic men or women. God has given us amazing capacity to accomplish incredible tasks. But there are limits to our energy and endurance.

Recently I played two-on-two basketball with some athletic, talented teenagers. What a rude awakening to the world of limitation! Spotting an opening to the basket, I thought about making a move I did pretty well when I was twenty-five. Driving toward the bucket, my mind signaled my body to spin and jump. My forty-something body told my mind, "You gotta be kidding!"

Needless to say, my "glory days" play never got off the ground.

Matter of fact, a smiling, strapping six-footer slapped the ball from my hands and left me looking at the tread on his sneakers as he stuffed the ball in the hoop.

I can't do what I used to do on the court. Even teenagers get tired after a while. (Though they'll never admit it!) There are limits to how many hours we can put in before we need to check out; limits to how much "midnight oil" we can burn; limits to how much pressure individuals can take. God has built boundaries into creation for our protection. Regularly exceeding reasonable limits puts us on a collision course with collapse.

We aren't invincible. We can't do everything. We can't always do what others can do. We have to make adjustments as life moves along. That's the way it is.

I have a fairly good handle on my limits. When I exceed them, I pay. It takes longer to recover from an hour of hoops than it used to, if you know what I mean!

There's nothing weak about knowing and acknowledging your personal limitations. Respect your body, family, friends and colleagues when they tell you it is time to back off. Take a break from the grind. Rest won't kill you. It will help you perform better.

The long haul is what matters. The Lord is looking for ministers and laymen who will cross the finish line (II Timothy 4:7), not fall out somewhere along the way.

11. Excel at what you do well.

A respected Christian leader said something at a conference that made a lot of sense to me. He said, "By the time you're forty, know who you are, what you do best, and spend the rest of your life doing it!" What a great burnout beater!

Focus is imperative for fruitfulness. Productivity creates energy. Spinning your wheels saps energy. Knowing who you are, what you do best, and then doing it is a highly efficient and satisfying strategy for successful living.

God hasn't called me to accomplish everything. He has gifted me for a specific task. No one can do what I do as well as I can when I am at my best. That's a fact. Each of us has a special place of service in the Kingdom. No one can fill our shoes.

Pastor, what are you good, really good, at? What ministry tasks do you do well and do you love doing more than anything else?

What do others say you excel at? What has your wife been telling you for years that you do best?

If you don't want to burn out, and you want to bring forth much fruit (John 15:16), become a specialist. Excel in what you do well. Spend the prime of your life doing what only you and God can do.

12. Allow others to minister to you.

Proverbs 27:17 states *"Iron sharpens iron, so one man sharpens another."* Lone Ranger ministers who isolate themselves from others unwittingly set themselves up for burnout. Men and women of God need each other.

No pastor has exclusive rights to God's Living Water. The Holy Spirit often ministers to us through others. During my recovery, the Lord brought healing via sermons, books, tapes and sharing times with brothers in the ministry.

The Lord loves His servants. God knows what we need, when we need it, how to meet the need, and through whom to deliver it. Time and time again the Spirit directed me and my wife to tune in to Christian programs. At the precise moment we needed encouragement, God used some preachers I had not listened to before to sharpen our spirits. Every message was right on the mark.

You can build a barrier against burnout by widening your circle of ministerial relationships. Open your heart to brothers and sisters in the Lord. Seek out clergy to fellowship with. Invite a pastor you would like to get to know out to lunch. Share your experiences. Pray for each other.

Cross denominational lines. It's okay. God is bigger than our narrowness. He has appointed people who may not be of your particular theological persuasion to bless you!

Read widely. Your library should include a broad range of outstanding, inspiring Christian authors. The Holy Spirit flows through many rich streams.

A great way to beat off the cynicism that burnout can produce is to allow positive pastors to minister to your spirit. Purposely sit under someone else's preaching once in a while. It will do you good. Ministers need to be ministered to, too! We can help each other beat burnout and at the same time build our ministries by joining our hearts and hands in Jesus's name.

13. Relax! Relax! Relax!

My journal entry from February 20, 1992 records these words:

"Walking in the woods early a.m. Waiting upon the Lord. Bundled up today with heavy coat. The late winter breeze cuts through my clothes. Doesn't matter. I am having a wonderful time singing, praising and rejoicing in the Lord. He has been so good to me. I feel increasing freedom in my spirit with each passing day.

"Compelled to be in the woods today. Couldn't wait to get out here to spend time with my Father. Strolled down by the creek. Sat on the bank. Threw sticks in the water. Watched the current carry them downstream. Oh, Lord, carry me in the flow of your Holy Spirit. Effortlessly, like that stick. Take me where you want me to go.

"Moved to the lower section of the acreage. Looked west to the higher ground of my prayer closet. Clouds moving swiftly above my head. A few cars pass by on the freeway in the background. As I lift my hands to the sky and praise Him, the Spirit spoke. Clearly. Powerfully. He said 'Be at peace with my pace.' I wrote it down on a scrap of paper. As I walked to the break in the fence line to exit the woods, the Spirit said it again, "Steve, be at peace with my pace."

Those words given to me three years ago by God revolutionized my thinking about God's timing. Everything is perfect in God's time. We get in trouble when we rush ahead of or lag behind His plan.

I have to work on patience. My wife and I joke that when I die she's going to put a bouquet of Impatiens flowers on my grave as a testimony of one of my strongest (not best) character traits. Sometimes I have burned out because I was running faster than God!

Be at peace with God's pace, pastor. Sometimes He moves rapidly. Sometimes He doesn't seem to be moving at all. Nonetheless, let Him set the pace. He knows where He's going and when He needs to get there. The best of all is — He wants to take us with Him!

Relax. God is in control. Burnout can't beat you when you rest in the Lord.

Chapter 13

The Future Is Forward

*For I know the plans that I have for you declares
the Lord, plans for welfare and not for calamity, to
give you a future and a hope.*

Jeremiah 29:11

Over twenty-one years ago, my bride and I headed up Highway 101 in California on our honeymoon. We traveled by car from San Diego to San Francisco.

Our first trip as Mr. and Mrs. Roll took us to places like Solvang, a delightfully detailed replica of a Dutch village, where we indulged ourselves with delicious Danish pastries while leisurely browsing through the quaint little shops on main street.

The next stop on our romantic journey was San Simeon and a tour of Hearst Castle. We marveled at the magnificent architecture and the one-of-a-kind collection of priceless artifacts displayed in the fortress-style home hidden in the hills. Every room contained some spectacular design, decorator touch or unique antique that kept us "oohing" and "aahing."

The Seventeen Mile Drive through Carmel left us dreaming about being rich and famous. Sunlight bouncing off the turquoise-blue water of Santa Barbara's breathtaking bay was beautiful beyond description.

Leaving the lowlands, we started up the scenic rim along the coastal mountains overlooking the Pacific Ocean. I have never seen such sensational scenery in all of my life!

The highway hugs the mountains as it weaves it's way through the rocky terrain. The winding roadbed rests hundreds of feet above the foamy ocean waves that rhythmically crash in on the deserted beaches below. Only a few precious feet of dirt and rusty safety rails separate you and your vehicle from a straight drop over the edge!

It seemed to take forever to make any progress on the two-lane roadway. But that was it's beauty. Each slow, sluggish mile was packed with unparalleled natural beauty that provided a bountiful feast for the senses. We pulled over at all the viewpoints to soak up the splendid sights.

Ocean breeze gently flowing across your face, playful seals frolicking offshore, distinctive rock formations jutting into a sea of blue that seems to stretch to eternity, and puffy, cotton candy clouds hovering over the distant horizon painted a picture of divine beauty that no man can duplicate.

I loved the road because you couldn't get bored. I felt like an explorer discovering virgin territory. What you left behind didn't matter. There was always something new and exciting around the next bend.

The coastal highway led us to the city where many people have left their hearts. We stayed at the historic Hotel San Francisco. We enjoyed strolling along the waterfront eating chunks of sourdough bread from Fisherman's Wharf. A ride on the world famous trolley cars made us feel like children again. Lombard Street, Chinatown, Alcatraz Island, Farmer's Market and many other novel and attractive sights and sounds produced a memorable adventure for two carefree lovebirds who had nothing to think about but tomorrow.

Departing the city by the bay, we drove across the sprawling Golden Gate Bridge toward the towering Redwoods of northern California. What an awesome and almost eerie experience driving through a forest where the trees stand so tall they block the sun's rays from reaching the earth. Those quiet giants rise so high it appears that their tops touch heaven. One tree is so huge that we actually drove our car through a tunnel carved in it's trunk!

Occasionally, I take out the now-tattered- and-torn photo album to retrace our honeymoon trip. It was a very special time in our lives that never fails to warm my heart when I reflect upon it.

Young and in love, we were beginning a new life together, enthusiastic about the plan God had for us. Each day we thanked God for our yesterdays, lived our today's to the fullest, and reached boldly for tomorrow, knowing that our future was forward.

Tomorrow was an exciting opportunity to be embraced, explored and enjoyed. It was fun pushing ahead to discover what lay around the next bend in the road of life.

A major backlash from burnout is preoccupation with the past. Satan likes nothing better than to keep the old fires of failure and heartache smoldering, with us sitting right in the middle of the ashes!

Yesterday is like a mighty magnet that pulls us backwards and prevents us from going forward. If the devil can keep us mired in the muck of the past, our setback becomes a tombstone instead of a stepping stone to a wonderful life of new opportunities God has prepared for us.

I have battled long and hard with yesterday's hurt. There are times when depression's long-reaching tentacles try to entangle me again in the pain of the past. Despair attempts to drag me back to the events that broke my heart. Resisting in the flesh has proved futile. When I forget to fight in the spirit, I find myself reliving the heart piercing pain, sorrow, and grief that almost destroyed me once before.

A few years ago a sister in Christ shared Jeremiah 29:11 with me. I have held on to this verse time and time again when I am tempted to look back and despair of life because of the past's dark shadows.

The nation of Judah had been taken captive by Nebuchadnezzar and exiled to Babylon. They had suffered horrendous heartbreak at the hands of their ruthless captors. God declared through the prophet Jeremiah that He had "plans for welfare, and not calamity" for His people.

The Lord had good things waiting for them, not disaster. He promised to be there for them, to restore their fortunes and bring them back home! (See verses 12-14.) Great days lay ahead for Judah!

Satan is a thief who comes to steal his victims' hope of better days. Burnout blinds them to the possibilities of the future by focusing their attention on the past. Judah did enjoy better days because they looked to the future. Instead of concentrating on the calamity of their captivity, they released yesterday and reached for tomorrow.

It's a law of life: There is no future in yesterday. No matter how hard we may try to resurrect and rearrange the events of the past, we can't. What has been done cannot be changed.

Hope lies in today and tomorrow. God's great promises of restoration and renewal await in His children's future. Reaching backwards prevents us from reaching forward to the new things God has planned for us. His richest blessings are mine when I possess a "don't look back," "full speed ahead" attitude.

A simple principle has helped me overcome the temptation to focus unduly on yesterday. I got it from the Apostle Paul. In Philippians 3, Paul discussed the goal of life. He used his own personal experience as an illustration of what is and what is not of value. After detailing what hadn't worked (verses 1-7) he declares what does work (verses 8-12). Without mincing words or wasting a single breath, he states emphatically what his desire is (verse 10-11).

Paul then moves boldly (verses 13-14) to tell his brothers and sisters in Christ of a major decision he has made. This decision directs all that he does.

> *Brethren, I do not regard myself as having laid hold of it yet; but one thing I do, forgetting what lies behind and reaching forward to what lies ahead.*
> *I press on toward the goal for the prize of the upward call of God in Christ Jesus.*

Paul boiled life down to one thing. One thing! The goal of life is the prize of fulfilling our call in Christ Jesus. Paul said "I press on." Those are going forward words. To press on, Paul had to practice the principle of releasing and reaching.

Release the past; reach for the future.

Paul discovered that the power of the principle of pressing on lies in the conscious effort on our part to be "forgetting (present tense continuous) what lies behind" (the past) and "reaching (present tense continuous again) forward to what lies ahead" (the future).

Present tense continuous is not a one time forgetting or reaching. It means to forget and reach over and over and over again.

If you have experienced burnout, you can count on one thing for certain. The enemy will prove himself ruthless and tireless in his efforts to haul you back to yesterday. We must be on guard continually and remain spiritually vigilant if we are to successfully repel his attacks (Zechariah 4:6).

I love Paul's dogged determination. He presses on. Keeps going forward, forgetting the past, reaching for what lies ahead.

The Lord taught me something about shutting the door on the past. Isaiah 58:8 records these encouraging words.

> *Then your light shall break out like the dawn and your healing will speedily spring forth; and your*

righteousness will go before you; the glory of the
Lord will be your rear guard.

There's some shouting stuff in that Scripture! When God's people do His work in His way as laid out in verses 1-7, then light breaks forth like the dawn of a new day, and healing comes quickly. Glory Hallelujah!

Note what then happens ahead of us and behind us. Our righteousness (right standing in God) goes before us and the glory of the Lord will be our rear guard. Righteousness opens future doors while the glory of the Lord as our rear guard keeps an eye on the closed door to the past.

When Israel left Egypt, the Lord guided them by going before them in a pillar of cloud by day and a pillar of fire by night (Exodus 13:21-22). Today the Holy Spirit is our cloud and fire who guides us in truth (John 16:13).

Something significant happened when Pharaoh's chariots caught up to Israel. Exodus 14:19 reads:

And the angel of God, who had been going before
the camp of Israel, moved and went behind them;
and the pillar of cloud moved from before them and
stood behind them.

Why did God move in between Egypt and Israel? He was their rear guard! The Lord was watching out for their backside! He was protecting them. From the cloud would come confusion and de-struction for Israel's enemy from the past.

I am learning (slowly but surely!) to close the door on the past and post the Lord Jesus as my personal sentry to keep it from opening again. The past can't sneak up on me when Jesus is on duty! The devil can't touch the glory of the Lord! The Psalmist tells us that "the Lord will guard your going out and your coming in, from this time forth and forever" (Psalm 121:8). God guards every part of my life everyday of my life.

"Forgetting what lies behind" is what slams the door on yesterday. With Jesus on guard against an assault from the rear by Satan, I am free to focus my energy on reaching for the glory that lies ahead.

Before I share what I have learned about reaching for the future,

I wonder if you have released the past? Have you consciously decided with the help of the Holy Spirit to forget about burnout and the pain it caused you?

I encourage you to stop right now. Make a list of the hurtful things you need to forget. Write every one of them down. Talk to the Lord about them. Release them to Him. Let go of past pain. Let go. Really let go.

Take your hands off yesterday. Put your hurt in the hands of Jesus. Slam the door on the past and see Jesus standing there as your rear guard. Thank Him for keeping the lid on yesterday so you can look to tomorrow.

Early one Sunday morning I was thinking about the future. The Spirit was stirring my spirit about dreaming again. I felt like I was supposed to turn on the television. Obeying the impulse, I flipped on the tube. Robert Schuller stood before me in all of his ecclesiastical splendor. The first words I heard from his mouth were, "Shape your dreams by your hopes, not by your hurts."

What a message. What truth. Dreams shaped by hurt never come to pass. Dreams shaped by hope do. I was attempting to dream again. That was good. But my dreams were bogged down with baggage from burnout. They didn't stand a chance of coming true as long as past pain was in the plan.

The Lord reminded me once again about His word to me from Isaiah 43:18. He told me not to dwell on yesterday because He was going to do something new. The "something new" was a fresh dream. A vision based on hope. A grand dream focused on the future.

In all honesty, I had spent so much time dwelling on what dashed the first dream that I had neglected to ask for a new one. James tells us in very simple language, "You do not have because you do not ask" (James 4:2).

When you ask God for something, He answers. He generally responds by sending us to the Bible. If my new dream was to be shaped by hope and not hurt, I needed to rediscover what my hope was.

Despite a serious bout with burnout, God's plan for Steve Roll remained the same. My future and hope was still grounded in some very basic goals that God had given me years before. Burnout's smoke had blocked them from my view, but now the smoke had cleared and I was ready to run again the race set before me. (Hebrews 12:1)

Once again, Paul provided the inspiration and instruction that helped me reach for the future. His farewell words to the faithful, in II Timothy 4:5-8, are dynamic dream shapers.

> *But you, be sober in all things, endure hardship, do the work of an evangelist, fulfill your ministry. For I am already being poured out as a drink offering, and the time of my departure is at hand. I have fought the good fight, I have finished the course, I have kept the faith; In the future, there is laid up for me the crown of righteousness, which the Lord, the righteous Judge, will award to me on that day; and not only to me, but also to all who have loved His appearing.*

Paul had done what he said he would do. He had faithfully "pressed on" to the end of his earthly life. The prize he sought was within sight. He was preparing to go home and receive his reward. Before he departed, he reminded those who love Jesus how they, too, can be assured of receiving their reward ("the crown of righteousness") when it's their time to go and be with the Lord.

Four things stand out in my mind from Paul's final words. The Lord gave them to me in the form of strong exhortations. They have revived my hope and energized the new dream that burns in my heart. Take these four thoughts into your spirit and see if you won't agree that the future is forward.

As Christians, we are in a war. Spiritual war. Heaven and hell. Eternal souls hang in the balance. How well we battle for the spirits of men directly influences their destiny. It's entirely possible to win a war by fighting the right battles. It's equally possible to lose a war by fighting the wrong battles.

In light of this truth and the importance of winning the lost to Christ, have you ever wondered if you were fighting the right fight? I have. More than once I have questioned whether some spiritual skirmish I was engaged in was that important. Did it really have any bearing on bringing victory to God's side?

We have to fight the right fight if we are to win. One of Satan's tricks is to sidetrack us from the main track of "fighting the good fight" (II Timothy 4:7a). What is the good fight? It's the good fight of faith. Paul clarifies what the faith fight is all about in I Timothy 6:12.

Fight the good fight of faith; take hold of the eternal
life to which you were called, and you made the good
confession in the presence of many witnesses.

When we were saved, God called us to eternal life. Our faith-walk began when we confessed Christ before men. Witnesses heard of our turning from trust in self to trust in the Savior. The Holy Spirit used our testimony to touch many people for the Kingdom. That's "the good fight of faith."

The devil designed my burnout and depression for the purpose of destroying my faith and silencing my witness. Battling burnout left me struggling to believe in God, the Gospel, myself, and men. The enemy tried to take this faith fighter out of action permanently.

Doubting drives you to silence. You don't boldly proclaim what you're struggling to believe. And that's exactly what the devil wants. Silenced believers.

Satan is out to quiet as many Christians as possible. His sinister strategy is to beat 'em up, burn 'em out, chew 'em up, and dump 'em out into some dark corner of disillusionment where no one will ever hear the name of Jesus from their lips again.

I started to flex my spiritual muscles again when I took hold of the eternal life to which I was called. God helped me to see anew the things that matter. Eternal things that I had spent my life faithfully confessing to others are what counts.

One afternoon when I was sitting in our backyard looking into the woods, the Lord gave me a vision. He showed me multitudes of people I had influenced for Him through my ministry. I saw a vast crowd of joyful faces peeking around trees and poking out of the bushes. I called out many of their names as I happily scanned the assembly of believers in the Church Among the Trees!

Then the Spirit said, "Steve, these are what it is all about. Souls who have come to faith. My son, the future is forward. I have given you a backward look so you will never forget where the real fight is. I have prepared your hands for war. Go forward now in My strength and fight to win the lost."

Jumping out of my lawn chair, I committed myself to never again waste one ounce of spiritual energy fighting the wrong fights. What are some of those wrong fights?

- Maneuvering for personal position, prominence and prestige in the Body of Christ.
- Theological hair-splitting.
- Interdenominational squabbling over petty differences in doctrine and polity.
- Wrangling over which wallpaper pattern to put in the fellowship hall.
- Trying to please everybody in the church.
- Participating in political power plays in God's house.

Satan loves it when the saints fight with each other instead of him. While we pick at each other, he picks off people and drags them to hell. We fight bloody battles over the color of bathroom walls while precious souls outside our four walls perish in the devil's grasp.

Time is too short, and eternity is too long for us to fight the wrong fight. If you want to get fired up again about ministry, think about battling for the things that are part of the right fight.

- Fight for Jesus reputation — not your own!
- Fight the devil — not people!
- Fight for what is right — not to be right!
- Fight for the Word of God — not the opinions of men!
- Fight to save souls — not to save face!
- Fight in his name — not in the name of your denomination!
- Fight to push back the gates of hell — not to extend your little corner of the kingdom!
- Fight to tear down Satan's strongholds — not to shore up your walls!
- Fight to set people free — not to set them straight!
- Fight for the glory of God and the good of men!

Eternity is what counts. Get back in the fight for the future. Fight for God! Fight for men! Fight for your vision! Fight for your dream! Put burnout in your rearview mirror and fight, fight, fight the right fight!

A close friend who knows my story asked me recently what kept me from leaving the ministry. I told him it was my calling. When my pain was the greatest, the Holy Spirit gently reminded me of God's call on my life.

My call is like a canopy or umbrella over my life. Everything comes under my divine appointment from God to be His servant. Satan wants ministers and lay Christian leaders to forget who they are and what they are called to do. If we lose sight of our call, we have lost sight of our purpose. Burnout finds easy targets in those who have drifted from God's grand design for their life.

Paul's parting words to Pastor Timothy pointed the young leader to the anchor that would hold him steady in the smooth and rough waters of the ministry. The Apostle couched his words in a charge.

> *I solemnly charge you in the presence of God and of Christ Jesus, who is to judge the living and the dead, and by His appearing and His kingdom; preach the Word; be ready in season and out of season; reprove, rebuke, exhort, with great patience and instruction. But you, be sober in all things, endure hardship, do the work of an evangelist, fulfill your ministry.*
>
> II Timothy 4:1-2, 5

Paul gave his son in the faith a solemn charge, not a casual suggestion. Before God, the battle hardened veteran of many ministry campaigns commanded Timothy to fulfill his ministry.

What was his ministry? Preaching the Word. When it was convenient and when it wasn't. Being sober and serious about God's business. Enduring hardship.

That's right young man. Ministry won't be easy. You have to hang in there through the rough times.

Your work is that of an evangelist. Proclaim the Good News in all you do. Instruct people how to find their way into the Kingdom. Teach them God's truth. Be very patient when you reprove, rebuke and exhort. Always remember as God's servant, your call is to win people to Jesus.

The Lord has a strategic ministry for each of His servants. Every calling is vital to the fulfillment of the big picture of redemption. That's why we must bounce back from burnout and break forth to complete our calling. There are people who won't be saved unless we get back in the battle again. We return to the battlefield by releasing the past and reaching for the future.

Take the fire of burnout and turn it into fire for God. Fall in love with Jesus all over again. Receive the Holy Spirit. Allow Him to re-ignite your call and set you ablaze with a fresh passion to preach the

Word and do the work of an evangelist.

Like me, you may have been hurt. But can't you feel that tug in your soul? That stirring from the Holy Spirit to do the work of the ministry? Don't let anything keep you from fulfilling your service to the Lord! God needs you and people need you.

Fix your eyes on the prize.

My son and I were watching an NBA playoff game between the New York Knicks and Indiana Pacers. The contest had been close and went into overtime. As the final seconds ticked off the clock in the extra period, Reggie Miller got his hands on the ball. In the clutch, he's simply amazing! Powering his way through the lane, he left two frantic defenders in the dust. Reggie then went airborne and electrified the Market Square Arena crowd with a two-handed stuff over the outstretched arms of Patrick Ewing. Game over. Pacers won by two points.

A big game was on the line. Reggie Miller didn't hesitate a second to make a strong move and take the ball to the basket. Why? Because he had his sights fixed on winning an NBA championship.

The previous season, the Pacers missed the finals and the chance to play for all the marbles by just one game. Miller was highly motivated to get to the finals and to play for the prize — the shiny silver trophy that signifies you're the best professional basketball team in the world.

Paul's eyes were fixed on "the crown of righteousness" waiting for him in the future (II Timothy 4:8). He was mightily motivated to fulfill his ministry and receive the crown (trophy) that had his name on it. The promise of the prize kept Paul going forward, toward the future.

You won't find the crown of righteousness in the past. You'll find it in the future. The prize awaits the faithful who have kept their eyes on Jesus and kept the faith. Tomorrow, not yesterday is where we will find God's trophy case.

Let me say it again. God's rewards aren't behind us, they're in front of us! And they are worth working and waiting for. Look what Paul says about what believers have to look forward to in Christ.

> *But as it is written, eye has not seen, nor ear heard,*
> *neither have entered into the heart of man, the things*
> *which God has prepared for them that love Him!*
> I Corinthians 2:9, KJV

Championships on earth are nothing in comparison with the spiritual treasures and trophies that God's champions of righteousness will receive at His appearing! The only way to claim ours is to walk toward tomorrow.

So fix your eyes on the prize! Keep looking forward. The Lord has shown me that life is not about me, it's about Him. It's not about what has happened in the past, it's about what is going to happen in the future. It's not about survival, it's all about revival!

Finish the course.

There is nothing more self-defeating than quitting. Burnout can turn us into quitters if we are not careful.

I know of pastors and lay leaders who got beat up in the course of their ministry. Now they're sitting on the bench watching the game. They decided that the gain is not worth the pain, so they hung up their cleats and called it quits.

Where would we be today if the Apostle Paul had decided after his stoning at Lystra (Acts 14) to give up being a missionary? How many thousands would have gone unsaved? Who would have planted the churches in Europe and Asia Minor? Who would the Holy Spirit have used to record thirteen books of the New Testament? Who would we look to for instruction in sound doctrine and an inspiring example of Christlike faith if Paul had hung it up because at times it was hard?

The Apostle of apostles didn't quit. He said with satisfaction, "I have finished the course" (II Timothy 4:7). Paul kept the faith. He didn't chuck the faith. He kept trucking towards tomorrow, trusting the One to whom He had committed everything.

> *For this reason I also suffer these things, but I am*
> *not ashamed; for I know whom I have believed and*
> *I am convinced that He is able to guard what I have*
> *entrusted to Him until that day.*
>
> II Timothy 2:12

I've taught my children a phrase that we often exhort one another with: Winners never quit. Quitters never win!

The headline in the sports section of the local newspaper read "Jansen's Years of Tears Turn to Gold." What sports fan will soon forget that dramatic moment when U.S. Olympic speed skater Dan Jansen shot across the finish line, smashing the world record for the

1,000 meters sprint in the games in Lillehammer, Norway. The emotionally charged victory earned him the gold medal and ended a decade of personal disappointment. I can still see Dan celebrating his win, circling the rink with jubilant tears streaming down his face and his little daughter lifted triumphantly above his head.

The real story is the story behind the story. Dan Jansen is probably the finest male speed skater of all time. When he takes to the ice and hit his stride, time and everyone else seems to stand still. Jansen competed in the '84, '88, '92 and '94 Winter Olympics. He placed and won medals, but not gold. Disappointment and tragedy stalked him at the Olympics. Slips, falls, and uncharacteristically slow times plagued his performance.

Tough times reached the pinnacle when Dan's beloved sister died during the '92 Olympics. He bravely skated in her memory, but everyone's heart was crushed when he fell coming out of a turn. Overcome with grief and disappointment, Dan left the games again without a gold medal.

The sports world thought Dan was finished. But Dan and his wife didn't. They decided to go forward. To try one more time. Dan kept skating and skating toward the future when he would have another shot at the gold in Norway. The rest is history.

Dan Jansen has a gold medal because he refused to quit. He went forward when it was tough. He kept skating. Standing on the podium receiving his prize before an adoring world finished his Olympic journey.

Winners in life don't quit the race. They keep heading toward the finish line. They complete the course.

Burnout may have beat you up, as it did me, but don't you quit. I was tempted to throw in the towel when burnout blurred my vision of God's promises. But glory to God! Jesus loves me and has great things for me to do. I can't quit, I won't quit because He hasn't quit on me!

Pharaoh was coming. The Red Sea was uncrossable. Israel was crying. The Lord told Moses to tell the people to "Go forward" (Exodus 13:15). It seems ridiculous, doesn't it?

Only if you forget what God was up to.

The Promised Land was God's goal for His children. Israel's future wasn't in Egypt, it was in Canaan. Slavery and bondage were not God's Will for His chosen people. Freedom and blessing were, and they were awaiting Israel on the other side of the seemingly impossible situation confronting them.

Faith moves forward, toward tomorrow. The Lord fought for Israel because Israel went forward. His mighty miracle of deliverance opened the door to the future. Everything Israel could ever dream of or desire was theirs as long as they kept going forward.

Biblical faith looks forward. Doubt looks back. Farther on down the road, the Israelites would forget what the Lord did for them at the Red Sea, and choose not to go forward at Kadesh-Barnea (Numbers 13-14). Their doubting led to their deaths in the desert. What a price to pay for not trusting the future to the Lord.

We will die spiritually, too, if we don't go forward. Burnout removed me from the battlefield of faith. I was a wounded warrior whose battered armor lay at his feet. Weary of warfare, I found myself wanting to go back to a time before I'd been blown out of the saddle. The good old days looked pretty good.

Going forward seemed so impossible. My faith was shattered. But "the Lord is near to the brokenhearted and saves those who are crushed in spirit" (Psalm 34:18). The Holy Spirit rushed to my side. He restored and renewed me. The Word of God restored my faith. I am now revived, rearmed, and re-enlisted in God's army!

The Lord Jesus Christ fights for us when we go forward. The most difficult decision I have had to make was to decide to go ahead when it would have been so easy to go back.

You might be there right now. At a critical crossroads of choice. Yesterday looks safe. Tomorrow looks scary. You fear the future.

Beloved brother or sister in Christ, in the name of Jesus, go forward. The future is forward. God is there. Good things are there. The victorious, Spirit-filled, Christian life you seek is straight ahead.

Don't delay another minute. Make a solid commitment to go forward by faith into the future. With the help of the Father, Son, and Holy Spirit, never look back again to the pain of the past. Look ahead to the promises of the future!

Proverbs 31:10-31 described the virtues of the worthy woman. I like what verse 25 says about her attitude toward tomorrow. *"Strength and dignity are her clothing, and she smiles at the future."*

If the godly woman can look forward to the future with a smile, so can you and I. Stop frowning and start smiling at the future, because the future is smiling at you!

Epilogue

Turning Burnout Into Blessing!

*"O Lord My God, I cried to Thee for help, and
Thou didst heal me."*

Psalm 30:2

His big, brown cow-eyes, soft, gentle paws, curly black coat, submissive spirit and constantly wagging "happy stick" stole our hearts. From the very first moment we laid our eyes on Cody, we knew he was the puppy for us. The tale of how this abandoned canine became a member of the Roll clan is nothing less than miraculous.

It was a Saturday morning. Jo Ann and the kids had gone shopping. I was in the woods praying. As I concluded my time with the Lord, I asked Him how we should spend our day. He said, "Do whatever the family wants to do." Sounded good to me.

I walked back to the house. As I opened the door, I was greeted by my three redheads. By the look on their faces, I could tell they were up to something. My daughter, who finds it very difficult to keep a secret, blurted out with wild-eyed enthusiasm, "Dad, we found a dog. He's so cute. We want you to go and look at him." I turned in the direction of my wife who was trying to act innocent. I gave her my what-have-you-guys-been-up-to look!

Jo Ann's plan to slowly break the news to Dad had just been blown out of the water. She had no choice now but to tell me what they were plotting. The "fam" hadn't been to the mall at all. They'd spent the morning at PetsMart, where the Adopt-a-Pet agency was displaying homeless animals. Sure enough — they fell in love with a little Lhasa Apso puppy. On the way home, my soft-hearted redheads discussed how to "work Dad over" so he would agree to an addition to our family.

I am one of those guys who does everything he can to stay out of pet stores. First, because I'm allergic to most animals. Second, because I'm a sucker. Just one look at those orphan puppies and their please-take-me-home-mister faces, and I'm ready to bust them out of their cages and turn our home into a pet farm! My family is well aware that Dad's a soft touch when it comes to puppies.

Normally, getting a dog is no big deal. We'd brought home a puppy twice before. But both of them had died. One as the result of an injury, the other, a brain tumor. Putting them to sleep had been hard on the family. Especially dad.

I wasn't ready for another dog. But God said to do whatever the family wanted to do today. So we headed to PetsMart. Of course, I told them I was just looking and they shouldn't get their hopes up. The final decision would be mine. Jo Ann dutifully told Adam and Stacy not to pressure their father.

All the way to the store, I was pummeled with things like, "He's so cute!" or "He took right to us, Daddy?" and "He's so soft and he cuddles right up on your lap!" and "He licked our faces and cried when we started to leave and they put him back in his cage!" and finally, "We know you'll love him!"

No pressure there.

The attendant brought out this adorable, fuzzy ball of energy and happiness that made a beeline to none other than dear old dad. He had a red ribbon in his hair. It was all over when he put his little white paws on my forearms, looked into my eyes and licked me on the cheek. The kids went nuts! "See Daddy, we told you. He likes you. Isn't he cute! Can we take him home? Can we, Dad?"

Emotionally the dog was ours. But I reminded the kids of the responsibilities. Then I started to sneeze.

The dog couldn't be taken home until Monday, so Jo Ann put our name on the interested list and got the address of the vetrenarian where he would be taken. I told the kids again that I would have to seriously think about this decision.

At home, we discussed the pros and cons. Jo Ann and the children were all "pro." I was the sole "con." When I refreshed the family's memory that I was allergic to curly haired dogs in particular, Stacy sprang into action. "Daddy," she said, "the allergies are no problem." Stepping boldly in my direction, she laid hands on me and declared, "Allergies, be gone. I rebuke you in Jesus's name. Thank you God for healing my daddy. Amen!"

Talk about out of the mouth of a babe. Wow! What's a dad to

do now? I certainly couldn't tell her I don't believe in healing, because I do. I've taught my children to boldly put their faith in action. She did. So I agreed with her, hoping I was healed for real.

My son was playing in a baseball tournament that afternoon. The game had gone down to the wire. Last inning. Two outs. Our team was at bat. We needed one run to tie, two to win. Two of Adam's teammates were on base as he stepped up to the plate. As he took a practice swing, without thinking, I hollered from the dugout, "Son, how bad do you want that dog?" His face lit up. "Bad Dad." I told him if he hit a double and drove in the winning runs, the puppy was his. You should have seen the determined look on that little leaguer's face!

The opposing pitcher never had a chance. Adam pounded the first pitch between left and center. One run scored. Two runs scored. Adam, legs pumping a hundred miles an hour, rounded third and crossed the plate safely on a throwing error. Our bench went crazy! The kids mobbed Adam as he returned to the dugout.

When the celebration subsided, my son sauntered over to me and gave me a high-five. A smug little smile beamed across his face. "Thanks for the dog dad!"

"You're welcome son," I responded. Then I looked toward heaven murmuring, "Lord, what did I just do?"

His answer was clear. "You got yourself a puppy."

It only took two seconds for Adam to announce to his mother and sister that Dad said we could have the dog. My wife nearly fainted. Stacy shouted and said, "Thank you, Jesus!" I began to prepare for the arrival of our next "man's best friend."

Early Monday morning, before daybreak, Jo Ann left for the vet's office. We weren't guaranteed that the dog would be ours. It was a first-come, first-serve sort of deal. But we were confident this dog had our name on it.

Slowed by a severe thunderstorm all the way across town, my wife arrived only to hear the young assistant say, "I'm sorry, Mrs. Roll. Someone has already come and claimed the dog. He's no longer available for adoption."

Jo Ann burst into tears.

It wasn't supposed to happen that way. We'd understood the procedure to be that the dog wasn't available until Monday. But someone had convinced the vet to release the dog on Sunday.

Deeply disappointed, Jo Ann returned to the car. It wouldn't

start. She and anothe rwoman stood in the darkness trying to
jumpstart a dead battery as the rain poured down. It was beginning
to look like one of those days!

Brokenhearted and soaked to the bone, Jo Ann called me at
home. The kids were glued to my side, awaiting the good news that
Mommy was heading home with our new puppy. She told me what
had happened. I concealed my personal disappointment as I drove
the kids to school. I didn't have the heart to tell them the dog was
gone, so I told them there had been a hitch in the process. We would
know more in the afternoon. I hugged them up and encouraged them
to have a good day, knowing they would be thinking about "their
puppy" all day.

When we shared the sad news after school, both kids cried their
eyes out. They were so disappointed. It broke my heart to see them
so disappointed. They cried all evening.

While tucking them in for the night, I did my best to comfort
their crushed spirits. Adam was hurt and confused. He couldn't
understand why a boy couldn't have a dog. He wept and wondered
why God let somebody else sneak in and take "his puppy."

When we said our prayers, Adam prayed that the guy who had
the dog would be allergic to him, not be able to sleep all night, and
return him to the vet! In the silent sanctuary of my spirit, I said a
hearty Amen!, hoping that might happen too!

Stacy was beside herself. Her heart was set on that particular
puppy. She had asked God for him, believed I was healed from my
allergies, and thought it was a miracle Dad said yes! She was upset
with God because she thought He had let her down and taken her dog
away. She finally fell asleep in her daddy's arms, worn out from
sobbing and sniffling.

Jo Ann and I went to bed, praying for the Lord to help our little
ones let go and look forward to another puppy in the future. But in
our hearts, we were pulling for a miracle that would deliver that
four-legged bundle of joy to our home.

Tuesday morning I met for prayer with a brother in Christ. I
shared our puppy story with him. We asked the Lord to comfort the
children, and agreed in faith if there was any way He might
supernaturally intervene for two little kids, that He would.

An hour later the phone rang. It was Jo Ann. "Sit down. You
won't believe this. The man who took the puppy sneezed and

coughed all night. Didn't sleep a wink. He returned the dog to the animal clinic because he's allergic to him! The vet called me at work and the dog is ours!"

I shouted Hallelujah! and then breathed a prayer of thanks to God. He had heard the cry of two precious little people who wanted a puppy. In just a few short hours, their dream of having a dog to love would come true.

I picked the kids up as usual from school, but I didn't tell them anything about the dog. When we drove up to the house, instead of parking the the car in the garage, I parked on the driveway. I told Adam and Stacy to go in the house through the front door. Shoulders sagging, they walked to the porch.

As their feet hit the threshold, the door opened and there stood Mom. She asked Adam and Stacy if they believed that God answers the prayers of little children. The hopeful glow in their eyes and the wishful words out of their mouths were, "Yes." Then Jo Ann opened the door wide and there stood a little black puppy, red hair-bow and all, tugging on his leash, wanting desperately to love on some kids. Stacy burst into an ear shattering scream of spontaneous delight! She squealed and squealed and squealed — thanking Jesus for her puppy.

Adam seemed to go into shock. He stood perfectly still, staring in unbelief. Then, suddenly, he turned around, went outside and ran circles in the frontyard! He was carried away with joy! He just circled and circled the yard, hilariously celebrating that Cody was ours!

Dreams do come true! If God cares about children and puppies, He cares about you and your heart's desires. The miracle you need in order to turn your burnout into blessing is just a prayer away.

The Psalmist cried to God for help, and the Lord heard him and healed him! If burnout has had you down in the dumps, isn't it time to look up and turn the table on the devil?

It isn't God's Will for you to remain in the grip of depression, discouragement or despair. Your victory is in Christ, not in your circumstances! Away with burnout! On to blessing! Look to Jesus, the healer of broken hearts.

You've read my story. The hardest and healthiest thing I've ever done was submitting myself to God and letting Him turn my burnout into blessing. Psalm 40:1-3 best captures the condition of my restored spirit:

I waited patiently for the Lord, and He inclined to
me, and heard my cry. He brought me out of the pit
of destruction, out of the miry clay; And He set my
feet upon a rock, making my footsteps firm. And He
put a new song in my mouth, a song of praise to our
God. Many will see and fear, and trust in the Lord.

The Holy Spirit has given me a new song to sing! I'm rejoicing in His great love for me! I'm excited about and smiling at the future! I'm praising the Lord for taking my broken life and making it whole again!

I pray that my story will help you to see that God can be trusted. Faith in Him is the key to turning brokenness into blessing.

Hopeful warrior, wait for the Lord. Be strong, and let your heart take courage. Wait for the Lord and He will renew your strength. You will rise up from the ashes of burnout to soar on the heights of blessing as you wait on Him.

May He grant you your heart's desire, and fulfill
all your dreams. We will sing for joy over your
victory, and in the name of our God. We will set up
our banners. May the Lord fulfill all your petitions.
Psalm 20:4-5